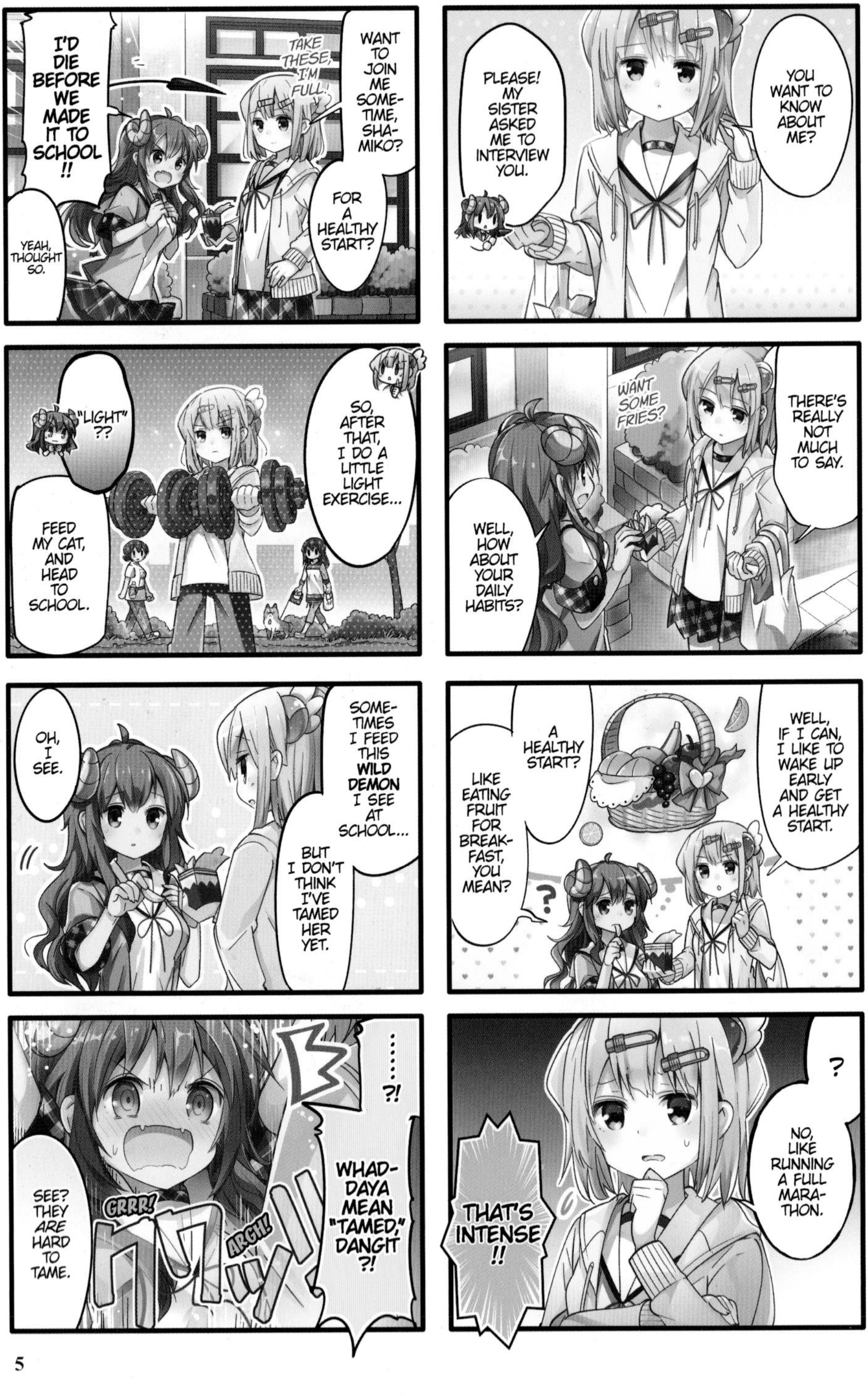
YOU WANT TO KNOW ABOUT ME?
PLEASE! MY SISTER ASKED ME TO INTERVIEW YOU.
THERE'S REALLY NOT MUCH TO SAY.
WANT SOME FRIES?
WELL, HOW ABOUT YOUR DAILY HABITS?
WELL, IF I CAN, I LIKE TO WAKE UP EARLY AND GET A HEALTHY START.
A HEALTHY START?
LIKE EATING FRUIT FOR BREAK-FAST, YOU MEAN?
?
?
NO, LIKE RUNNING A FULL MARA-THON.
THAT'S INTENSE!!
WANT TO JOIN ME SOME-TIME, SHA-MIKO?
TAKE THESE, I'M FULL!
FOR A HEALTHY START?
I'D DIE BEFORE WE MADE IT TO SCHOOL!!
YEAH, THOUGHT SO.
SO, AFTER THAT, I DO A LITTLE LIGHT EXERCISE...
"LIGHT"??
FEED MY CAT, AND HEAD TO SCHOOL.
SOME-TIMES I FEED THIS WILD DEMON I SEE AT SCHOOL...
BUT I DON'T THINK I'VE TAMED HER YET.
OH, I SEE.
......?!
WHAD-DAYA MEAN "TAMED," DANGIT?!
ARGH!
GRRR!
SEE? THEY ARE HARD TO TAME.

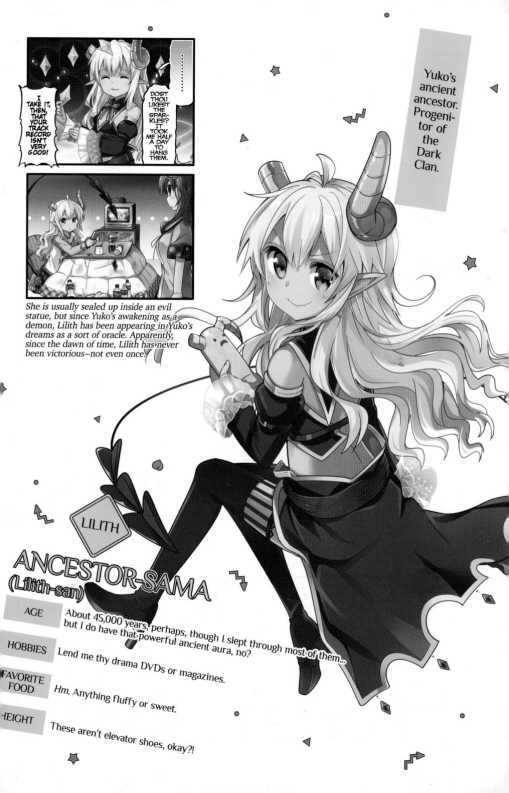

Yuko's ancient ancestor. Progenitor of the Dark Clan.

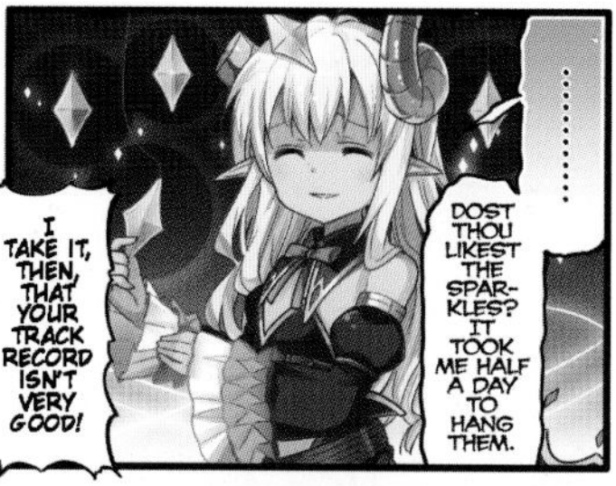

....
DOST THOU LIKEST THE SPARKLES? IT TOOK ME HALF A DAY TO HANG THEM.
I TAKE IT, THEN, THAT YOUR TRACK RECORD ISN'T VERY GOOD!

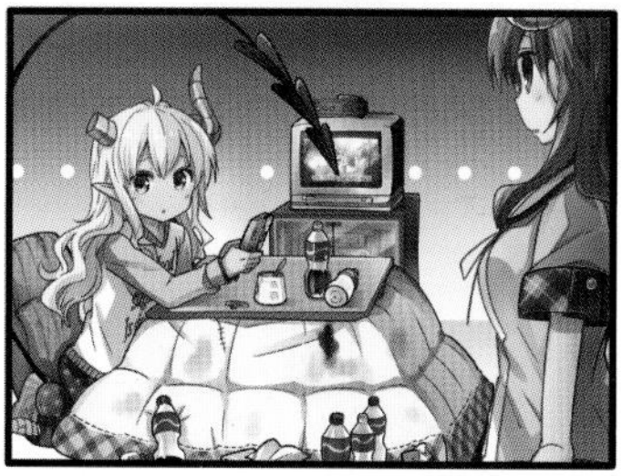

She is usually sealed up inside an evil statue, but since Yuko's awakening as a demon, Lilith has been appearing in Yuko's dreams as a sort of oracle. Apparently, since the dawn of time, Lilith has never been victorious—not even once.

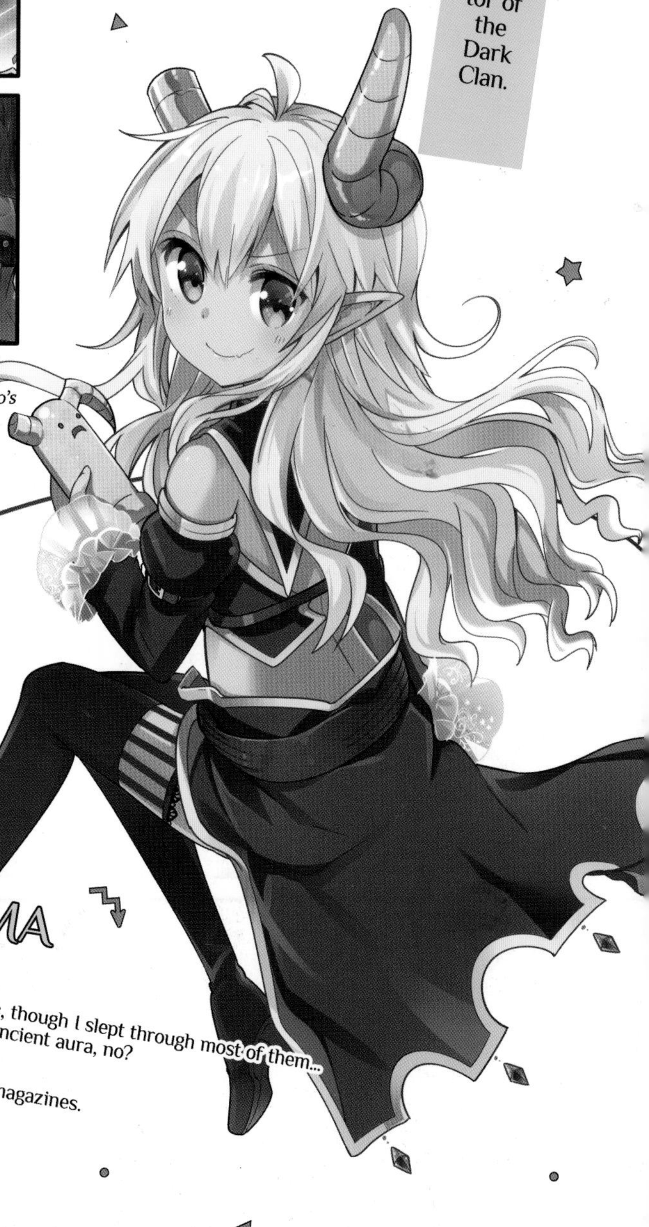

LILITH

ANCESTOR-SAMA
(Lilith-san)

AGE	About 45,000 years, perhaps, though I slept through most of them... but I do have that powerful ancient aura, no?
HOBBIES	Lend me thy drama DVDs or magazines.
FAVORITE FOOD	Hm. Anything fluffy or sweet.
HEIGHT	These aren't elevator shoes, okay?!

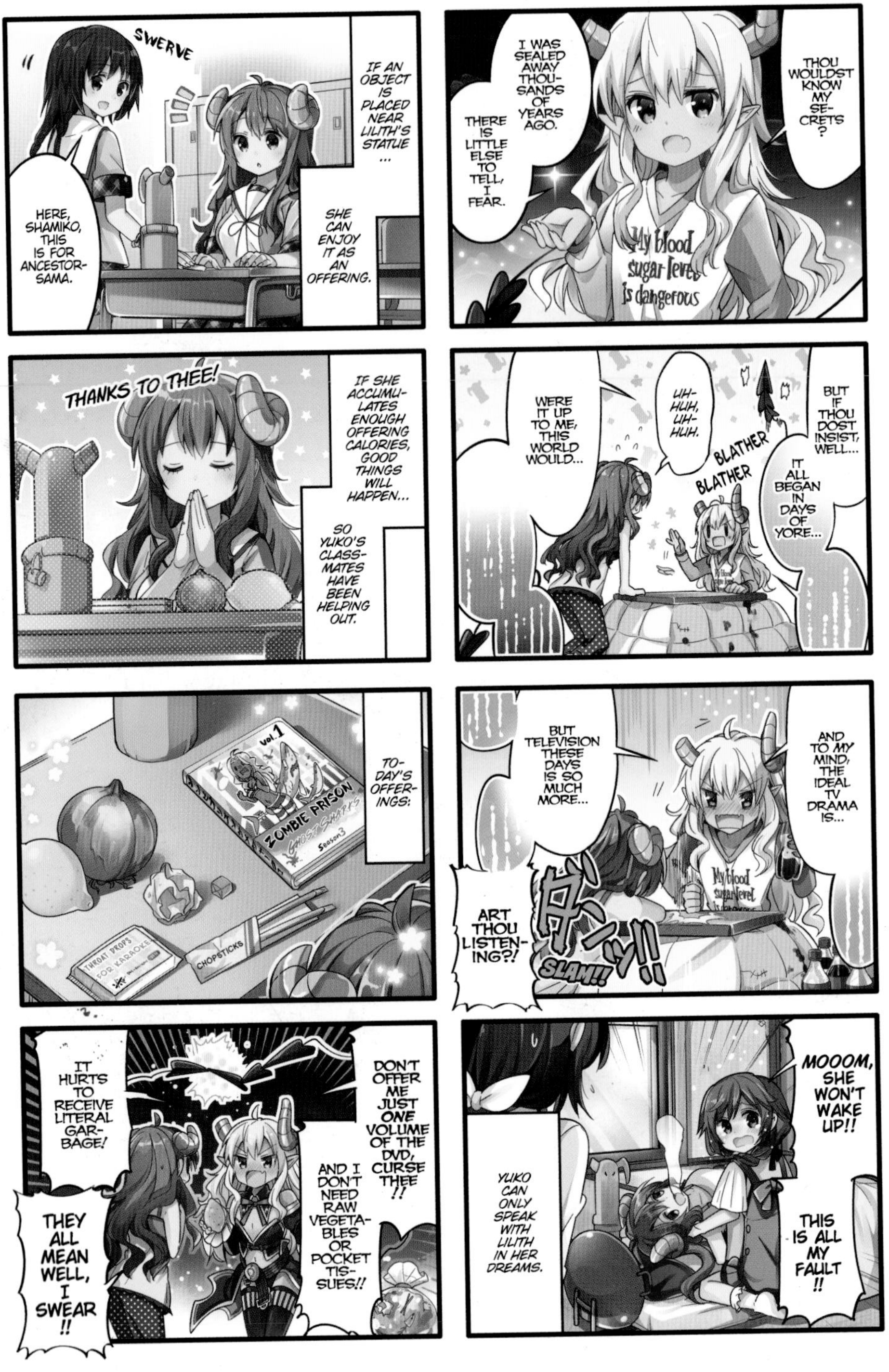
THOU WOULDST KNOW MY SE-CRETS?
I WAS SEALED AWAY THOU-SANDS OF YEARS AGO.
THERE IS LITTLE ELSE TO TELL, I FEAR.
My blood sugar level is dangerous
BUT IF THOU DOST INSIST, WELL...
IT ALL BEGAN IN DAYS OF YORE...
BLATHER
BLATHER
UH-HUH, UH-HUH.
WERE IT UP TO ME, THIS WORLD WOULD...
AND TO MY MIND, THE IDEAL TV DRAMA IS...
BUT TELEVISION THESE DAYS IS SO MUCH MORE...
SLAM!!
ART THOU LISTEN-ING?!
MOOOM, SHE WON'T WAKE UP!!
THIS IS ALL MY FAULT!!
YUKO CAN ONLY SPEAK WITH LILITH IN HER DREAMS.
IF AN OBJECT IS PLACED NEAR LILITH'S STATUE...
SWERVE
HERE, SHAMIKO, THIS IS FOR ANCESTOR-SAMA.
SHE CAN ENJOY IT AS AN OFFERING.
IF SHE ACCUMU-LATES ENOUGH OFFERING CALORIES, GOOD THINGS WILL HAPPEN...
THANKS TO THEE!
SO YUKO'S CLASS-MATES HAVE BEEN HELPING OUT.
TO-DAY'S OFFER-INGS:
vol.1
ZOMBIE PRISON
GHOST SHARKS
Season3
THROAT DROPS FOR KARAOKE
CHOPSTICKS
DON'T OFFER ME JUST ONE VOLUME OF THE DVD, CURSE THEE!!
AND I DON'T NEED RAW VEGETA-BLES OR POCKET TIS-SUES!!
IT HURTS TO RECEIVE LITERAL GAR-BAGE!
THEY ALL MEAN WELL, I SWEAR!!

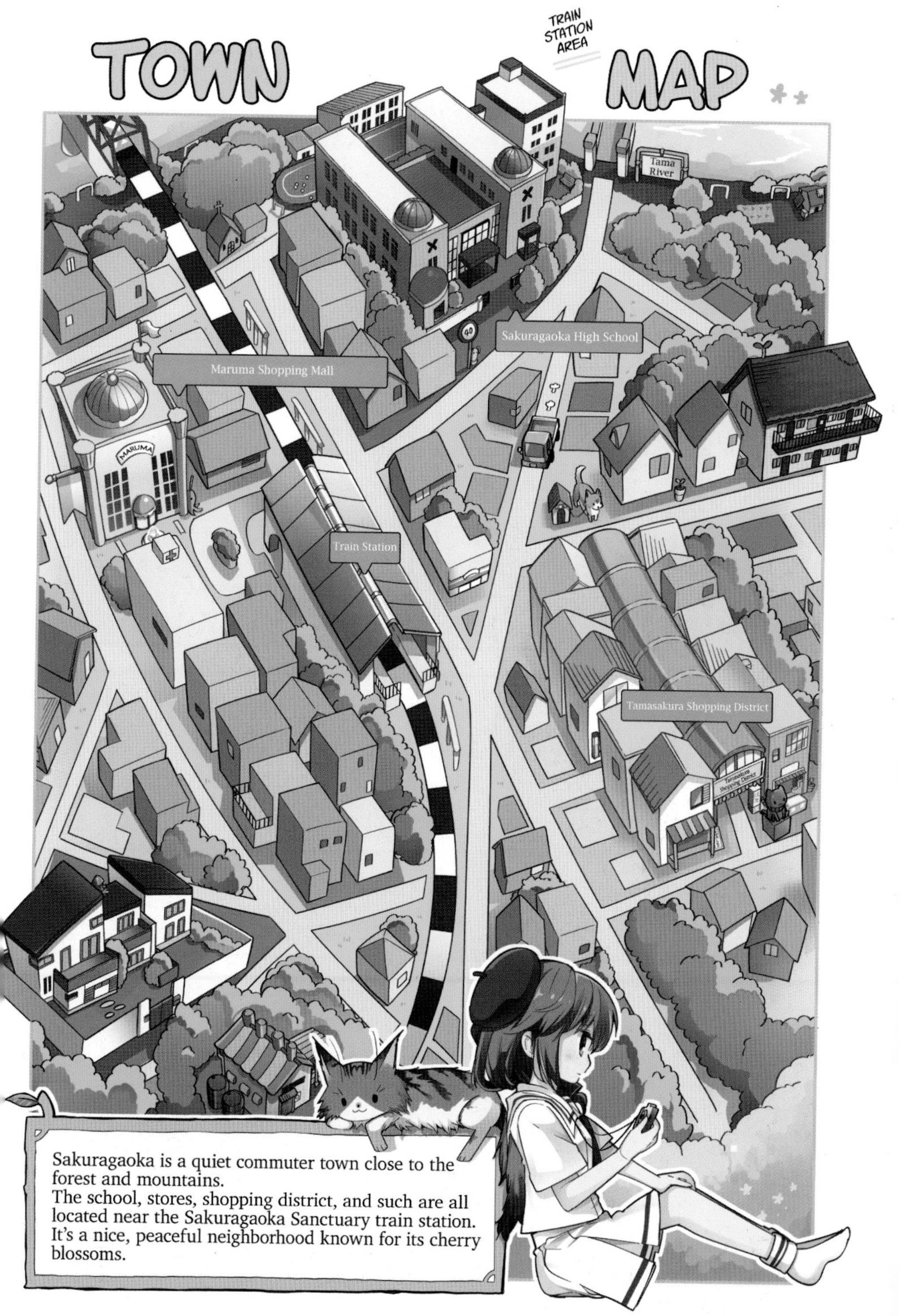
TOWN
TRAIN STATION AREA
MAP
Tama River
Sakuragaoka High School
40
Maruma Shopping Mall
MARUMA
Train Station
Tamasakura Shopping District

Sakuragaoka is a quiet commuter town close to the forest and mountains.
The school, stores, shopping district, and such are all located near the Sakuragaoka Sanctuary train station.
It's a nice, peaceful neighborhood known for its cherry blossoms.

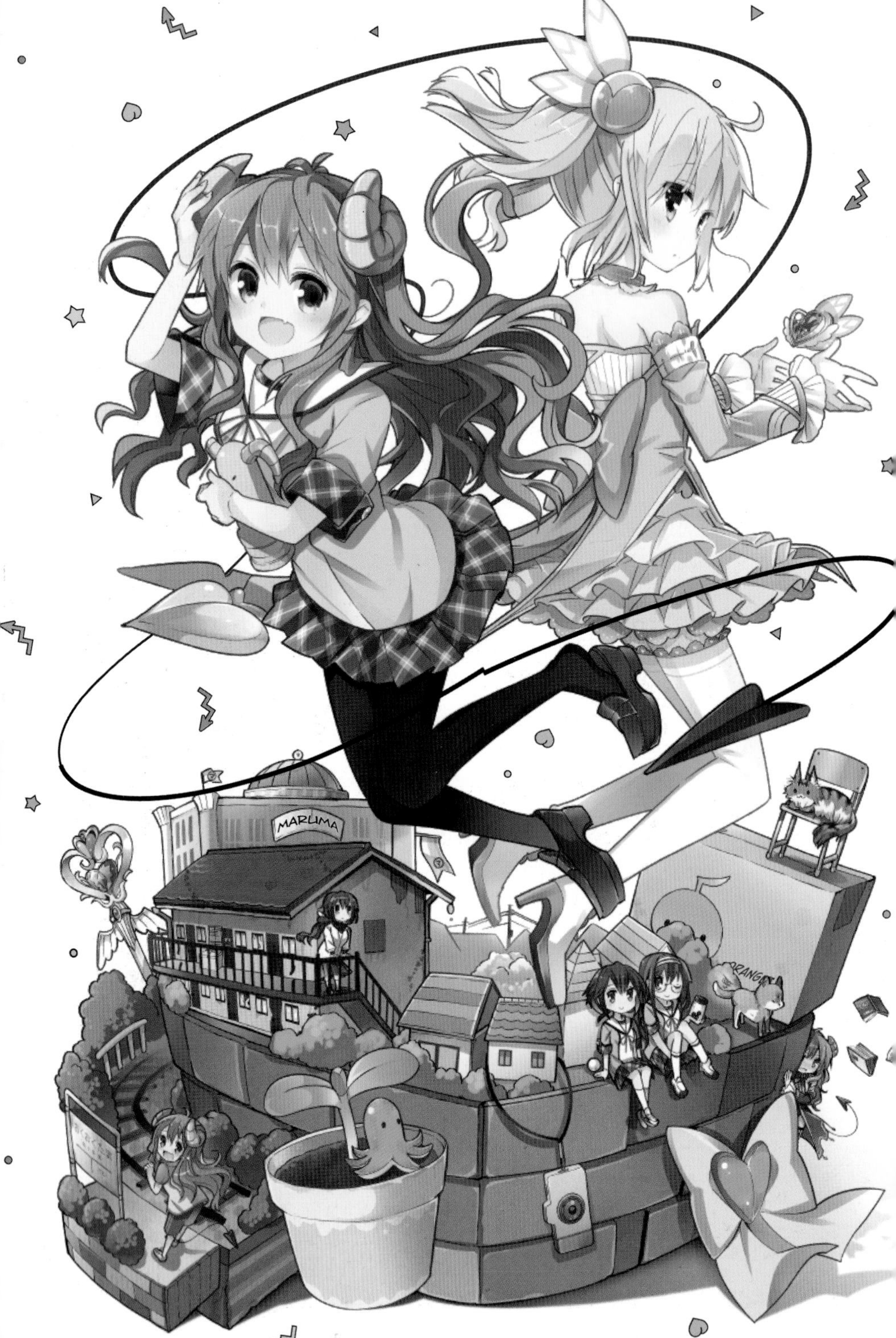
MARUMA

The Demon Girl Next Door 01

story & art by **Izumo Ito**

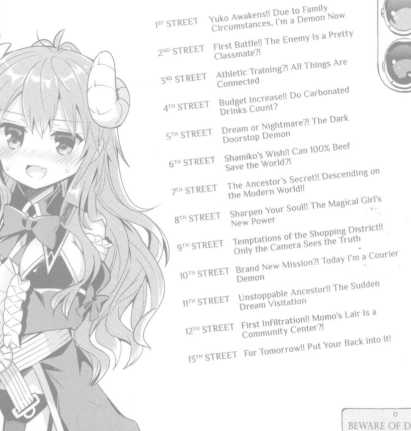

1ST STREET — Yuko Awakens!! Due to Family Circumstances, I'm a Demon Now

2ND STREET — First Battle!! The Enemy Is a Pretty Classmate?!

3RD STREET — Athletic Training?! All Things Are Connected

4TH STREET — Budget Increase!! Do Carbonated Drinks Count?

5TH STREET — Dream or Nightmare?! The Dark Doorstop Demon

6TH STREET — Shamiko's Wish!! Can 100% Beef Save the World?!

7TH STREET — The Ancestor's Secret!! Descending on the Modern World!!

8TH STREET — Sharpen Your Soul!! The Magical Girl's New Power

9TH STREET — Temptations of the Shopping District!! Only the Camera Sees the Truth

10TH STREET — Brand New Mission?! Today I'm a Courier Demon

11TH STREET — Unstoppable Ancestor!! The Sudden Dream Visitation

12TH STREET — First Infiltration!! Momo's Lair Is a Community Center?!

13TH STREET — For Tomorrow!! Put Your Back into It!

Izumo presents ★

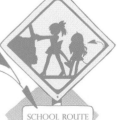

SCHOOL ROUTE

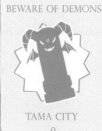

BEWARE OF DEMONS

TAMA CITY

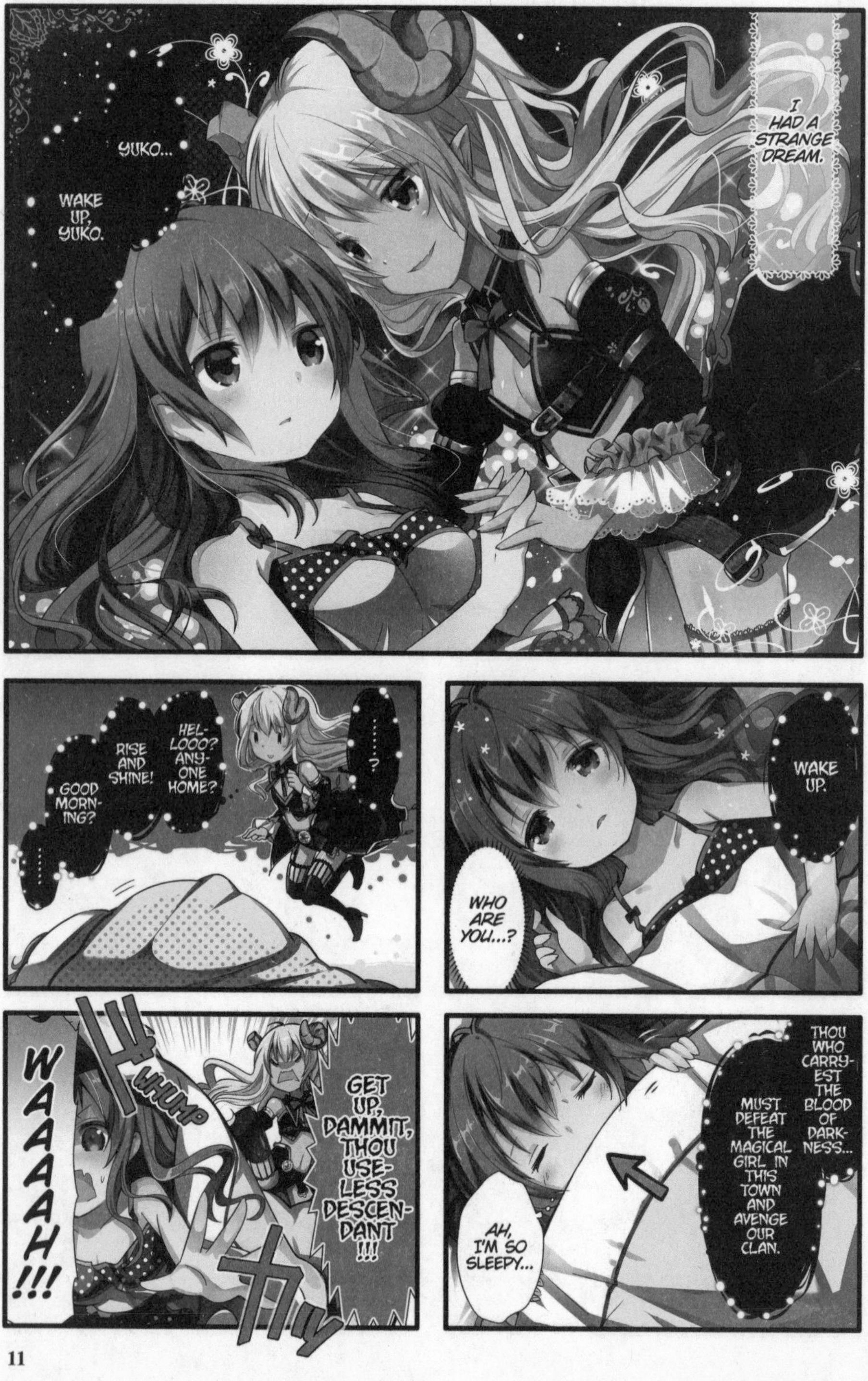
I HAD A STRANGE DREAM.
YUKO...
WAKE UP, YUKO.
WAKE UP.
WHO ARE YOU...?
......?
HEL-LOOO? ANY-ONE HOME?
RISE AND SHINE!
GOOD MORN-ING?
......
THOU WHO CARRY-EST THE BLOOD OF DARK-NESS...
MUST DEFEAT THE MAGICAL GIRL IN THIS TOWN AND AVENGE OUR CLAN.
AH, I'M SO SLEEPY...
GET UP, DAMMIT, THOU USE-LESS DESCEN-DANT!!!
WHUMP
WAAAAAH!!!

YUKO-SAN AWAKENS

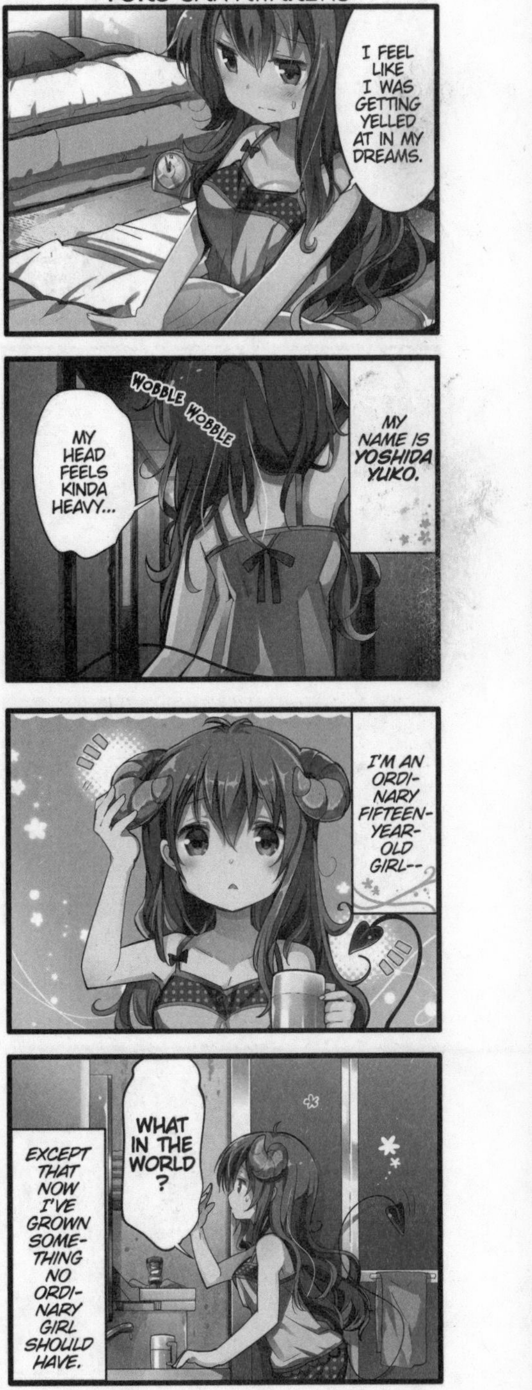
I FEEL LIKE I WAS GETTING YELLED AT IN MY DREAMS.
MY NAME IS YOSHIDA YUKO.
WOBBLE WOBBLE
MY HEAD FEELS KINDA HEAVY...
I'M AN ORDINARY FIFTEEN-YEAR-OLD GIRL--
WHAT IN THE WORLD ?
EXCEPT THAT NOW I'VE GROWN SOMETHING NO ORDINARY GIRL SHOULD HAVE.

LEARNING THROUGH EXPERIENCE

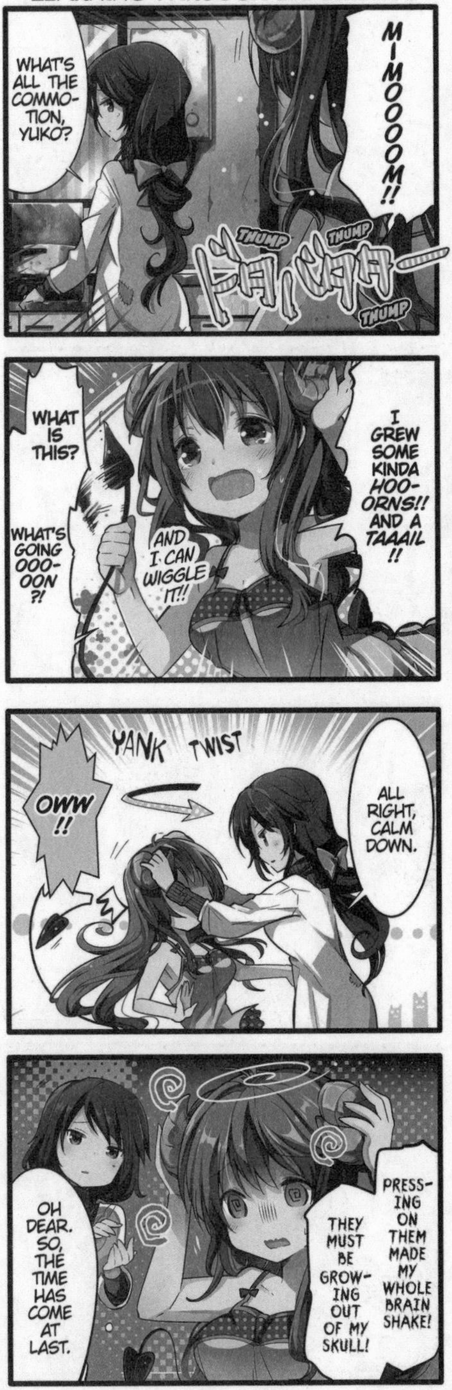
MIMOOOOOM!!
WHAT'S ALL THE COMMOTION, YUKO?
THUMP THUMP THUMP THUMP
I GREW SOME KINDA HOO-ORNS!! AND A TAAAIL!!
AND I CAN WIGGLE IT!!
WHAT IS THIS?
WHAT'S GOING OOOO-OON?!
ALL RIGHT, CALM DOWN.
YANK TWIST
OWW!!
PRESSING ON THEM MADE MY WHOLE BRAIN SHAKE!
THEY MUST BE GROWING OUT OF MY SKULL!
OH DEAR. SO, THE TIME HAS COME AT LAST.

THE YOSHIDA FAMILY SECRET REVEALED!

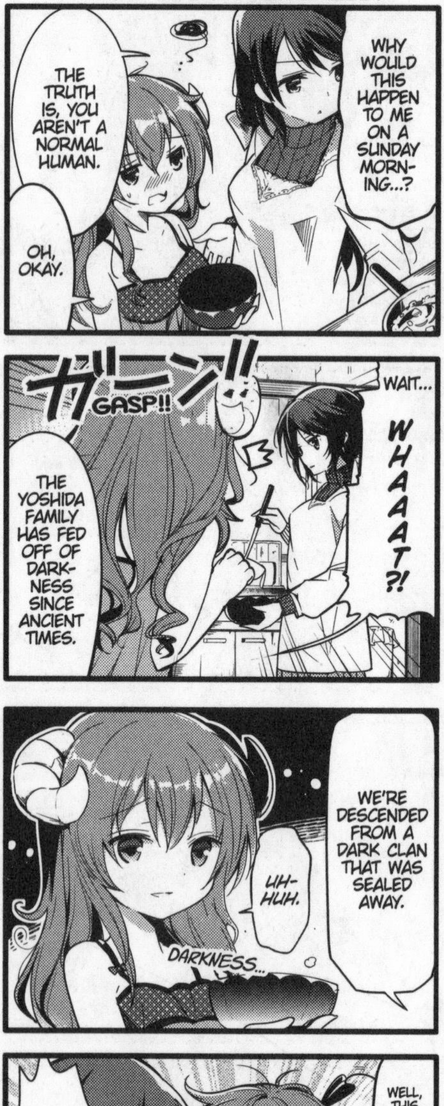
WHY WOULD THIS HAPPEN TO ME ON A SUNDAY MORNING...?
THE TRUTH IS, YOU AREN'T A NORMAL HUMAN.
OH, OKAY.
WAIT...
WHHAAAAT?!
ガーン!!
GASP!!
THE YOSHIDA FAMILY HAS FED OFF OF DARKNESS SINCE ANCIENT TIMES.
WE'RE DESCENDED FROM A DARK CLAN THAT WAS SEALED AWAY.
UH-HUH.
DARKNESS...
WELL, THIS JUST HAS TO BE A WEIRD DREAM.
I'LL GO BACK TO BED
FACE FACTS, CHILD!!
OW, MY BRAINS!!
ぐい
TUG

IT'S ALL THEIR FAULT

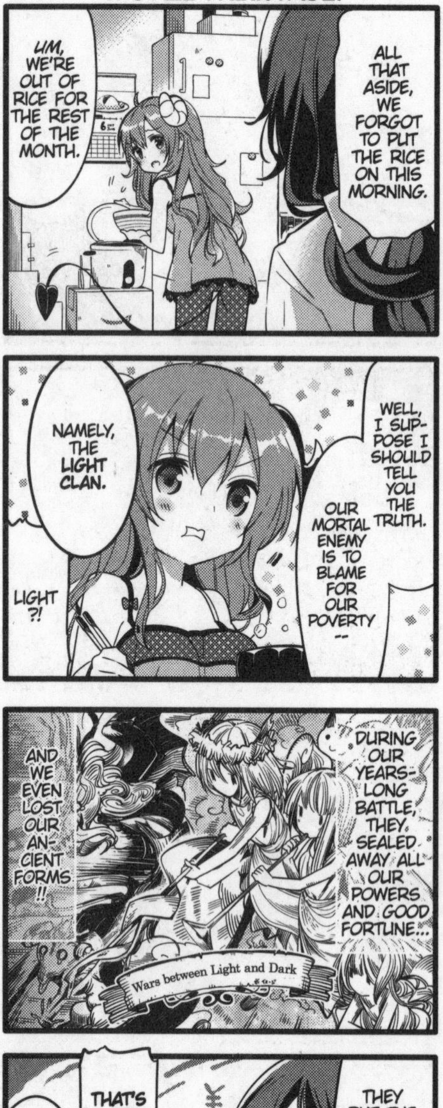
ALL THAT ASIDE, WE FORGOT TO PUT THE RICE ON THIS MORNING.
UM, WE'RE OUT OF RICE FOR THE REST OF THE MONTH.
WELL, I SUPPOSE I SHOULD TELL YOU THE TRUTH.
OUR MORTAL ENEMY IS TO BLAME FOR OUR POVERTY--
NAMELY, THE LIGHT CLAN.
LIGHT?!
DURING OUR YEARS-LONG BATTLE, THEY SEALED AWAY ALL OUR POWERS AND GOOD FORTUNE...
AND WE EVEN LOST OUR ANCIENT FORMS!!
Wars between Light and Dark
THEY PUT THE "FEEDING A FAMILY OF FOUR ON FORTY THOUSAND YEN A MONTH" CURSE ON US, TOO.
THEY TOOK EVERYTHING FROM US.
THAT'S SO SPECIFIC!!
¥
WELL, BY THAT POINT, WE HAD NOTHING ELSE LEFT FOR THEM TO SEAL AWAY.
MORE, PLEASE.

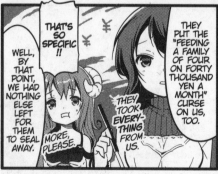

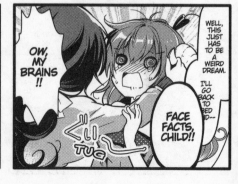

IT WON'T GET *THAT* MUCH BETTER

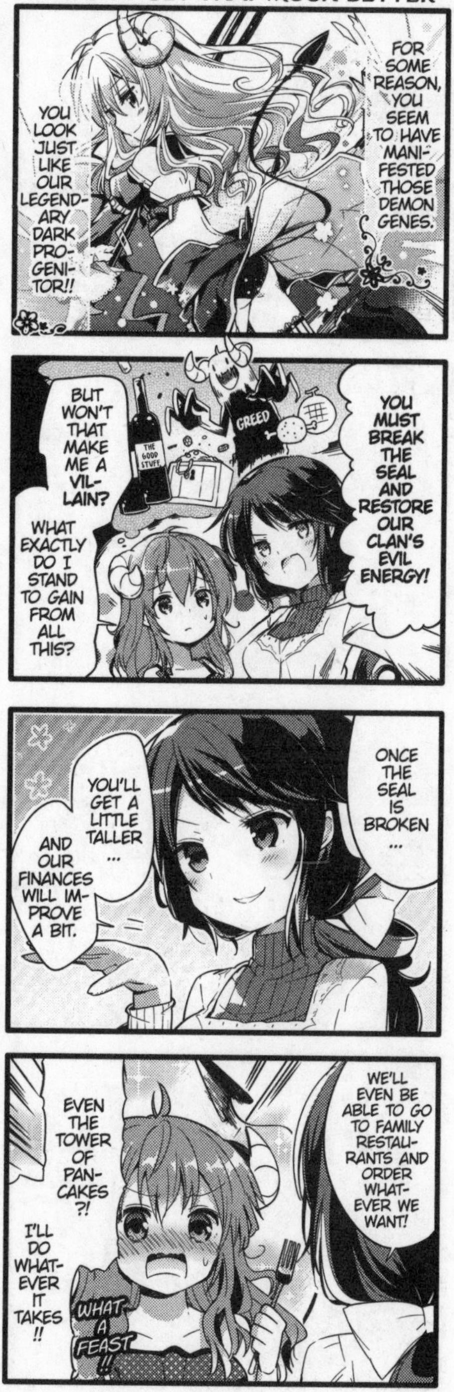
FOR SOME REASON, YOU SEEM TO HAVE MANIFESTED THOSE DEMON GENES.
YOU LOOK JUST LIKE OUR LEGENDARY DARK PROGENITOR!!
YOU MUST BREAK THE SEAL AND RESTORE OUR CLAN'S EVIL ENERGY!
GREED
THE GOOD STUFF
BUT WON'T THAT MAKE ME A VILLAIN?
WHAT EXACTLY DO I STAND TO GAIN FROM ALL THIS?
ONCE THE SEAL IS BROKEN ...
YOU'LL GET A LITTLE TALLER ...
AND OUR FINANCES WILL IMPROVE A BIT.
WE'LL EVEN BE ABLE TO GO TO FAMILY RESTAURANTS AND ORDER WHATEVER WE WANT!
EVEN THE TOWER OF PANCAKES?!
I'LL DO WHATEVER IT TAKES!!
WHAT A FEAST!!

THE YOSHIDA FAMILY'S ENEMY, REVEALED!

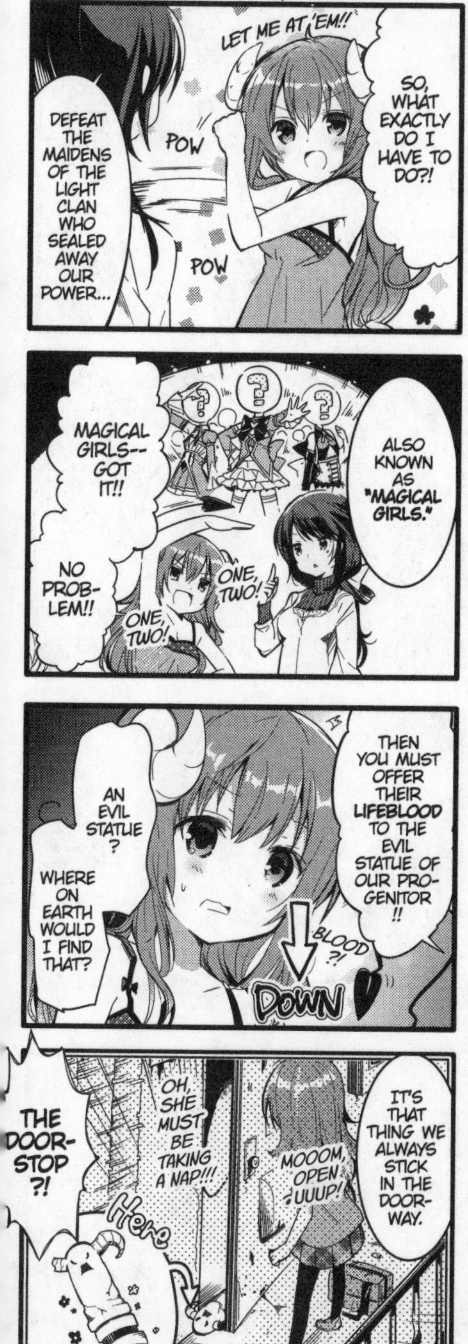
SO, WHAT EXACTLY DO I HAVE TO DO?!
LET ME AT 'EM!!
POW
POW
DEFEAT THE MAIDENS OF THE LIGHT CLAN WHO SEALED AWAY OUR POWER...
ALSO KNOWN AS "MAGICAL GIRLS."
ONE, TWO!
MAGICAL GIRLS--GOT IT!!
NO PROBLEM!!
ONE, TWO!
THEN YOU MUST OFFER THEIR LIFEBLOOD TO THE EVIL STATUE OF OUR PROGENITOR!!
BLOOD?!
DOWN
AN EVIL STATUE?
WHERE ON EARTH WOULD I FIND THAT?
IT'S THAT THING WE ALWAYS STICK IN THE DOORWAY.
MOOOM, OPEN UUUP!
OH, SHE MUST BE TAKING A NAP!!!
Here
THE DOORSTOP?!

THE QUEEN OF DARKNESS APPEARS!

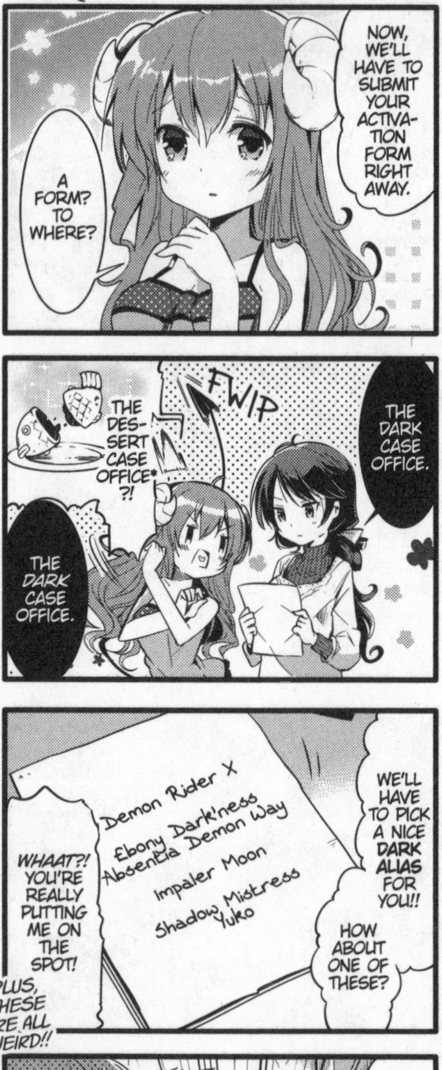
NOW, WE'LL HAVE TO SUBMIT YOUR ACTIVATION FORM RIGHT AWAY.
A FORM? TO WHERE?
FWIP
THE DARK CASE OFFICE.
THE DESSERT CASE OFFICE*?!
THE DARK CASE OFFICE.
WE'LL HAVE TO PICK A NICE DARK ALIAS FOR YOU!!
HOW ABOUT ONE OF THESE?
Demon Rider X
Ebony Dark'ness
Absentia Demon Way
Impaler Moon
Shadow Mistress Yuko
WHAAT?! YOU'RE REALLY PUTTING ME ON THE SPOT!
PLUS, THESE ARE ALL WEIRD!!
OKAY, WE'LL PUT DOWN "SHADOW MISTRESS YUKO (TEMP)."
TIME TO SEND THE FAX!
BREE
BREE
THIS IS HAPPENING WAY TOO FAST!!

SPD: -15, DEX: -8

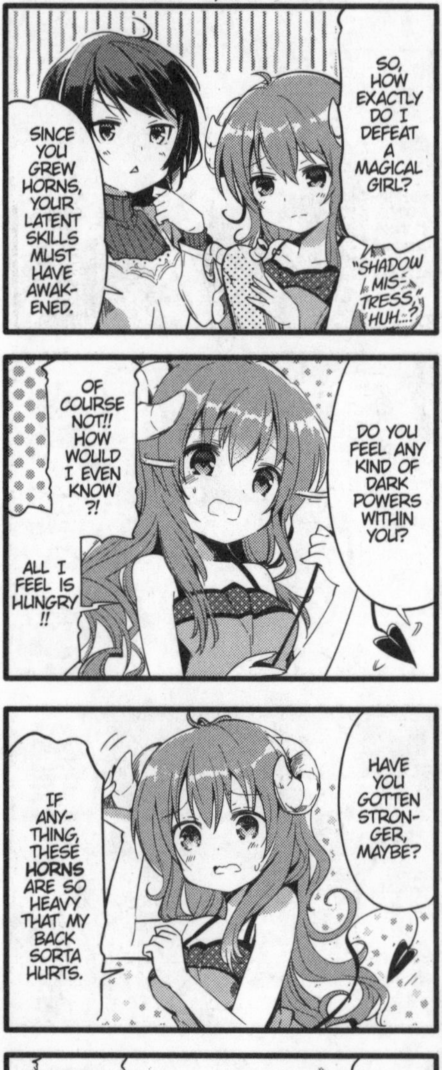
SO, HOW EXACTLY DO I DEFEAT A MAGICAL GIRL?
"SHADOW MISTRESS," HUH...?
SINCE YOU GREW HORNS, YOUR LATENT SKILLS MUST HAVE AWAKENED.
DO YOU FEEL ANY KIND OF DARK POWERS WITHIN YOU?
OF COURSE NOT!! HOW WOULD I EVEN KNOW?!
ALL I FEEL IS HUNGRY!!
HAVE YOU GOTTEN STRONGER, MAYBE?
IF ANYTHING, THESE HORNS ARE SO HEAVY THAT MY BACK SORTA HURTS.
I GUESS NOTHING'S CHANGED, THEN.
EXCEPT THAT MY CENTER OF GRAVITY'S BEEN THROWN OFF!!
I'VE GOTTEN WEAKER!!

*Mom says ankoku yakusho ("Darkness Office"), which Yuko misinterprets as anko kuyakusho ("Red Bean Paste Ward Office"), hence the picture of taiyaki (a dessert filled with red bean paste).

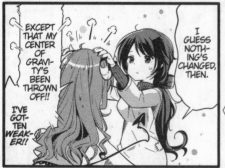

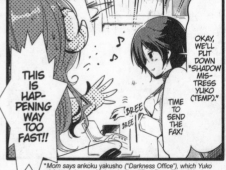

AROUND TOWN WITH THE EVIL STATUE

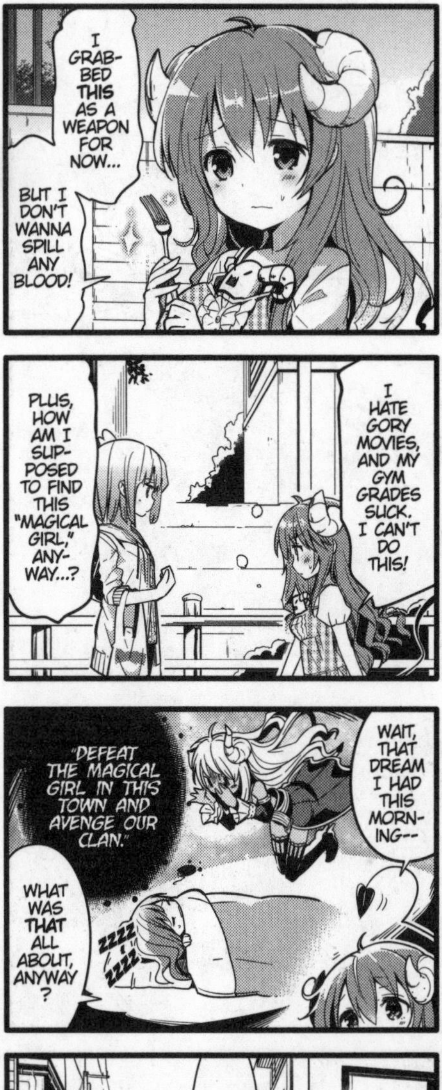
I GRABBED THIS AS A WEAPON FOR NOW...
BUT I DON'T WANNA SPILL ANY BLOOD!
I HATE GORY MOVIES, AND MY GYM GRADES SUCK. I CAN'T DO THIS!
PLUS, HOW AM I SUPPOSED TO FIND THIS "MAGICAL GIRL," ANYWAY...?
WAIT, THAT DREAM I HAD THIS MORNING--
"DEFEAT THE MAGICAL GIRL IN THIS TOWN AND AVENGE OUR CLAN."
ZZZZ ZZZZ
WHAT WAS THAT ALL ABOUT, ANYWAY?
"IN THIS TOWN"?
HORNS...?
SO, SHE'S AROUND HERE?

REFLEXES SEALED

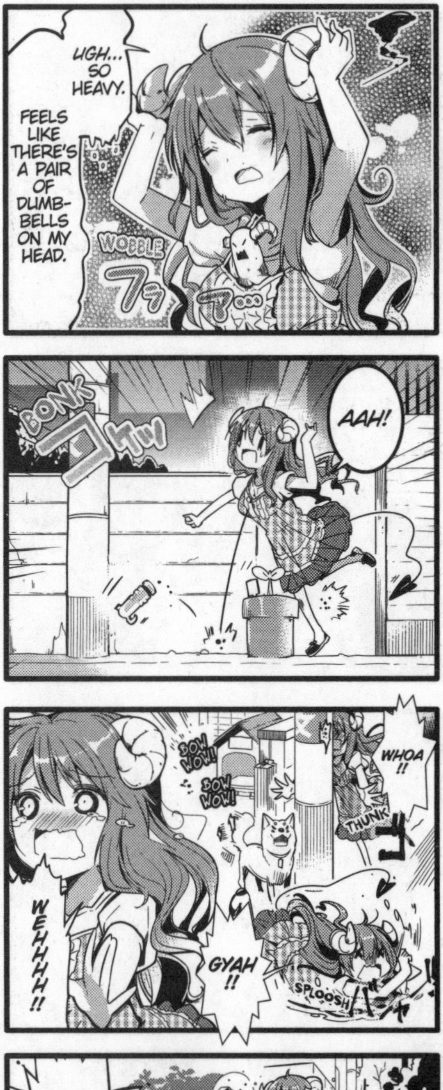
UGH... SO HEAVY.
FEELS LIKE THERE'S A PAIR OF DUMBBELLS ON MY HEAD.
WOBBLE
AAH!
BONK
WHOA!!
THUNK
BOW WOW!
BOW WOW!
WEHHHHH!!
GYAH!!
SPLOOSH
OH NO! MY SEALED-UP ANCESTOR!!
KA-THUNK
KA-THUNK
THUNK

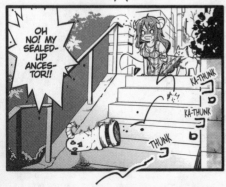

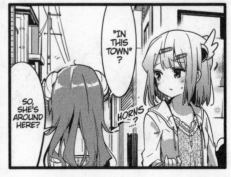

MOVEMENT ALSO SEALED

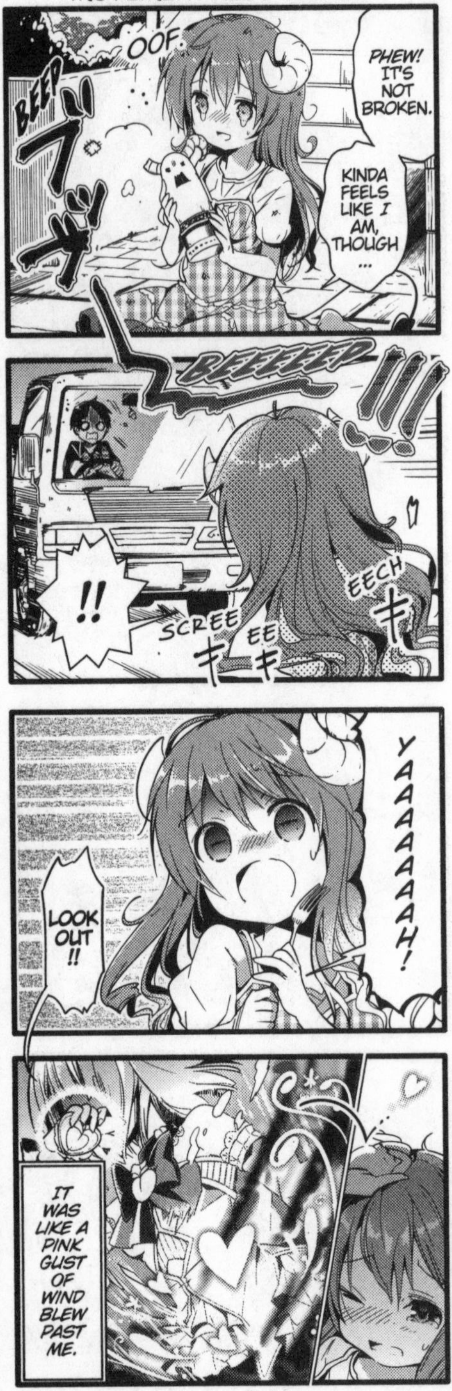
PHEW! IT'S NOT BROKEN.
OOF
BEEP
KINDA FEELS LIKE I AM, THOUGH ...
BEEEEEP!!!
!!
EECH
SCREE EE
YAAAAAAAAAH!
LOOK OUT!!
IT WAS LIKE A PINK GUST OF WIND BLEW PAST ME.

FIRST CONTACT

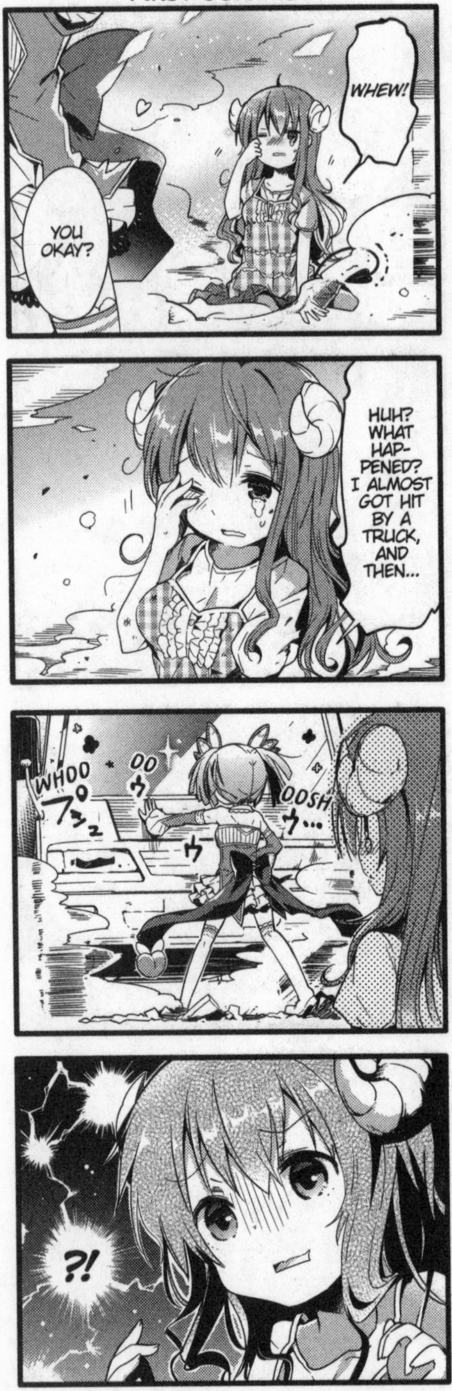
WHEW!
YOU OKAY?
HUH? WHAT HAP-PENED? I ALMOST GOT HIT BY A TRUCK, AND THEN...
OOSH
OO
WHOO
?!

UNNATURALLY FRILLY PERSON

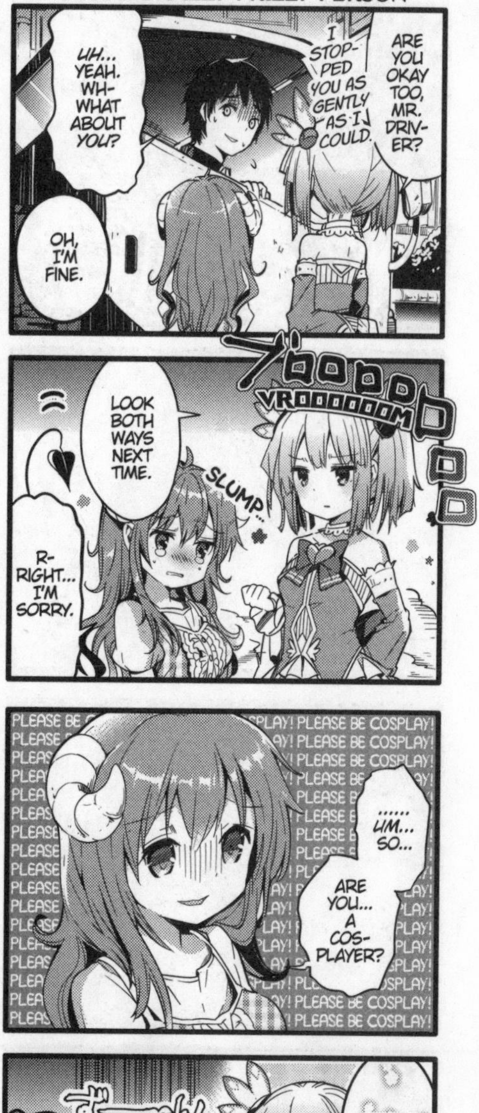
ARE YOU OKAY TOO, MR. DRIVER?
I STOP-PED YOU AS GENTLY AS I COULD.
UH... YEAH. WH-WHAT ABOUT YOU?
OH, I'M FINE.
VROOOOOOOM
LOOK BOTH WAYS NEXT TIME.
SLUMP...
R-RIGHT... I'M SORRY.
PLEASE BE COSPLAY!
...... UM... SO...
ARE YOU... A COS-PLAYER?
NOPE. MAGICAL GIRL.
NOOOOO!
OF COURSE. YOU DID STOP A DUMP TRUCK WITH ONE HAND.
NO KIDDING.

PREPARE YOUR WEAPON

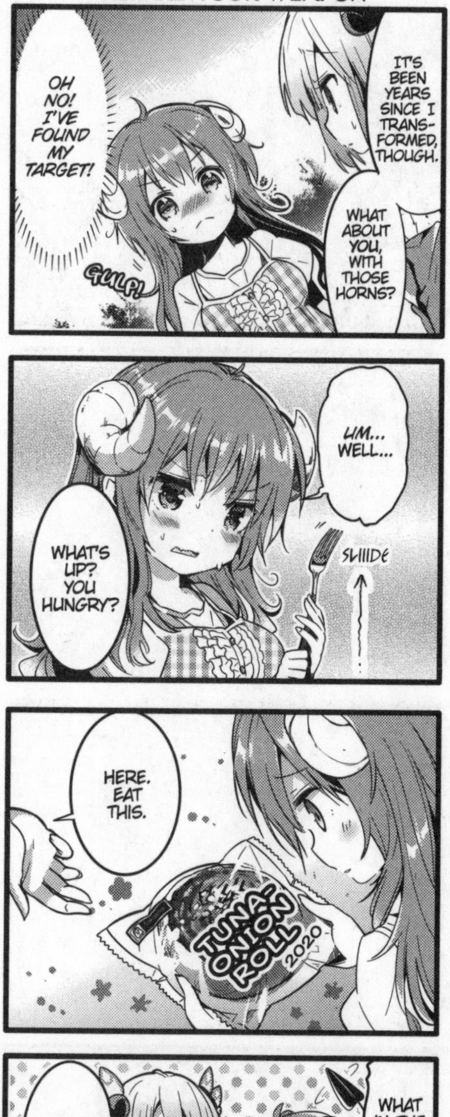
IT'S BEEN YEARS SINCE I TRANS-FORMED, THOUGH.
WHAT ABOUT YOU, WITH THOSE HORNS?
OH NO! I'VE FOUND MY TARGET!
GULP!
UM... WELL...
WHAT'S UP? YOU HUNGRY?
SLIIIDE
HERE. EAT THIS.
TUNA-ONION ROLL 2020
WHAT IN THE WORLD IS THIS?
IT'S A PASTRY.
I DON'T GET IT.

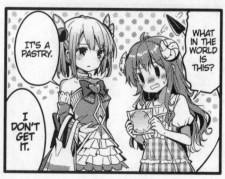

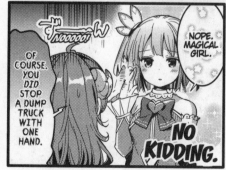

NATURAL-BORN GIVER

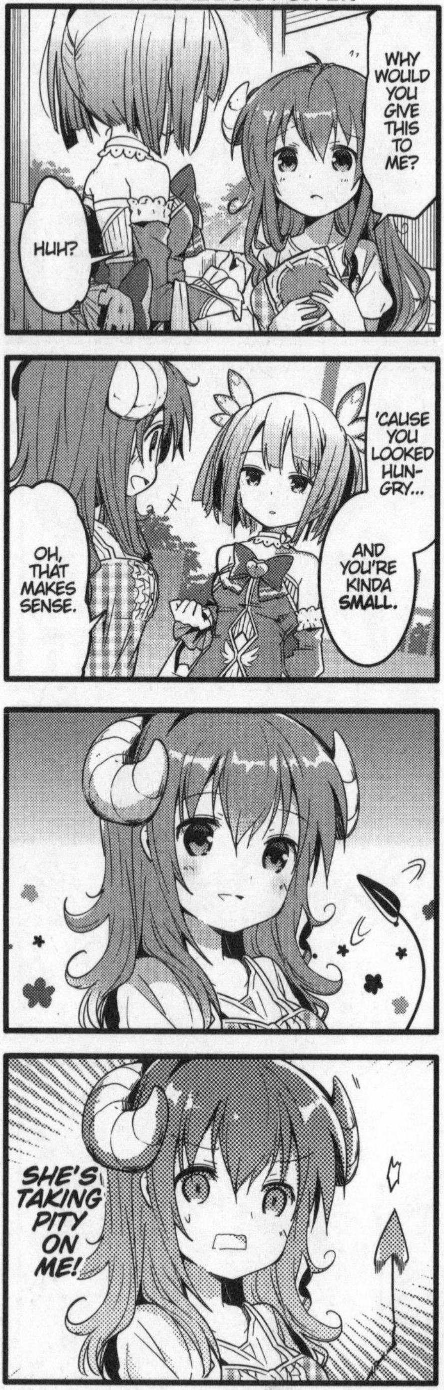
WHY WOULD YOU GIVE THIS TO ME?
HUH?
'CAUSE YOU LOOKED HUN-GRY...
AND YOU'RE KINDA **SMALL.**
OH, THAT MAKES SENSE.
SHE'S TAKING PITY ON ME!

FAILURE TASTES LIKE SNACKS

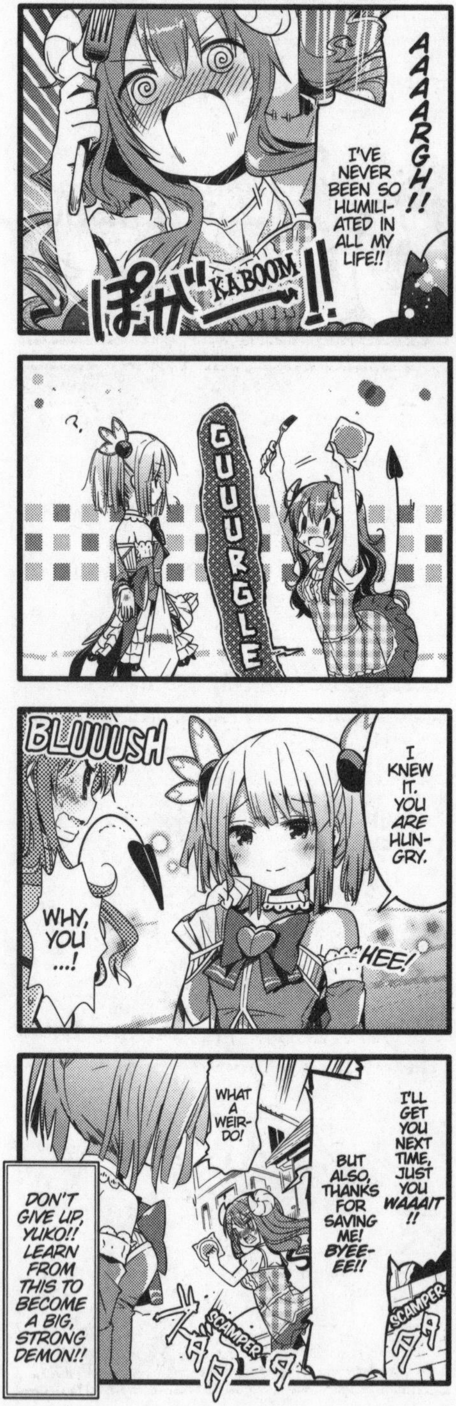
AAAAARGH!!
I'VE NEVER BEEN SO HUMILI-ATED IN ALL MY LIFE!!
ぽがー KA BOOM !!
GUUURGLE
BLUUUSH
I KNEW IT. YOU *ARE* HUN-GRY.
HEE!
WHY, YOU ...!
I'LL GET YOU NEXT TIME, JUST YOU *WAAAIT*!!
BUT ALSO, THANKS FOR SAVING ME! BYEEE-EE!!
WHAT A WEIR-DO!
SCAMPER
SCAMPER
DON'T GIVE UP, YUKO!! LEARN FROM THIS TO BECOME A BIG, STRONG DEMON!!

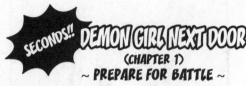

SECONDS!! DEMON GIRL NEXT DOOR
(CHAPTER 1)
~ PREPARE FOR BATTLE ~

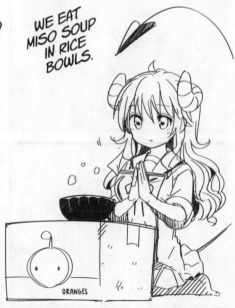

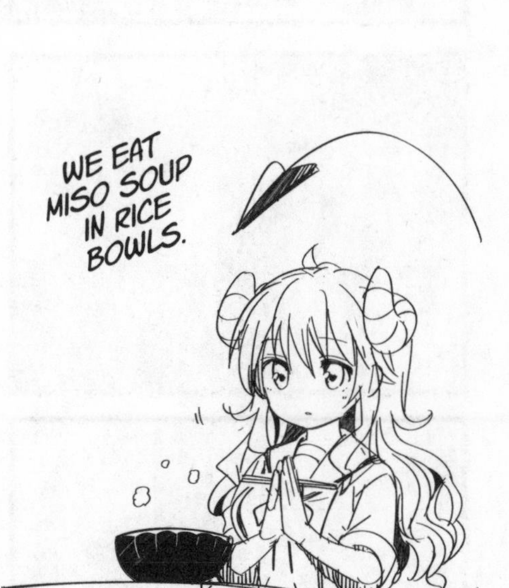
WE EAT MISO SOUP IN RICE BOWLS.
ORANGES

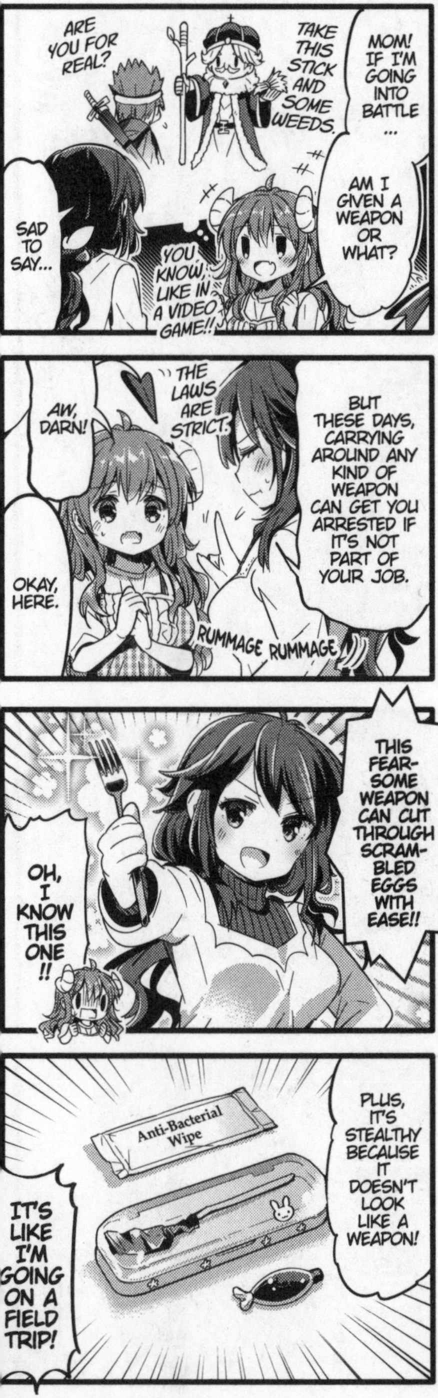
MOM! IF I'M GOING INTO BATTLE ...
AM I GIVEN A WEAPON OR WHAT?
TAKE THIS STICK AND SOME WEEDS.
ARE YOU FOR REAL?
YOU KNOW, LIKE IN A VIDEO GAME!!
SAD TO SAY...
BUT THESE DAYS, CARRYING AROUND ANY KIND OF WEAPON CAN GET YOU ARRESTED IF IT'S NOT PART OF YOUR JOB.
THE LAWS ARE STRICT.
AW, DARN!
OKAY, HERE.
RUMMAGE RUMMAGE
THIS FEARSOME WEAPON CAN CUT THROUGH SCRAMBLED EGGS WITH EASE!!
OH, I KNOW THIS ONE !!
PLUS, IT'S STEALTHY BECAUSE IT DOESN'T LOOK LIKE A WEAPON!
Anti-Bacterial Wipe
IT'S LIKE I'M GOING ON A FIELD TRIP!

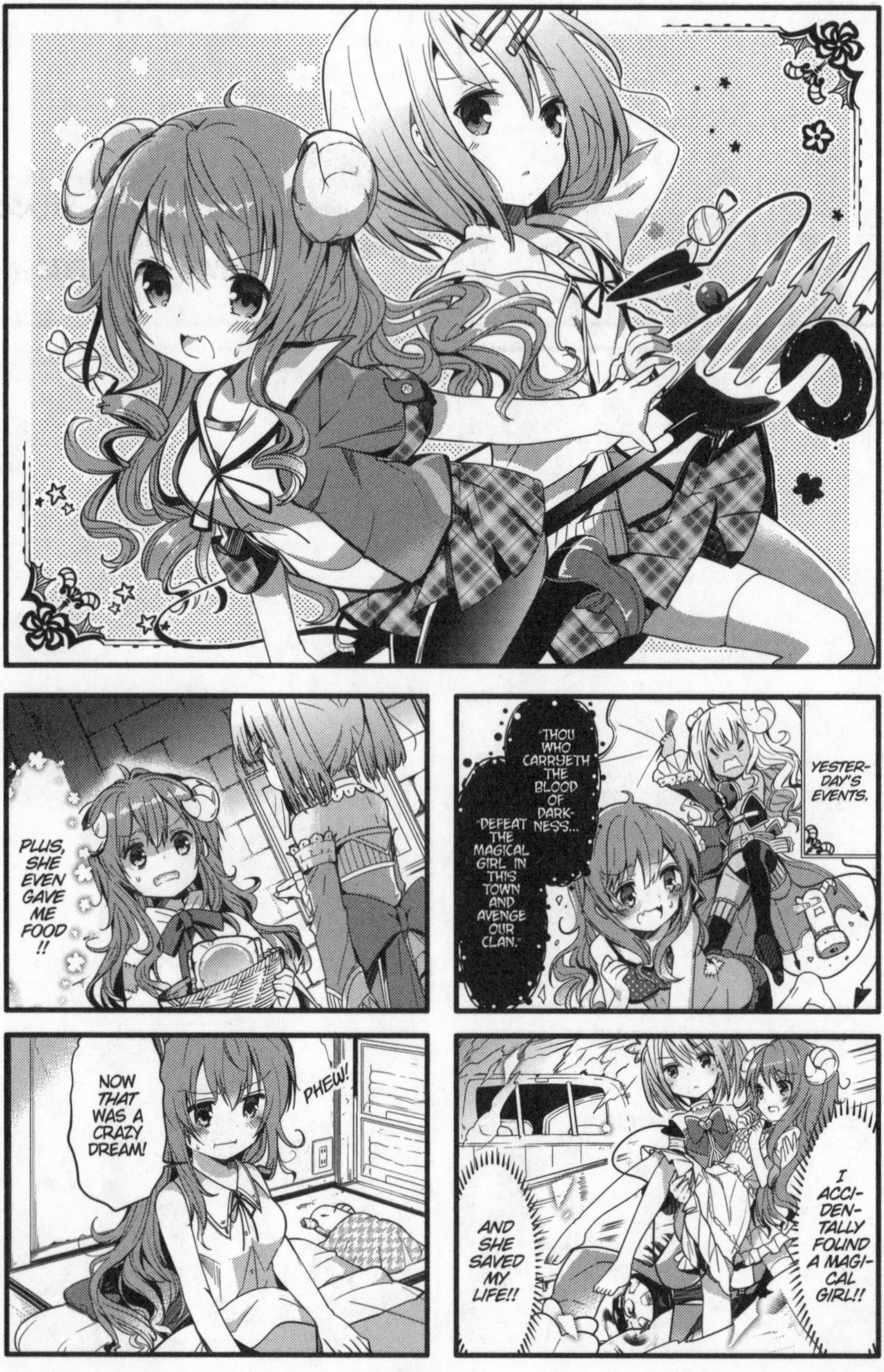

YESTERDAY'S EVENTS.
"THOU WHO CARRYETH THE BLOOD OF DARKNESS...
"DEFEAT THE MAGICAL GIRL IN THIS TOWN AND AVENGE OUR CLAN."
I ACCIDENTALLY FOUND A MAGICAL GIRL!!
AND SHE SAVED MY LIFE!!
PLUS, SHE EVEN GAVE ME FOOD!!
PHEW!
NOW THAT WAS A CRAZY DREAM!

YOU CAN SEE THEM, TOO?

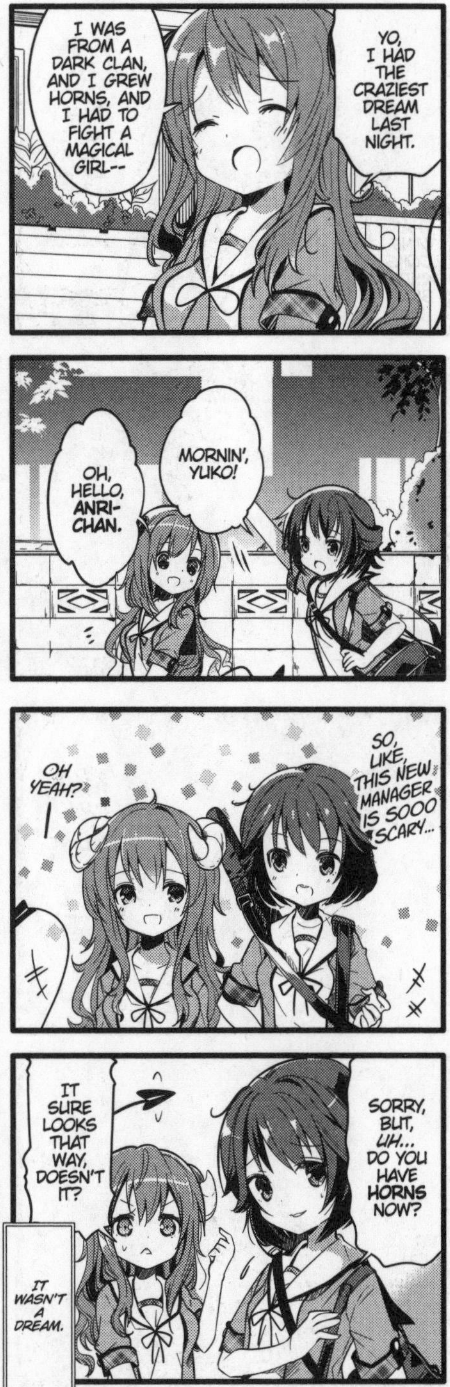
YO, I HAD THE CRAZIEST DREAM LAST NIGHT.
I WAS FROM A DARK CLAN, AND I GREW HORNS, AND I HAD TO FIGHT A MAGICAL GIRL--
MORNIN', YUKO!
OH, HELLO, ANRI-CHAN.
SO, LIKE, THIS NEW MANAGER IS SOOO SCARY...
OH YEAH?
SORRY, BUT, UH... DO YOU HAVE HORNS NOW?
IT SURE LOOKS THAT WAY, DOESN'T IT?
IT WASN'T A DREAM.

TOWN SECRET

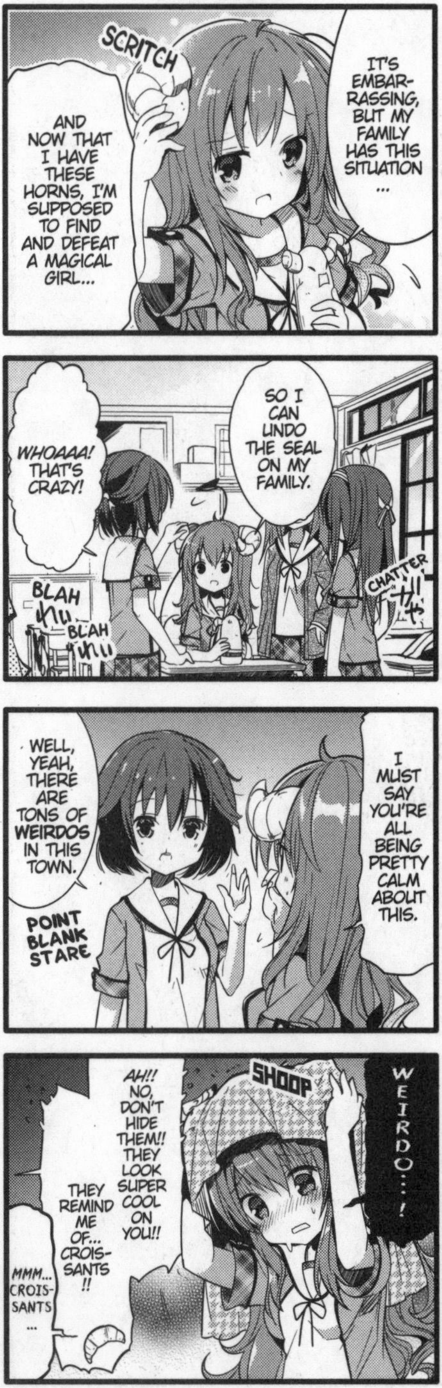
IT'S EMBAR-RASSING, BUT MY FAMILY HAS THIS SITUATION ...
SCRITCH
AND NOW THAT I HAVE THESE HORNS, I'M SUPPOSED TO FIND AND DEFEAT A MAGICAL GIRL...
SO I CAN UNDO THE SEAL ON MY FAMILY.
CHATTER
WHOAAA! THAT'S CRAZY!
BLAH
BLAH
I MUST SAY YOU'RE ALL BEING PRETTY CALM ABOUT THIS.
WELL, YEAH, THERE ARE TONS OF WEIRDOS IN THIS TOWN.
POINT BLANK STARE
WEIRDO...!
SHOOP
AH!! NO, DON'T HIDE THEM!! THEY LOOK SUPER COOL ON YOU!!
THEY REMIND ME OF... CROIS-SANTS !!
MMM... CROIS-SANTS ...

LEARNING THROUGH EXPERIENCE, PART 2

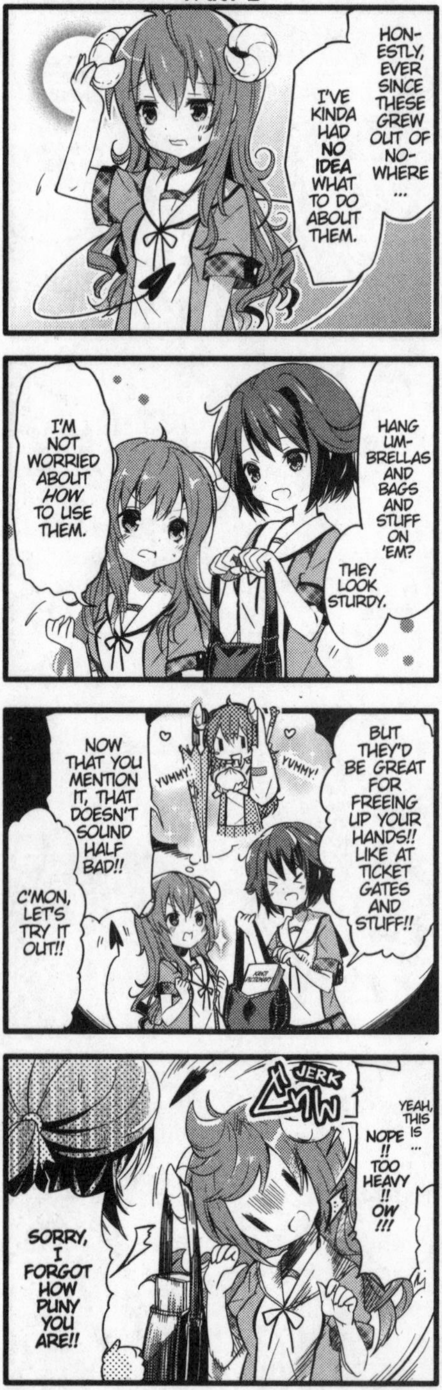
HONESTLY, EVER SINCE THESE GREW OUT OF NOWHERE...
I'VE KINDA HAD **NO IDEA** WHAT TO DO ABOUT THEM.
HANG UMBRELLAS AND BAGS AND STUFF ON 'EM?
THEY LOOK STURDY.
I'M NOT WORRIED ABOUT *HOW* TO USE THEM.
BUT THEY'D BE GREAT FOR FREEING UP YOUR HANDS!! LIKE AT TICKET GATES AND STUFF!!
YUMMY!
YUMMY!
NOW THAT YOU MENTION IT, THAT DOESN'T SOUND HALF BAD!!
C'MON, LET'S TRY IT OUT!!
YEAH, THIS IS ...
NOPE!! TOO HEAVY!! OW!!!
JERK
SORRY, I FORGOT HOW PUNY YOU ARE!!

FOUND IN SECONDS

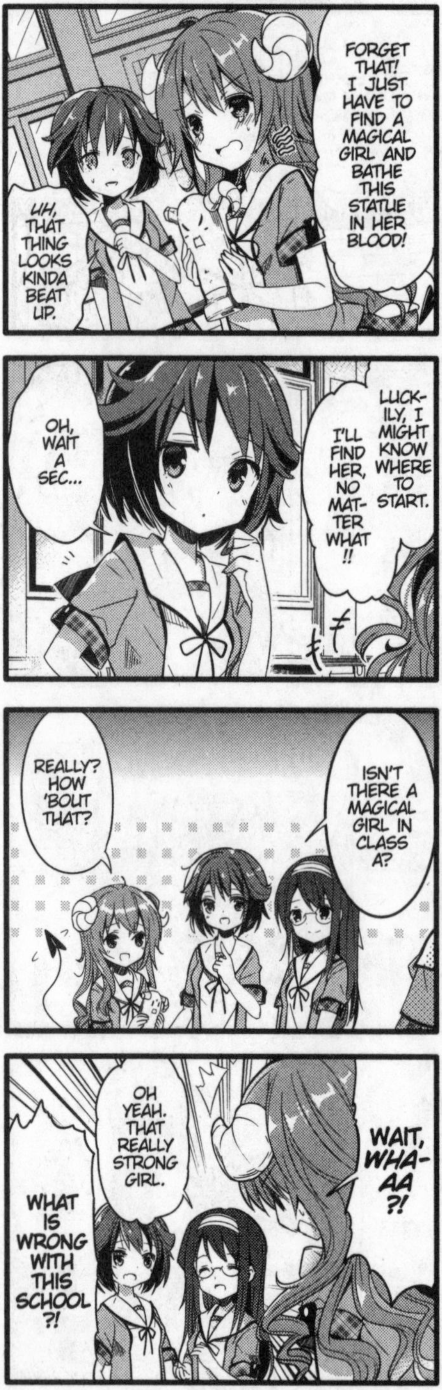
FORGET THAT! I JUST HAVE TO FIND A MAGICAL GIRL AND BATHE THIS STATUE IN HER BLOOD!
UH, THAT THING LOOKS KINDA BEAT UP.
LUCKILY, I MIGHT KNOW WHERE TO START.
I'LL FIND HER, NO MATTER WHAT!!
OH, WAIT A SEC...
ISN'T THERE A MAGICAL GIRL IN CLASS A?
REALLY? HOW 'BOUT THAT?
WAIT, WHAAA?!
OH YEAH. THAT REALLY STRONG GIRL.
WHAT IS WRONG WITH THIS SCHOOL?!

DUMP TRUCK GIRL

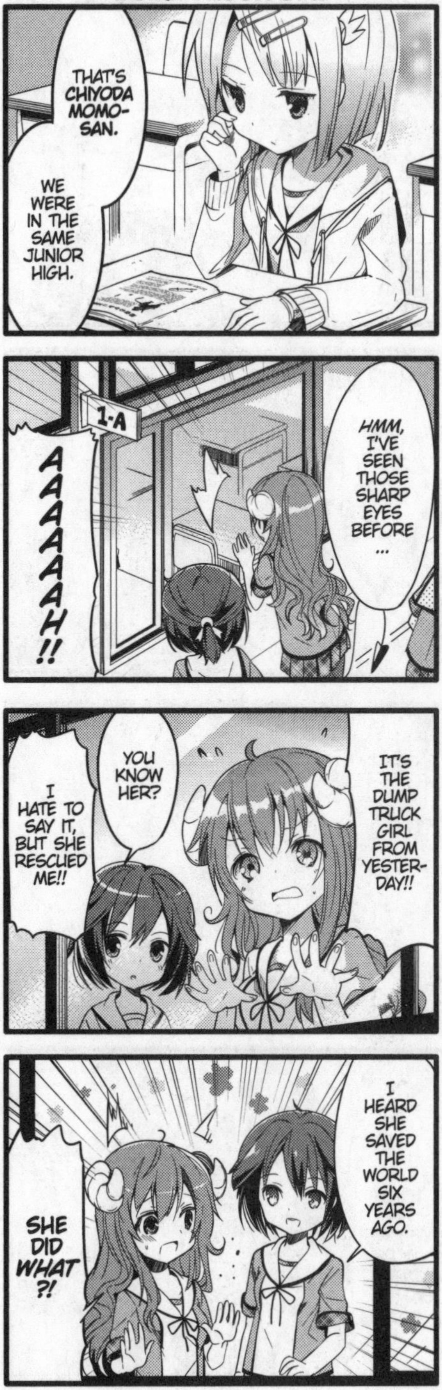
THAT'S CHIYODA MOMO-SAN.
WE WERE IN THE SAME JUNIOR HIGH.
HMM, I'VE SEEN THOSE SHARP EYES BEFORE ...
1-A
AAAAAAAH!!
IT'S THE DUMP TRUCK GIRL FROM YESTER-DAY!!
YOU KNOW HER?
I HATE TO SAY IT, BUT SHE RESCUED ME!!
I HEARD SHE SAVED THE WORLD SIX YEARS AGO.
SHE DID WHAT?!

SHE HAD TO USE THREE OF THEM

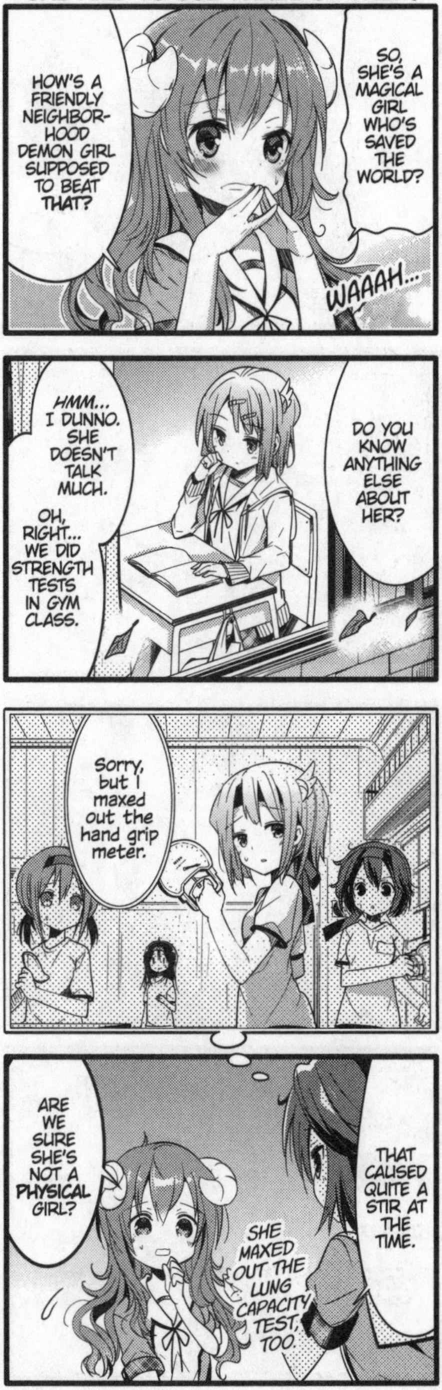
SO, SHE'S A MAGICAL GIRL WHO'S SAVED THE WORLD?
HOW'S A FRIENDLY NEIGHBOR-HOOD DEMON GIRL SUPPOSED TO BEAT THAT?
WAAAH...
DO YOU KNOW ANYTHING ELSE ABOUT HER?
HMM... I DUNNO. SHE DOESN'T TALK MUCH.
OH, RIGHT... WE DID STRENGTH TESTS IN GYM CLASS.
Sorry, but I maxed out the hand grip meter.
THAT CAUSED QUITE A STIR AT THE TIME.
SHE MAXED OUT THE LUNG CAPACITY TEST, TOO.
ARE WE SURE SHE'S NOT A PHYSICAL GIRL?

WITHOUT A PADDLE

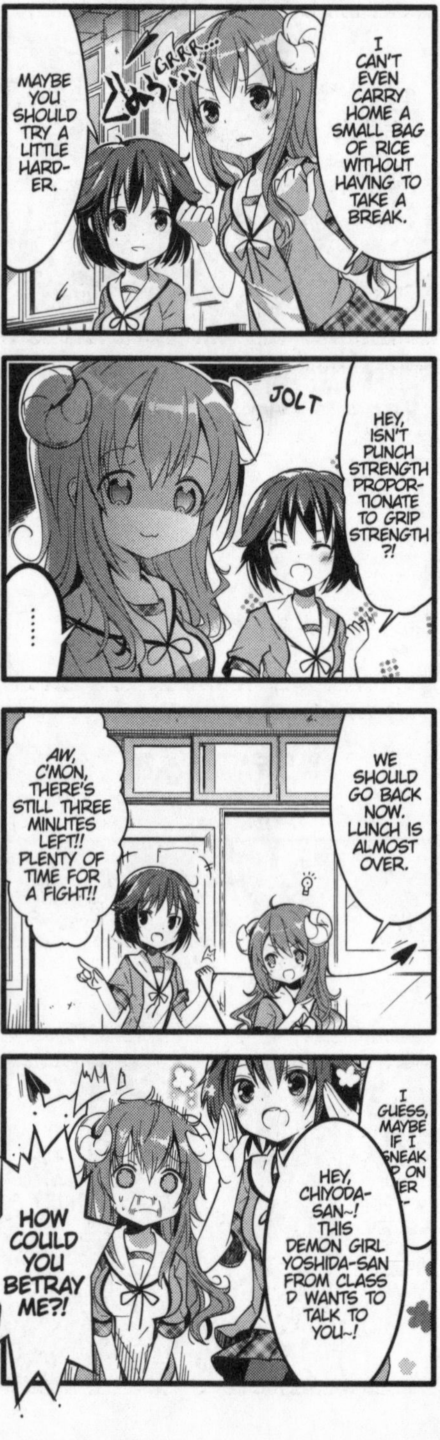
I CAN'T EVEN CARRY HOME A SMALL BAG OF RICE WITHOUT HAVING TO TAKE A BREAK.
GRRR...
MAYBE YOU SHOULD TRY A LITTLE HARDER.
HEY, ISN'T PUNCH STRENGTH PROPORTIONATE TO GRIP STRENGTH?!
JOLT
......
WE SHOULD GO BACK NOW. LUNCH IS ALMOST OVER.
AW, C'MON, THERE'S STILL THREE MINUTES LEFT!! PLENTY OF TIME FOR A FIGHT!!
I GUESS, MAYBE IF I
HEY, CHIYODA-SAN~! THIS DEMON GIRL YOSHIDA-SAN FROM CLASS D WANTS TO TALK TO YOU~!
HOW COULD YOU BETRAY ME?!

WHAT DO YOU MEAN, SMALL?!

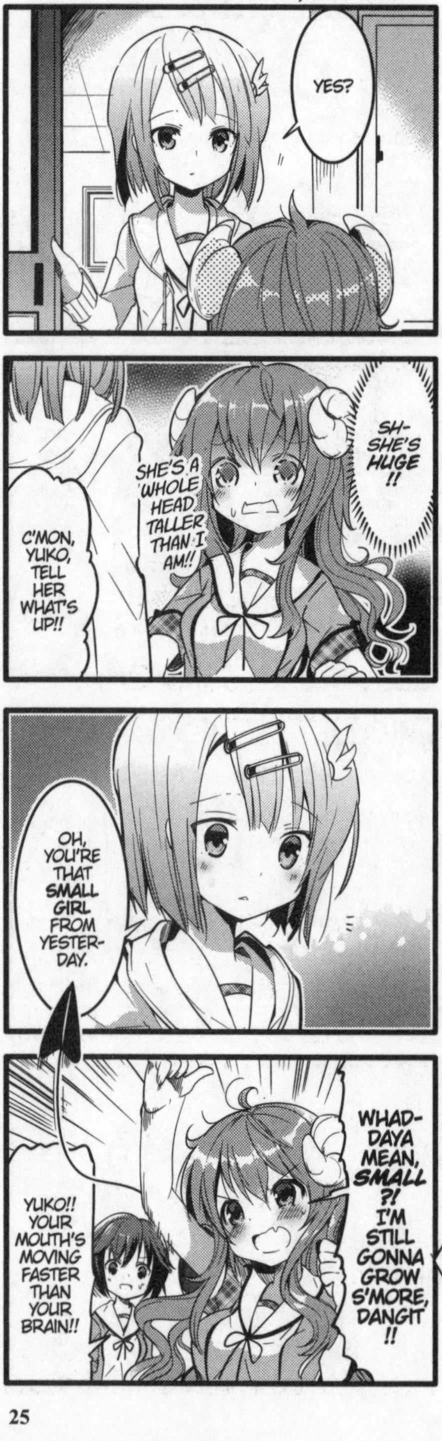
YES?
SH-SHE'S HUGE!!
SHE'S A WHOLE HEAD TALLER THAN I AM!!
C'MON, YUKO, TELL HER WHAT'S UP!!
OH, YOU'RE THAT SMALL GIRL FROM YESTERDAY.
WHADDAYA MEAN, SMALL?! I'M STILL GONNA GROW S'MORE, DANGIT!!
YUKO!! YOUR MOUTH'S MOVING FASTER THAN YOUR BRAIN!!

SHAMIKO

SORRY. I DIDN'T MEAN ANY HARM, REALLY. YOU JUST LOOK SO SMALL TO ME.
AAARGH
PICKING A FIGHT, HUH?! WELL, I'M RARING TO GO NOW!!
I AM SHAMI-- I MEAN, SHADOW MISTRESS YUKO!!
OKAY.
OKAY.
I'VE COME TO RESTORE MY SEALED CLAN AND WIN WORLD DENOM... DOMINATION... (WHEEZE) BY DEFEATING A MAGICAL GIRL !!
O... KAY.
SO... THERE YOU HAVE IT.
OUT OF FUEL.
OKAY, GOT IT.
UM, YOU MESSED UP YOUR SPEECH A COUPLA TIMES.
ONLY 'CAUSE YOUR INTERRUPTIONS KEPT THROWING ME OFF!!
WANNA TRY IT AGAIN?

DIDN'T WARM UP ENOUGH

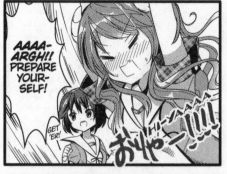

HI-YAAAA--!!!!
おりゃー
AAAA-ARGH!! PREPARE YOURSELF!
GET 'ER!
PAFF PAFF PAFF PAFF PAFF PAFF PAFF PAFF PAFF PAFF (Haa) PAFF PAFF PAFF
PAFF PAFF...PA... FF...
MY... MY SIDES HURT...
AND MY WRISTS.
WHEEZE
WHEEZE
YOU'RE EVEN MORE FRAGILE THAN I THOUGHT !!

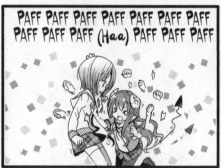

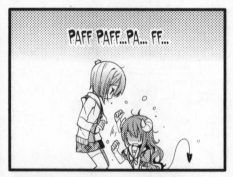

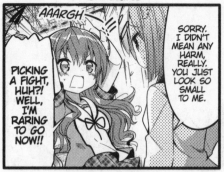

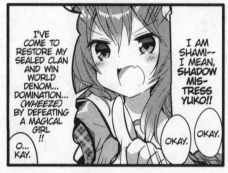

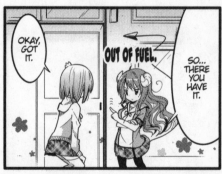

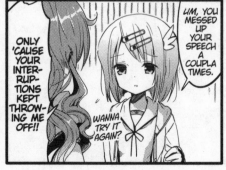

CAN'T HELP THROWING HER A BONE

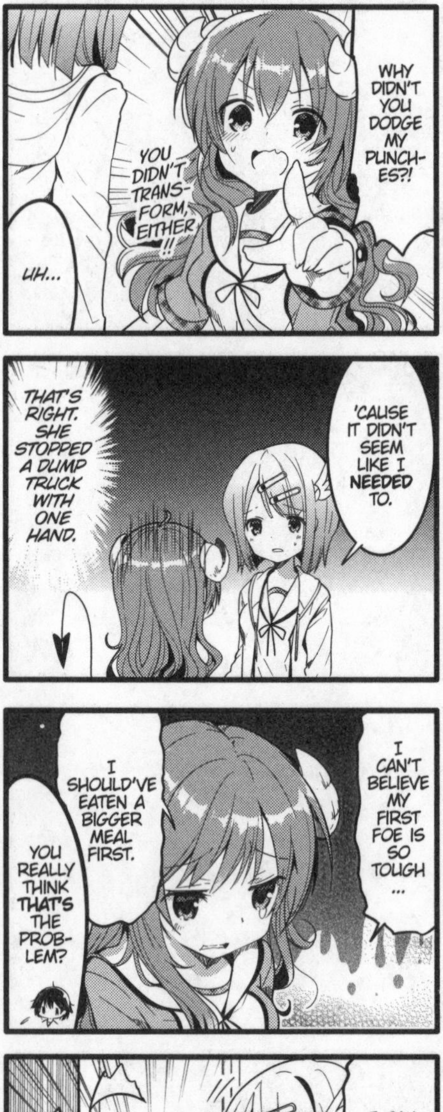
WHY DIDN'T YOU DODGE MY PUNCHES?!
YOU DIDN'T TRANSFORM, EITHER!!
UH...
'CAUSE IT DIDN'T SEEM LIKE I NEEDED TO.
THAT'S RIGHT. SHE STOPPED A DUMP TRUCK WITH ONE HAND.
I CAN'T BELIEVE MY FIRST FOE IS SO TOUGH ...
I SHOULD'VE EATEN A BIGGER MEAL FIRST.
YOU REALLY THINK THAT'S THE PROBLEM?
I CAN GIVE YOU A PASTRY--
CLATTER
NO!! IF YOU PITY ME ANY MORE, I'M GONNA CRY!!

FIRST APOLOGY

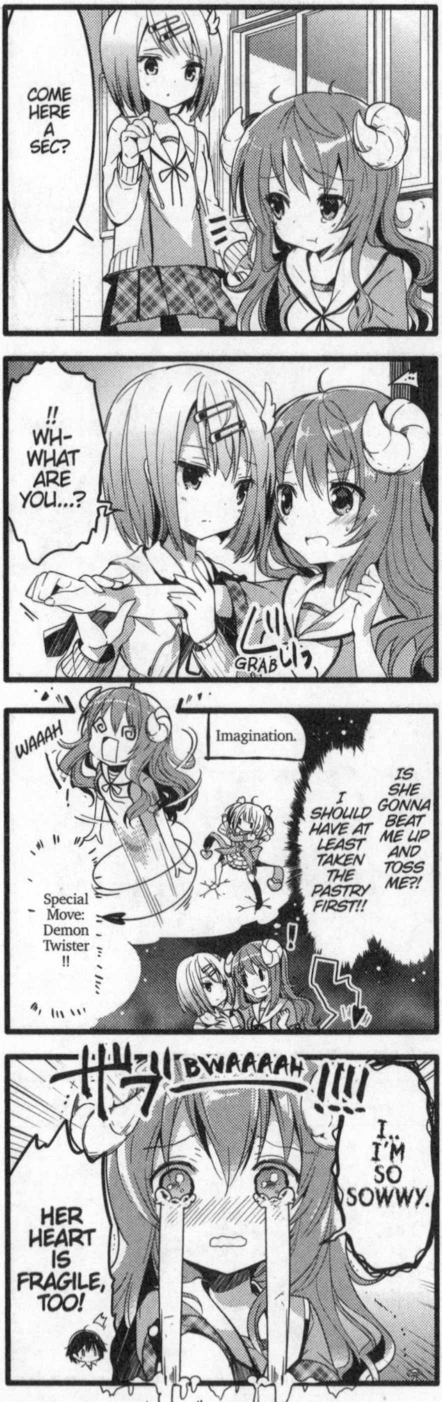
COME HERE A SEC?
!! WH-WHAT ARE YOU...?
GRAB
Imagination.
IS SHE GONNA BEAT ME UP AND TOSS ME?!
I SHOULD HAVE AT LEAST TAKEN THE PASTRY FIRST!!
WAAAH
Special Move: Demon Twister !!
BWAAAAAH !!!!
I... I'M SO SOWWY.
HER HEART IS FRAGILE, TOO!

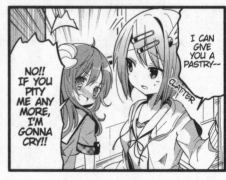

MAGICAL GIRL PUNCHING CLASS: THE BASICS

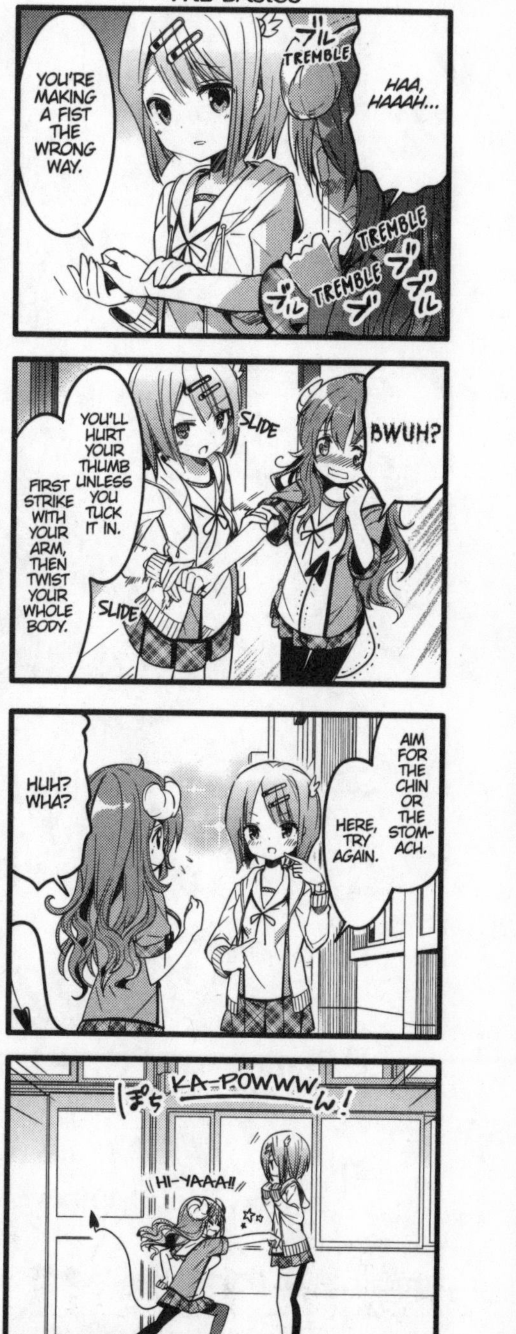
HAA, HAAAH...
TREMBLE
YOU'RE MAKING A FIST THE WRONG WAY.
TREMBLE TREMBLE
BWUH?
YOU'LL HURT YOUR THUMB UNLESS YOU TUCK IT IN.
SLIDE
FIRST STRIKE WITH YOUR ARM, THEN TWIST YOUR WHOLE BODY.
SLIDE
AIM FOR THE CHIN OR THE STOMACH.
HERE, TRY AGAIN.
HUH? WHA?
ぽち KA-POWWWん!
HI-YAAA!!

SHE CAN'T SAY, "YOU SUCK"

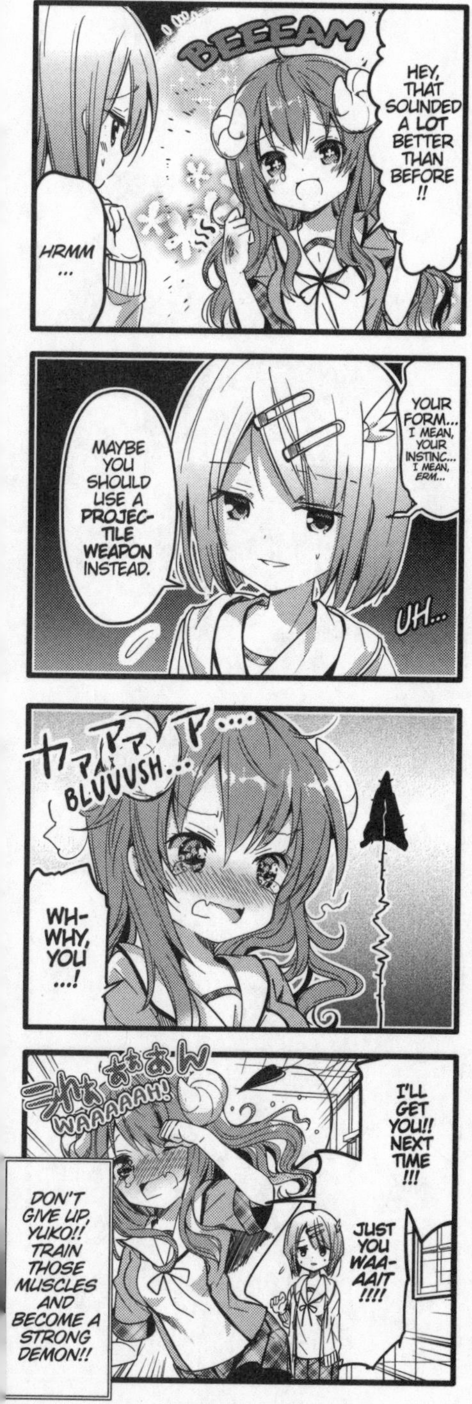
HEY, THAT SOUNDED A LOT BETTER THAN BEFORE!!
BEEEAM
HRMM...
YOUR FORM... I MEAN, YOUR INSTINC... I MEAN, ERM...
MAYBE YOU SHOULD USE A PROJECTILE WEAPON INSTEAD.
UH...
BLUUUSH...
WH-WHY, YOU...!
I'LL GET YOU!! NEXT TIME!!!
JUST YOU WAAAAIT!!!!
WAAAAAH!
DON'T GIVE UP, YUKO!! TRAIN THOSE MUSCLES AND BECOME A STRONG DEMON!!

The Demon Girl Next Door

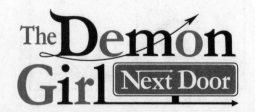

The Demon Girl Next Door

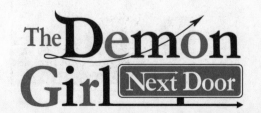

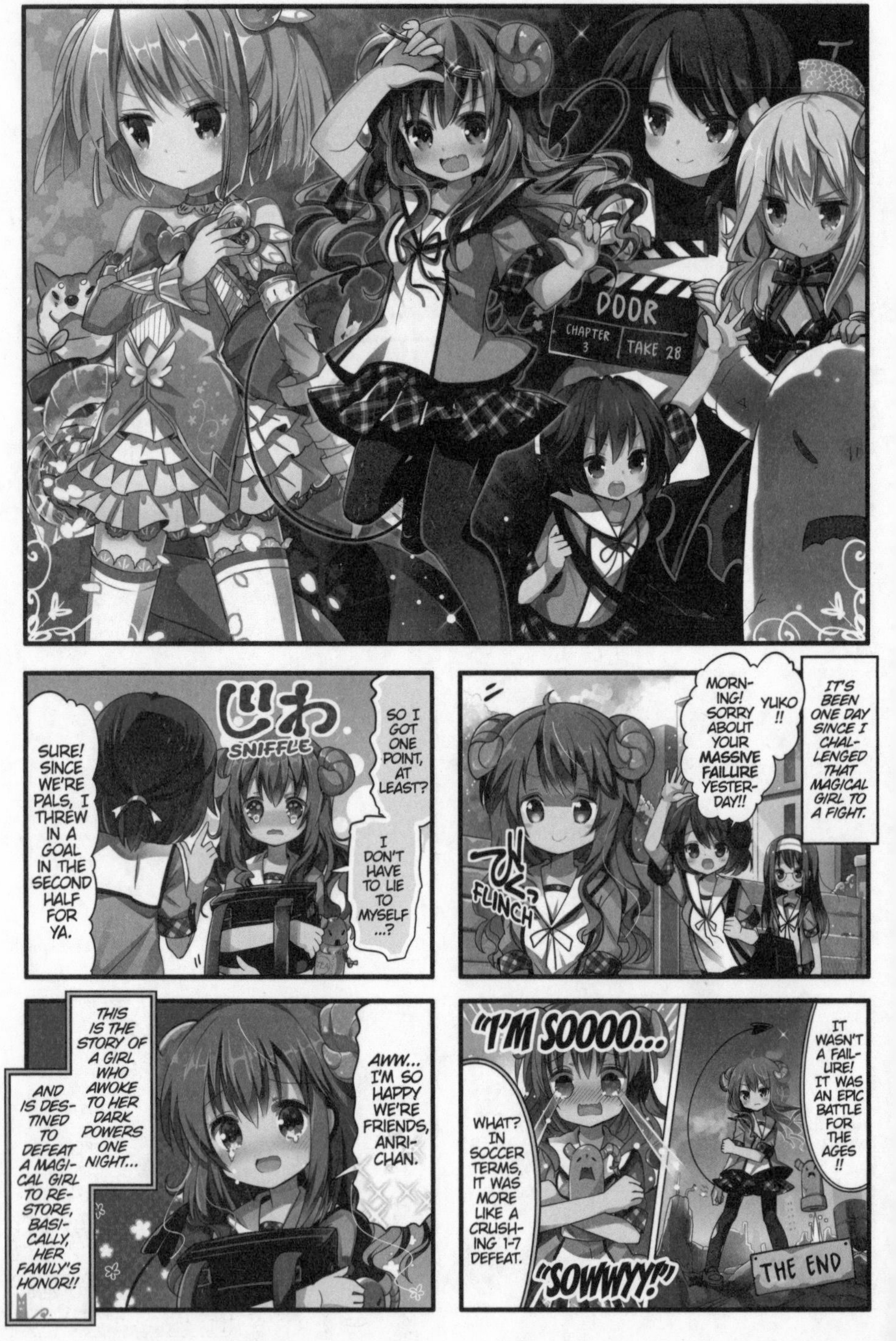
DOOR
CHAPTER 3
TAKE 28
IT'S BEEN ONE DAY SINCE I CHALLENGED THAT MAGICAL GIRL TO A FIGHT.
YUKO!!
MORNING! SORRY ABOUT YOUR MASSIVE FAILURE YESTERDAY!!
FLINCH
SO I GOT ONE POINT, AT LEAST?
I DON'T HAVE TO LIE TO MYSELF ...?
じわ
SNIFFLE
SURE! SINCE WE'RE PALS, I THREW IN A GOAL IN THE SECOND HALF FOR YA.
IT WASN'T A FAILURE! IT WAS AN EPIC BATTLE FOR THE AGES!!
WHAT? IN SOCCER TERMS, IT WAS MORE LIKE A CRUSHING 1-7 DEFEAT.
"I'M SOOOO..."
"SOWWYY!"
THE END
AWW... I'M SO HAPPY WE'RE FRIENDS, ANRI-CHAN.
THIS IS THE STORY OF A GIRL WHO AWOKE TO HER DARK POWERS ONE NIGHT...
AND IS DESTINED TO DEFEAT A MAGICAL GIRL TO RESTORE, BASICALLY, HER FAMILY'S HONOR!!

DUN DUN DUN!

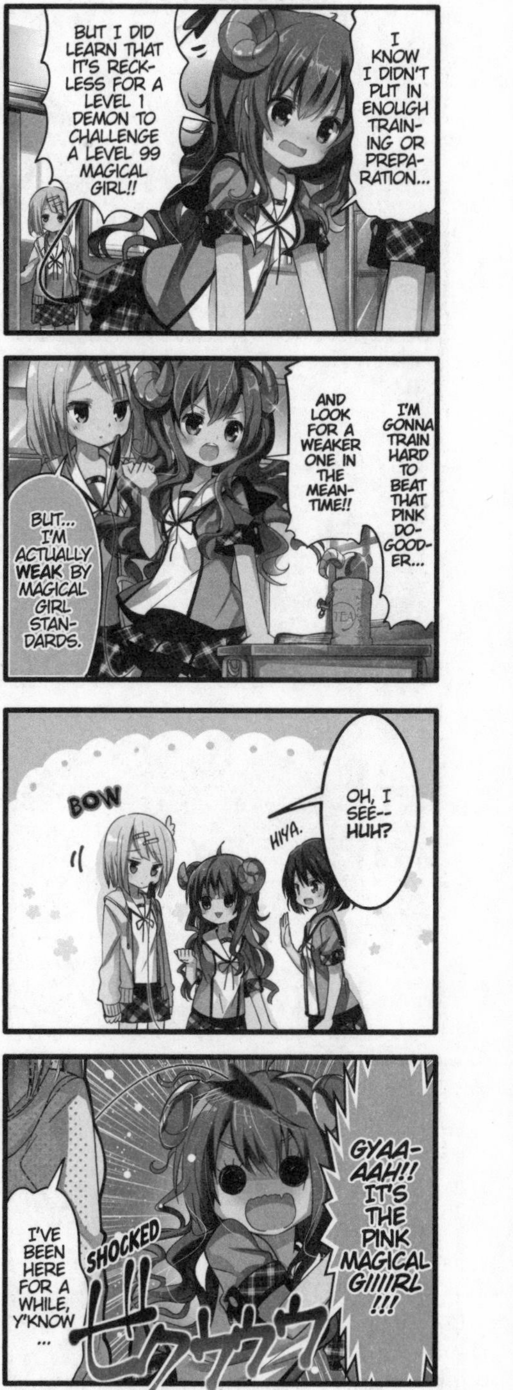
I KNOW I DIDN'T PUT IN ENOUGH TRAINING OR PREPARATION...
BUT I DID LEARN THAT IT'S RECKLESS FOR A LEVEL 1 DEMON TO CHALLENGE A LEVEL 99 MAGICAL GIRL!!
I'M GONNA TRAIN HARD TO BEAT THAT PINK DO-GOODER...
AND LOOK FOR A WEAKER ONE IN THE MEANTIME!!
BUT... I'M ACTUALLY WEAK BY MAGICAL GIRL STANDARDS.
TEA
OH, I SEE-- HUH?
HIYA.
BOW
GYAAAAH!! IT'S THE PINK MAGICAL GIIIIIRL!!!
SHOCKED
I'VE BEEN HERE FOR A WHILE, Y'KNOW ...

ALL THIS PINK WORKED BETTER IN FULL COLOR

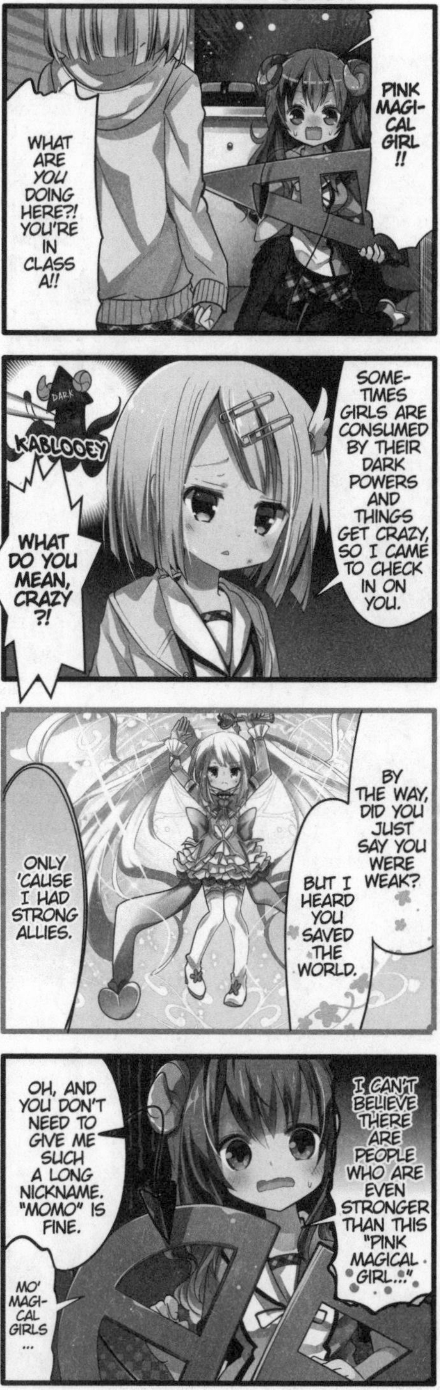
PINK MAGICAL GIRL!!
WHAT ARE YOU DOING HERE?! YOU'RE IN CLASS A!!
SOMETIMES GIRLS ARE CONSUMED BY THEIR DARK POWERS AND THINGS GET CRAZY, SO I CAME TO CHECK IN ON YOU.
DARK
KABLOOEY
WHAT DO YOU MEAN, CRAZY?!
BY THE WAY, DID YOU JUST SAY YOU WERE WEAK?
BUT I HEARD YOU SAVED THE WORLD.
ONLY 'CAUSE I HAD STRONG ALLIES.
I CAN'T BELIEVE THERE ARE PEOPLE WHO ARE EVEN STRONGER THAN THIS "PINK MAGICAL GIRL..."
OH, AND YOU DON'T NEED TO GIVE ME SUCH A LONG NICKNAME. "MOMO" IS FINE.
MO' MAGICAL GIRLS ...

JUMPING ON THE BANDWAGON

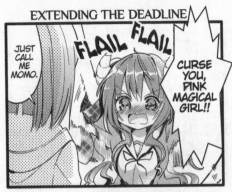

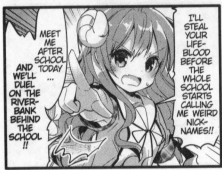

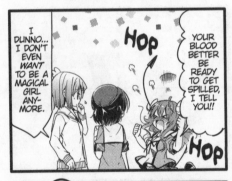

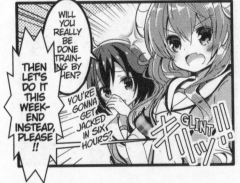

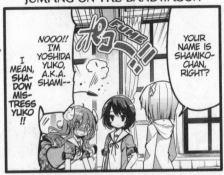

YOUR NAME IS SHAMIKO-CHAN, RIGHT?
FUME
NOOO!! I'M YOSHIDA YUKO, A.K.A. SHAMI--
I MEAN, SHADOW MISTRESS YUKO!!
......
GUESS I'LL STICK WITH SHAMIKO.
HEH.
D-DON'T LAUGH AT MEEE!
DON'T YOU WORRY ABOUT YOUR SLIP-UPS, SHAMMY!!
YEAH!!
QUIT GIVING ME NICKNAMES ALREADY!!
SHAMIRIN.*
GLARE
HUH?! WHAT WAS THAT?!
OH, NOTHING.

Mirin: a sweet rice wine used in Japanese cooking.

EXTENDING THE DEADLINE

CURSE YOU, PINK MAGICAL GIRL!!
FLAIL FLAIL
JUST CALL ME MOMO.
I'LL STEAL YOUR LIFEBLOOD BEFORE THE WHOLE SCHOOL STARTS CALLING ME WEIRD NICKNAMES!!
MEET ME AFTER SCHOOL TODAY...
AND WE'LL DUEL ON THE RIVERBANK BEHIND THE SCHOOL!!
YOUR BLOOD BETTER BE READY TO GET SPILLED, I TELL YOU!!
HOP
HOP
I DUNNO... I DON'T EVEN WANT TO BE A MAGICAL GIRL ANYMORE.
WILL YOU REALLY BE DONE TRAINING BY THEN?
YOU'RE GONNA GET JACKED IN SIX HOURS?
GLINT
THEN LET'S DO IT THIS WEEKEND INSTEAD, PLEASE!!

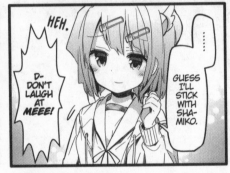

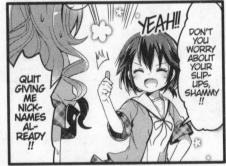

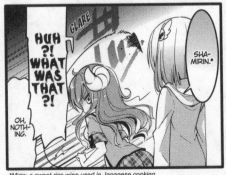

PINK DUMBBELLS

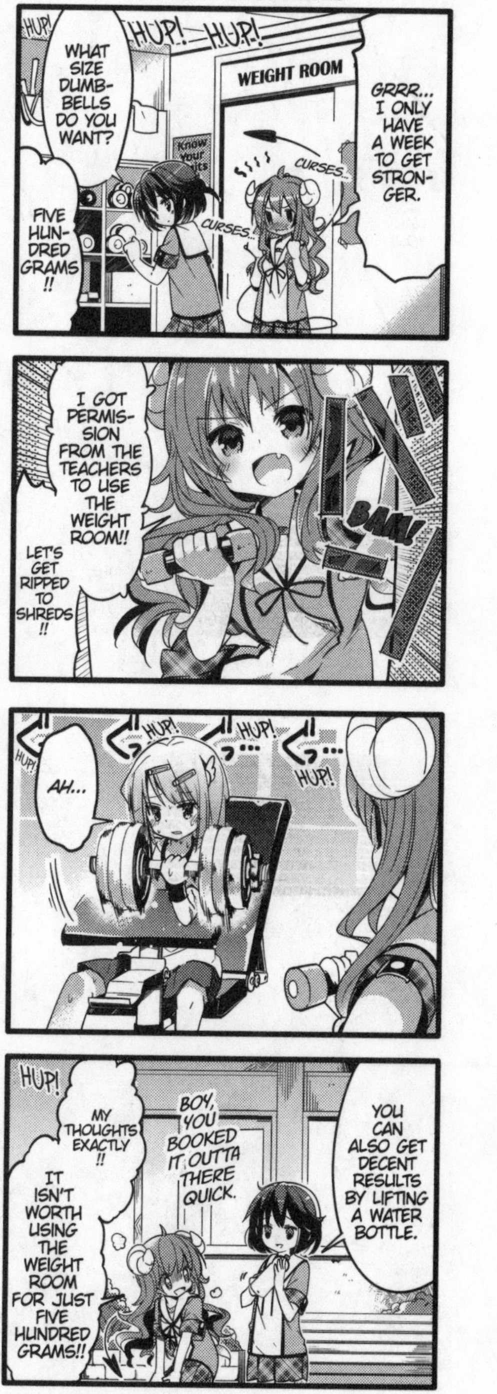
HUP! HUP!
WEIGHT ROOM
GRRR... I ONLY HAVE A WEEK TO GET STRONGER.
CURSES...
CURSES...
WHAT SIZE DUMBBELLS DO YOU WANT?
HUP!
FIVE HUNDRED GRAMS!!
BAM!
I GOT PERMISSION FROM THE TEACHERS TO USE THE WEIGHT ROOM!!
LET'S GET RIPPED TO SHREDS!!
HUP!
HUP!
HUP!
AH...
HUP!
YOU CAN ALSO GET DECENT RESULTS BY LIFTING A WATER BOTTLE.
BOY, YOU BOOKED IT OUTTA THERE QUICK.
MY THOUGHTS EXACTLY!!
IT ISN'T WORTH USING THE WEIGHT ROOM FOR JUST FIVE HUNDRED GRAMS!!
HUP!

LANDLINE PHONE

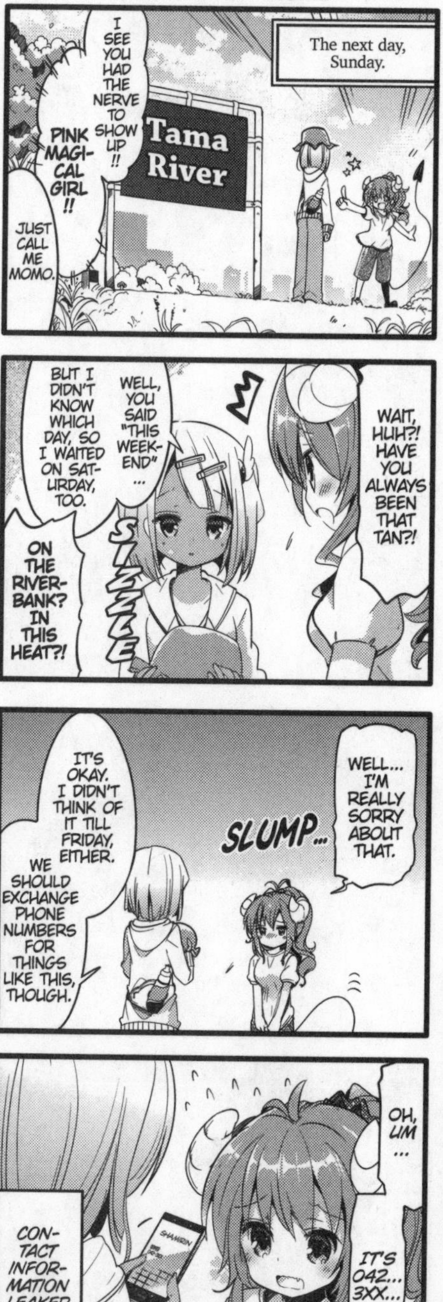
The next day, Sunday.
Tama River
I SEE YOU HAD THE NERVE TO SHOW UP!!
PINK MAGICAL GIRL!!
JUST CALL ME MOMO.
WAIT, HUH?! HAVE YOU ALWAYS BEEN THAT TAN?!
WELL, YOU SAID "THIS WEEKEND"...
BUT I DIDN'T KNOW WHICH DAY, SO I WAITED ON SATURDAY, TOO.
SIZZLE
ON THE RIVERBANK? IN THIS HEAT?!
WELL... I'M REALLY SORRY ABOUT THAT.
SLUMP...
IT'S OKAY. I DIDN'T THINK OF IT TILL FRIDAY, EITHER.
WE SHOULD EXCHANGE PHONE NUMBERS FOR THINGS LIKE THIS, THOUGH.
OH, UM...
IT'S 042... 3XX...
CONTACT INFORMATION LEAKED TO THE ENEMY!

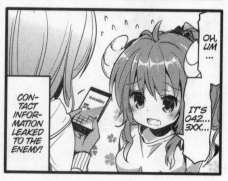

LIKE THE BACK OF HER HAND

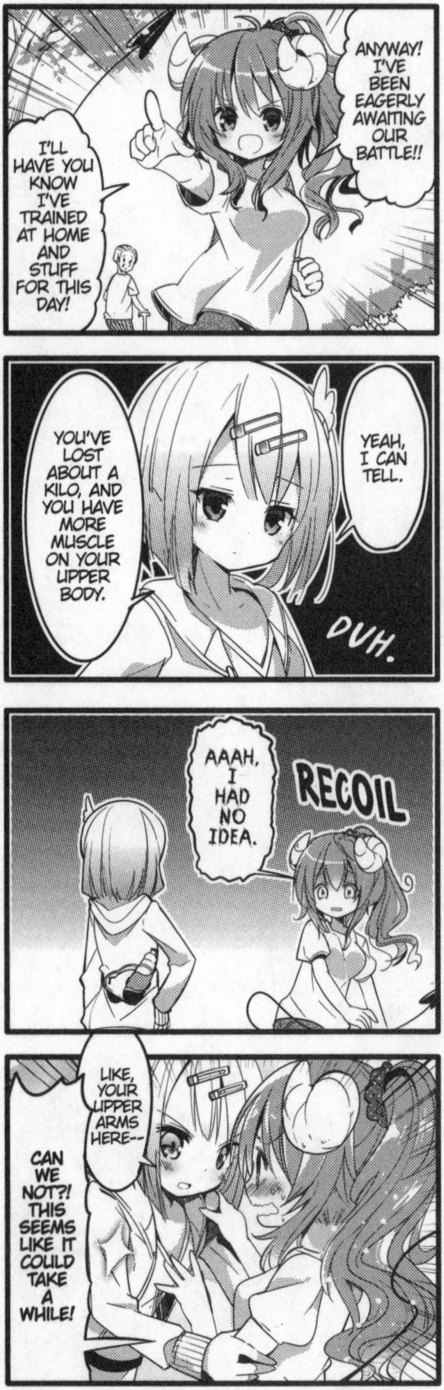
ANYWAY! I'VE BEEN EAGERLY AWAITING OUR BATTLE!!
I'LL HAVE YOU KNOW I'VE TRAINED AT HOME AND STUFF FOR THIS DAY!
YEAH, I CAN TELL.
YOU'VE LOST ABOUT A KILO, AND YOU HAVE MORE MUSCLE ON YOUR UPPER BODY.
DUH.
RECOIL
AAAH, I HAD NO IDEA.
LIKE, YOUR UPPER ARMS HERE--
CAN WE NOT?! THIS SEEMS LIKE IT COULD TAKE A WHILE!

TAIL LIGAMENT?

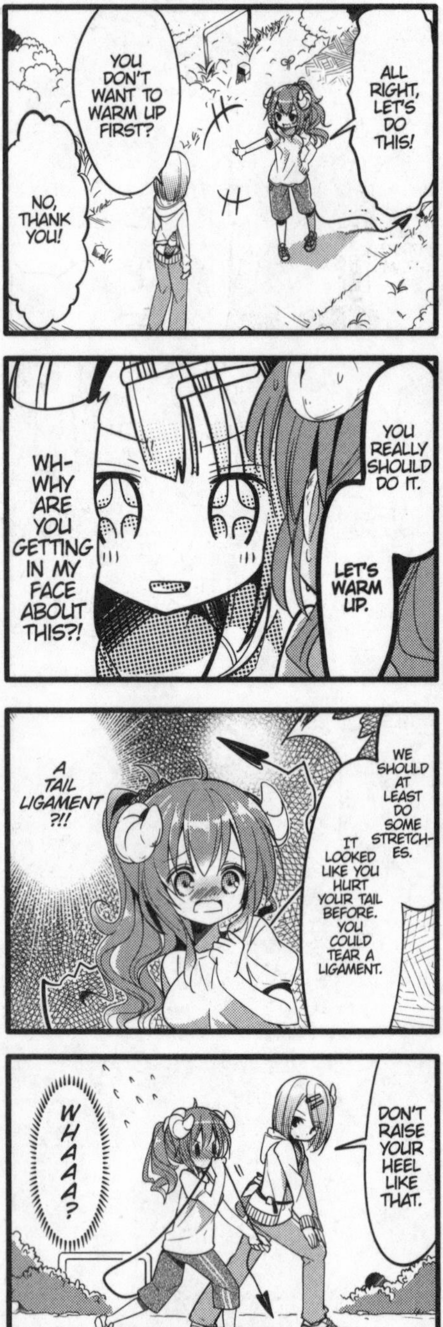
ALL RIGHT, LET'S DO THIS!
YOU DON'T WANT TO WARM UP FIRST?
NO, THANK YOU!
YOU REALLY SHOULD DO IT.
LET'S WARM UP.
WH-WHY ARE YOU GETTING IN MY FACE ABOUT THIS?!
WE SHOULD AT LEAST DO SOME STRETCH-ES.
IT LOOKED LIKE YOU HURT YOUR TAIL BEFORE. YOU COULD TEAR A LIGAMENT.
A TAIL LIGAMENT?!!
DON'T RAISE YOUR HEEL LIKE THAT.
WHAAAA?

IS THAT REALLY A WARM-UP?

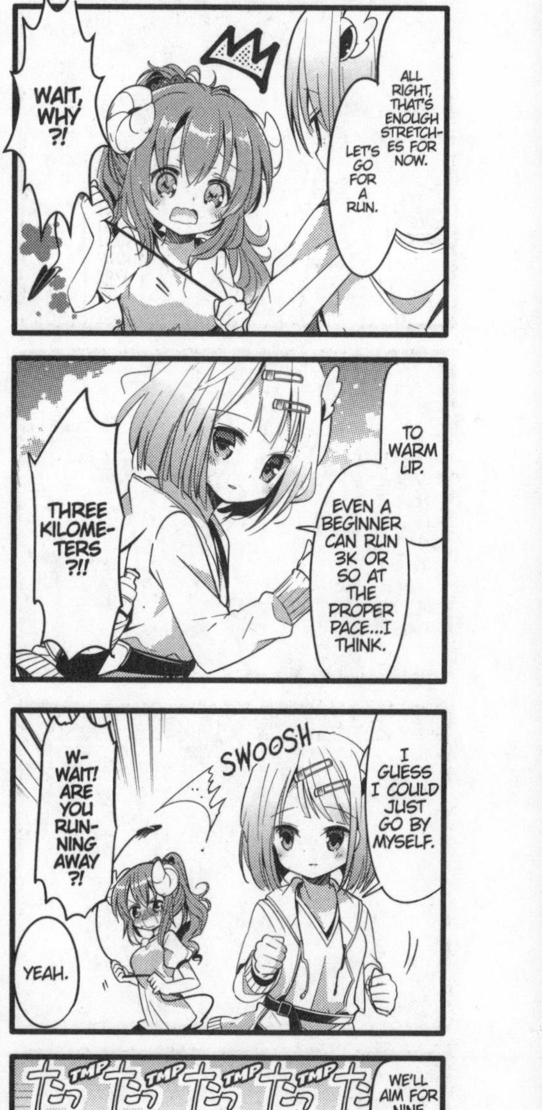
ALL RIGHT, THAT'S ENOUGH STRETCHES FOR NOW.
LET'S GO FOR A RUN.
WAIT, WHY?!
TO WARM UP.
THREE KILOMETERS?!!
EVEN A BEGINNER CAN RUN 3K OR SO AT THE PROPER PACE...I THINK.
I GUESS I COULD JUST GO BY MYSELF.
SWOOSH
W-WAIT! ARE YOU RUNNING AWAY?!
YEAH.
WE'LL AIM FOR NINE MINUTES FOR THE FIRST KILOMETER...
THEN SEVEN AND A HALF FROM THE SECOND ONE ON.
TMP TMP TMP TMP TMP
?
WH-WHAAAT??

BREAK ON THROUGH

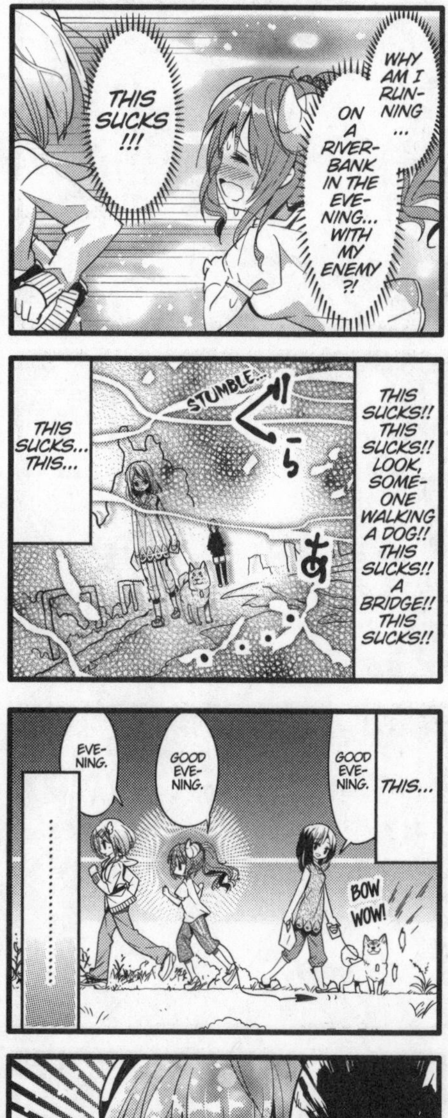
WHY AM I RUNNING...
ON A RIVERBANK IN THE EVENING... WITH MY ENEMY?!
THIS SUCKS!!!
THIS SUCKS!! THIS SUCKS!! LOOK, SOMEONE WALKING A DOG!! THIS SUCKS!! A BRIDGE!! THIS SUCKS!!
STUMBLE...
THIS SUCKS... THIS...
THIS...
GOOD EVENING.
BOW WOW!
GOOD EVENING.
EVENING.
....
CHANGE IS CONSTANT AND UNIVERSAL!
YUKO IS EXPERIENCING HER FIRST RUNNER'S HIGH.

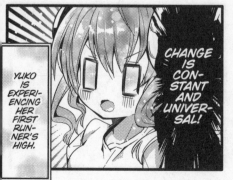

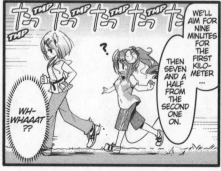

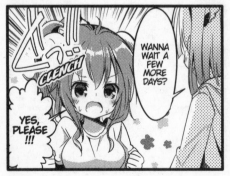

JUST ADD FORTY MORE

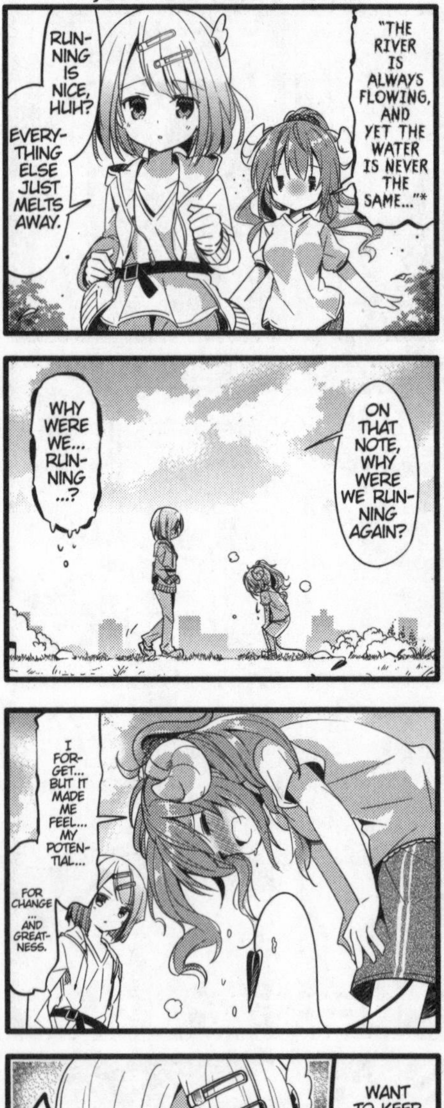
"THE RIVER IS ALWAYS FLOWING, AND YET THE WATER IS NEVER THE SAME..."*
RUNNING IS NICE, HUH?
EVERYTHING ELSE JUST MELTS AWAY.
ON THAT NOTE, WHY WERE WE RUNNING AGAIN?
WHY WERE WE... RUNNING...?
I FORGET... BUT IT MADE ME FEEL... MY POTENTIAL...
FOR CHANGE... AND GREATNESS.
WANT TO KEEP RUNNING TILL WE REACH THE OCEAN, THEN?
SMILE
AREN'T WE WAY UP IN THE MOUNTAINS?!

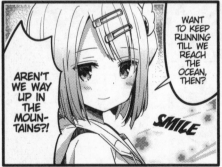

*This is the first line of the Hojoki, a classical Japanese text published in the year 1212. It's a famous passage about the transience of all things.

INSTANT RESPONSE

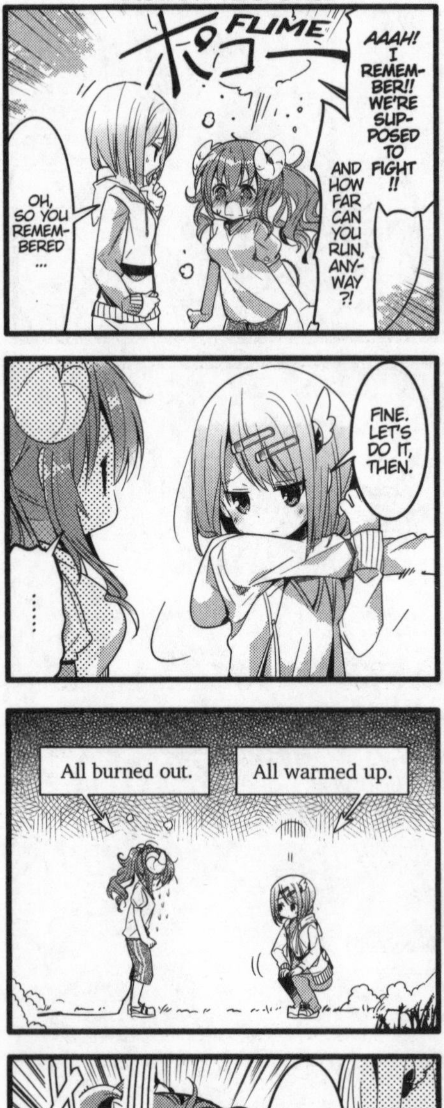
AAAH! I REMEMBER!! WE'RE SUPPOSED TO FIGHT!!
FLUME
AND HOW FAR CAN YOU RUN, ANYWAY?!
OH, SO YOU REMEMBERED...
FINE. LET'S DO IT, THEN.
......
All warmed up.
All burned out.
WANNA WAIT A FEW MORE DAYS?
CLENCH
YES, PLEASE!!!

PINK TRAINING LEVEL 1

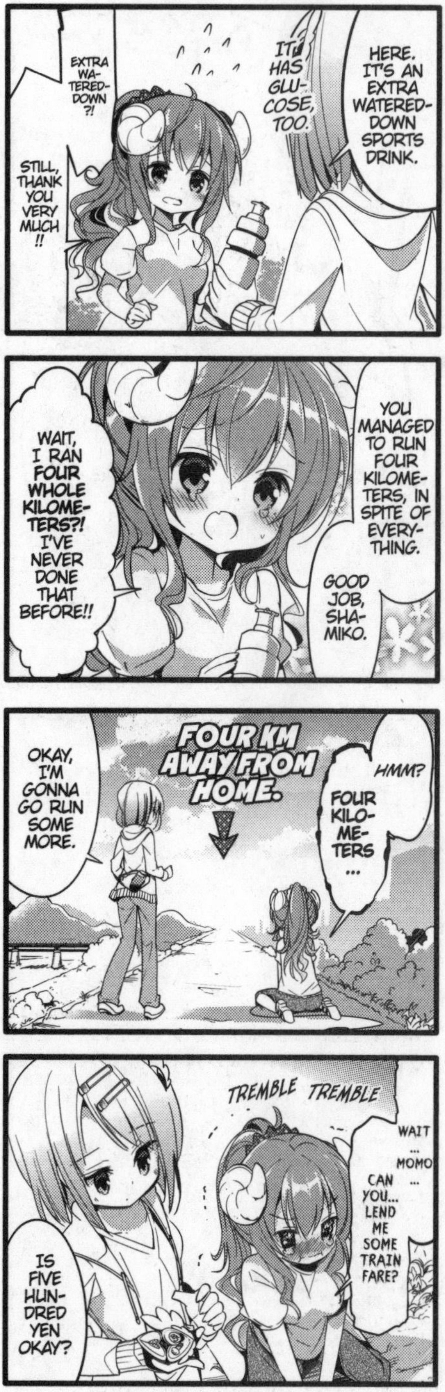
HERE. IT'S AN EXTRA WATERED-DOWN SPORTS DRINK.
IT HAS GLUCOSE, TOO.
EXTRA WATERED-DOWN?!
STILL, THANK YOU VERY MUCH!!
YOU MANAGED TO RUN FOUR KILOMETERS, IN SPITE OF EVERYTHING.
GOOD JOB, SHAMIKO.
WAIT, I RAN FOUR WHOLE KILOMETERS?! I'VE NEVER DONE THAT BEFORE!!
HMM? FOUR KILOMETERS...
FOUR KM AWAY FROM HOME.
OKAY, I'M GONNA GO RUN SOME MORE.
TREMBLE TREMBLE
WAIT... MOMO... CAN YOU... LEND ME SOME TRAIN FARE?
IS FIVE HUNDRED YEN OKAY?

UNEXPLORED PART OF THE CITY

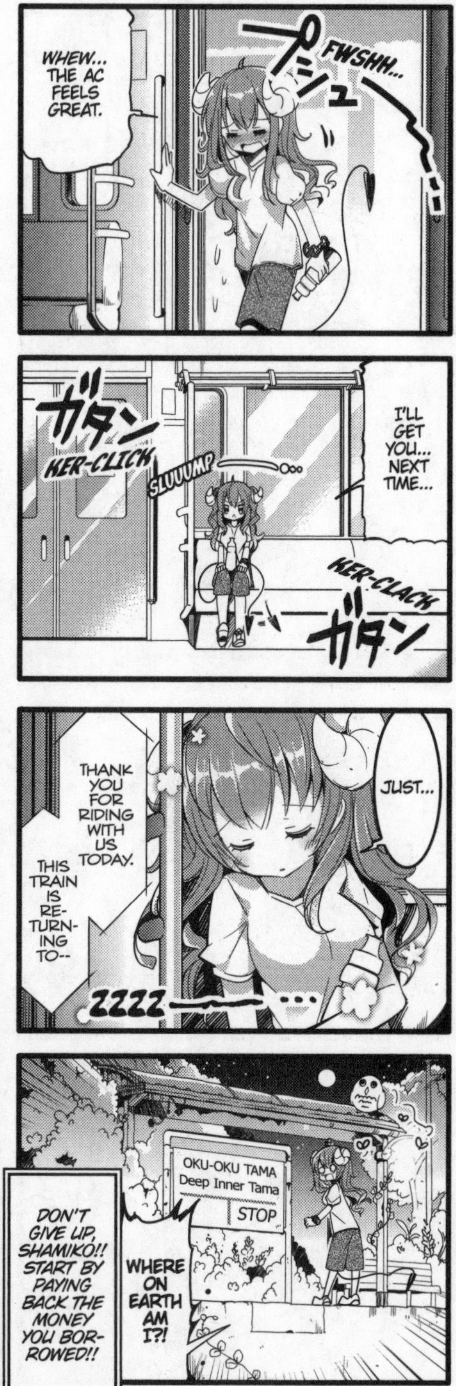
プシュ
FWSHH...
WHEW... THE AC FEELS GREAT.
I'LL GET YOU... NEXT TIME...
ガタン
KER-CLICK
SLUUUMP
KER-CLACK
ガタン
JUST...
THANK YOU FOR RIDING WITH US TODAY.
THIS TRAIN IS RETURNING TO--
ZZZZ...
OKU-OKU TAMA
Deep Inner Tama
STOP
WHERE ON EARTH AM I?!
DON'T GIVE UP, SHAMIKO!! START BY PAYING BACK THE MONEY YOU BORROWED!!

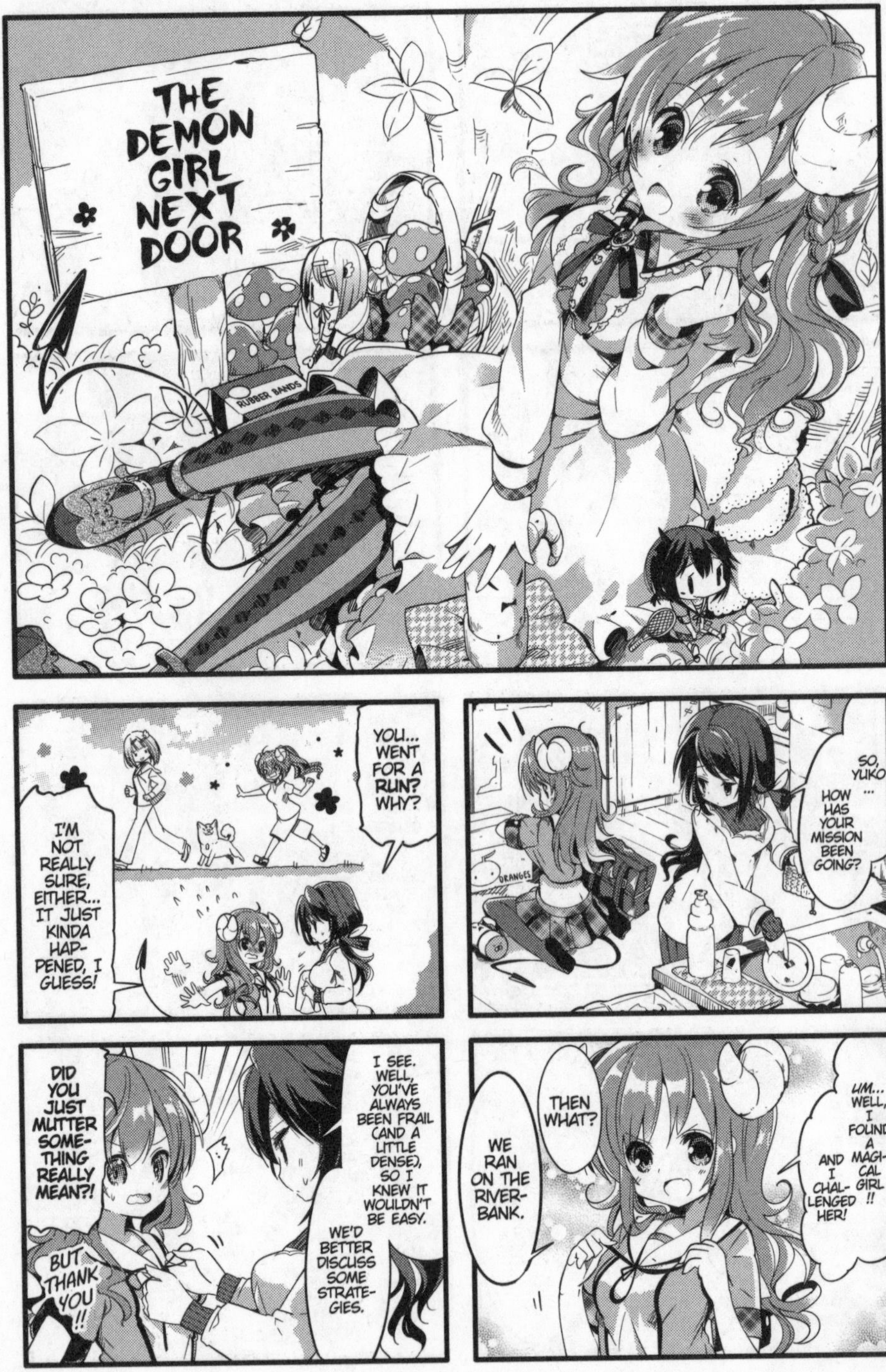
THE DEMON GIRL NEXT DOOR
RUBBER BANDS
SO, YUKO... HOW HAS YOUR MISSION BEEN GOING?
ORANGES
YOU... WENT FOR A RUN? WHY?
I'M NOT REALLY SURE, EITHER... IT JUST KINDA HAPPENED, I GUESS!
UM... WELL, I FOUND A MAGICAL GIRL!!
AND I CHALLENGED HER!
THEN WHAT?
WE RAN ON THE RIVERBANK.
I SEE. WELL, YOU'VE ALWAYS BEEN FRAIL (AND A LITTLE DENSE), SO I KNEW IT WOULDN'T BE EASY.
DID YOU JUST MUTTER SOMETHING REALLY MEAN?!
WE'D BETTER DISCUSS SOME STRATEGIES.
BUT THANK YOU!!

IN SPITE OF THE FAMILY'S CURSE

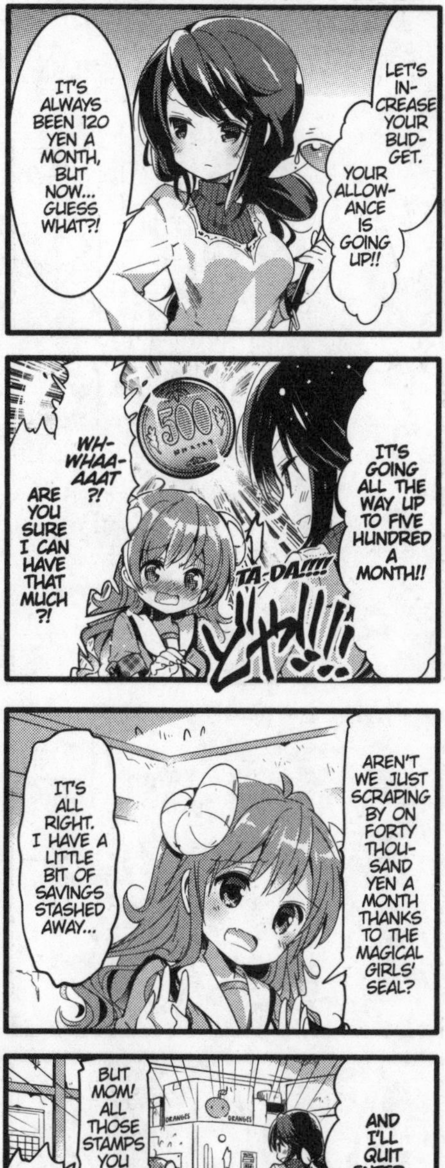
LET'S IN-CREASE YOUR BUD-GET.
YOUR ALLOW-ANCE IS GOING UP!!
IT'S ALWAYS BEEN 120 YEN A MONTH, BUT NOW... GUESS WHAT?!
IT'S GOING ALL THE WAY UP TO FIVE HUNDRED A MONTH!!
TA-DA!!!!
WH-WHAAA-AAAT ?!
ARE YOU SURE I CAN HAVE THAT MUCH ?!
AREN'T WE JUST SCRAPING BY ON FORTY THOU-SAND YEN A MONTH THANKS TO THE MAGICAL GIRLS' SEAL?
IT'S ALL RIGHT. I HAVE A LITTLE BIT OF SAVINGS STASHED AWAY...
AND I'LL QUIT ENTER-ING THOSE CON-TESTS I NEVER WIN!
BUT MOM! ALL THOSE STAMPS YOU SAVED UP!!
THEY ARE JUST WAST-ED IF I DON'T WIN!!

ADD SNACKS TO THE BUDGET

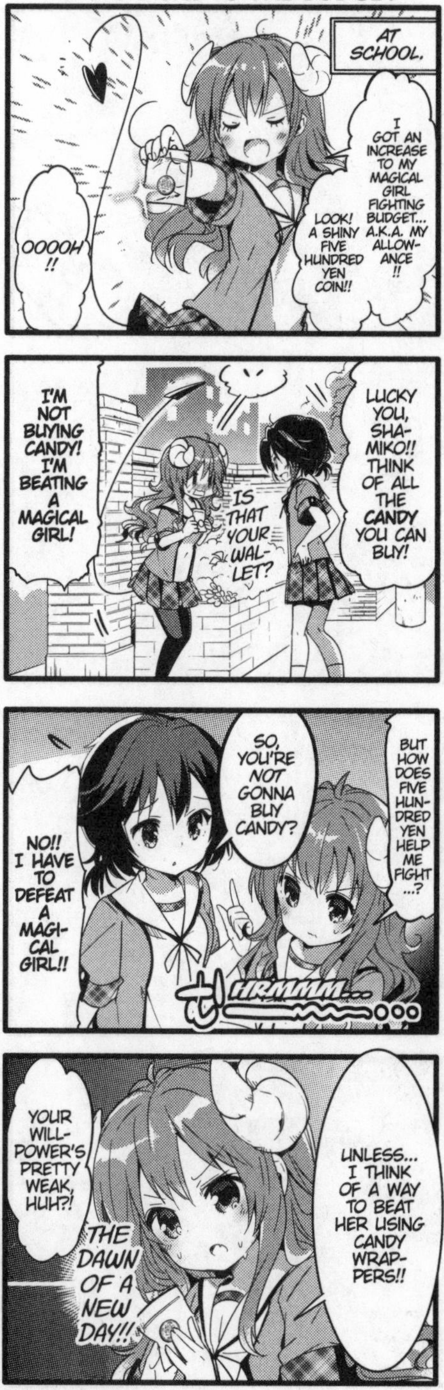
AT SCHOOL.
I GOT AN INCREASE TO MY MAGICAL GIRL FIGHTING BUDGET... A.K.A. MY ALLOW-ANCE !!
LOOK! A SHINY FIVE HUNDRED YEN COIN!!
OOOOH !!
LUCKY YOU, SHA-MIKO!! THINK OF ALL THE CANDY YOU CAN BUY!
IS THAT YOUR WAL-LET?
I'M NOT BUYING CANDY! I'M BEATING A MAGICAL GIRL!
BUT HOW DOES FIVE HUN-DRED YEN HELP ME FIGHT ...?
SO, YOU'RE NOT GONNA BUY CANDY?
NO!! I HAVE TO DEFEAT A MAGI-CAL GIRL!!
HRMMM...
UNLESS... I THINK OF A WAY TO BEAT HER USING CANDY WRAP-PERS!!
YOUR WILL-POWER'S PRETTY WEAK, HUH?!
THE DAWN OF A NEW DAY!!

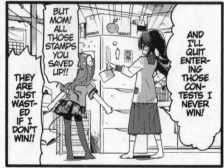

SO MUCH FOR THAT

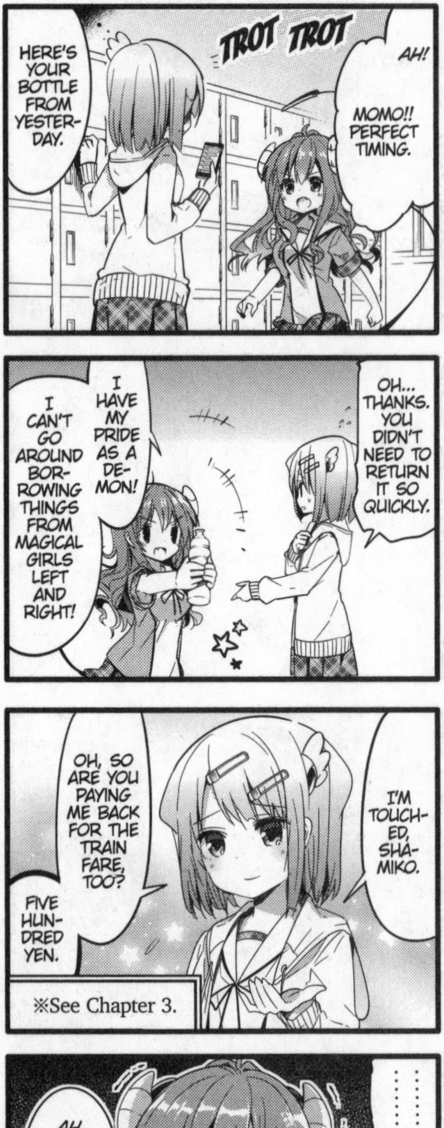
AH!
MOMO!! PERFECT TIMING.
TROT TROT
HERE'S YOUR BOTTLE FROM YESTERDAY.
OH... THANKS. YOU DIDN'T NEED TO RETURN IT SO QUICKLY.
I HAVE MY PRIDE AS A DEMON!
I CAN'T GO AROUND BORROWING THINGS FROM MAGICAL GIRLS LEFT AND RIGHT!
I'M TOUCHED, SHAMIKO.
OH, SO ARE YOU PAYING ME BACK FOR THE TRAIN FARE, TOO?
FIVE HUNDRED YEN.
※See Chapter 3.
......
I HAVE IT ON ME NOW, BUT I'M AFRAID ...
AH, NEVER MIND! I'M SORRY.
SHAKE

JUST A LITTLE DEMON JUICE

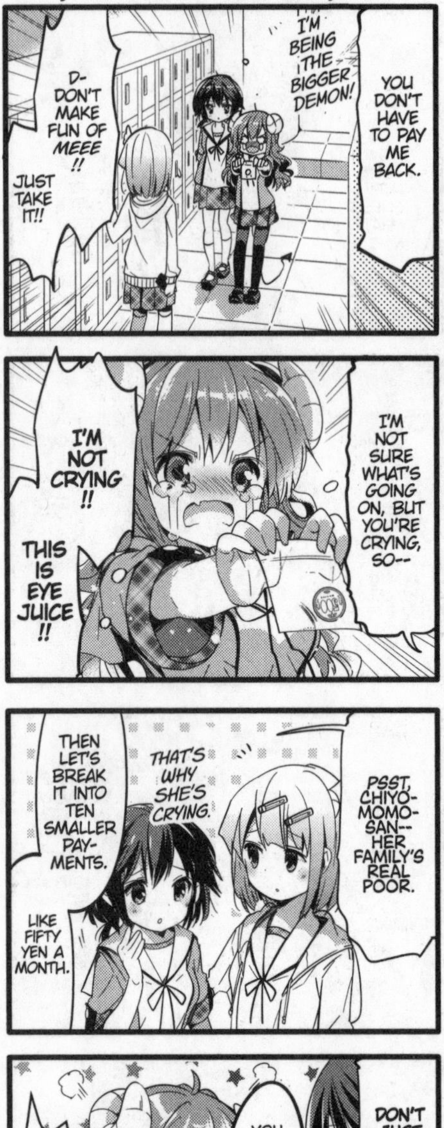
YOU DON'T HAVE TO PAY ME BACK.
I'M BEING THE BIGGER DEMON!
D-DON'T MAKE FUN OF MEEE!!
JUST TAKE IT!!
I'M NOT SURE WHAT'S GOING ON, BUT YOU'RE CRYING, SO--
I'M NOT CRYING!!
THIS IS EYE JUICE!!
PSST, CHIYOMOMO-SAN--HER FAMILY'S REAL POOR.
THAT'S WHY SHE'S CRYING.
THEN LET'S BREAK IT INTO TEN SMALLER PAYMENTS.
LIKE FIFTY YEN A MONTH.
DON'T JUST DECIDE THINGS FOR ME!!
YOU CAN STILL BUY CANDY.
OKAY, I'M GOOD WITH THAT!
SLIDE

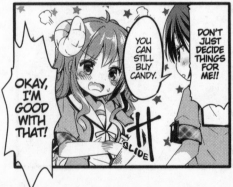

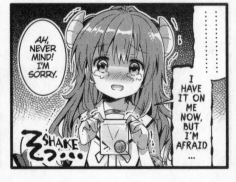

I WANT TO BE AN UNBEATABLE DEMON

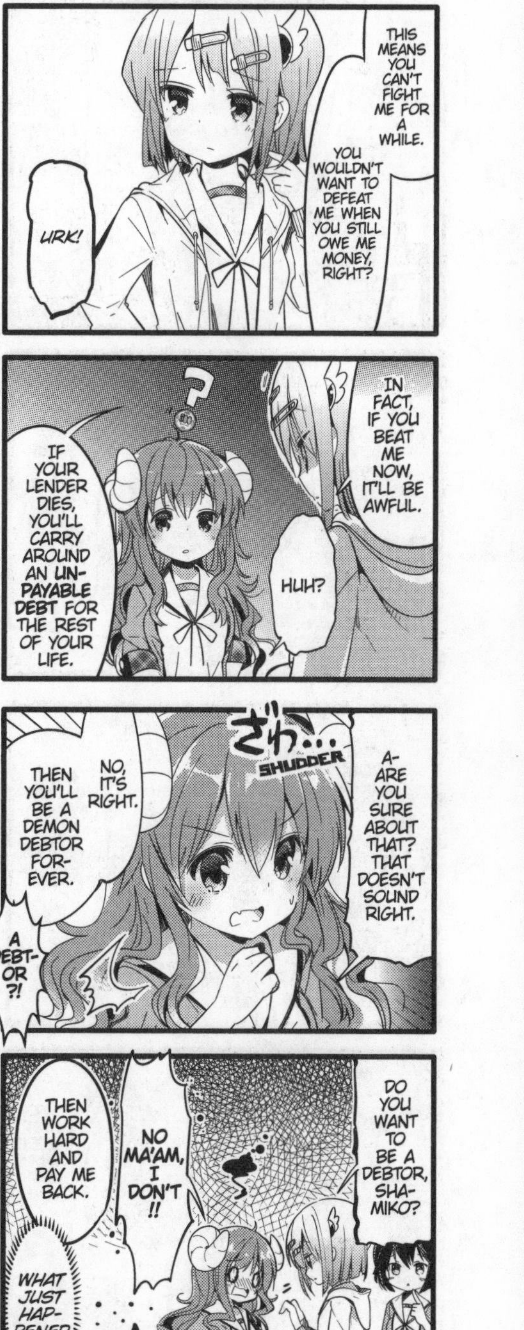
THIS MEANS YOU CAN'T FIGHT ME FOR A WHILE.
YOU WOULDN'T WANT TO DEFEAT ME WHEN YOU STILL OWE ME MONEY, RIGHT?
URK!
IN FACT, IF YOU BEAT ME NOW, IT'LL BE AWFUL.
HUH?
?
IF YOUR LENDER DIES, YOU'LL CARRY AROUND AN UN-PAYABLE DEBT FOR THE REST OF YOUR LIFE.
ざわ…
SHUDDER
A- ARE YOU SURE ABOUT THAT? THAT DOESN'T SOUND RIGHT.
NO, IT'S RIGHT.
THEN YOU'LL BE A DEMON DEBTOR FOR-EVER.
A DEBT-OR ?!
DO YOU WANT TO BE A DEBTOR, SHA-MIKO?
NO MA'AM, I DON'T !!
THEN WORK HARD AND PAY ME BACK.
WHAT JUST HAP-PENED ...?

ALL BARK, NO BITE

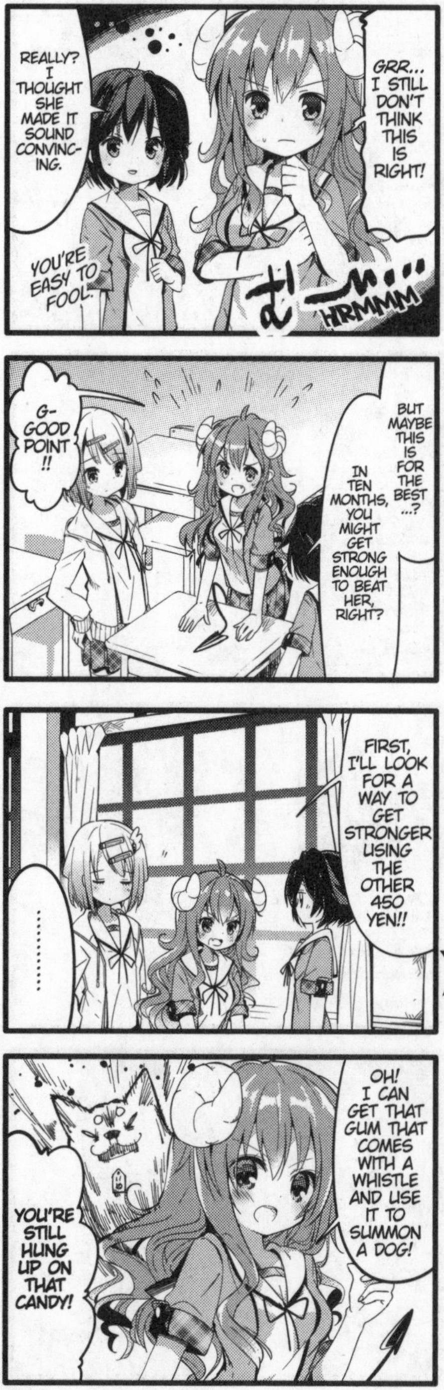
GRR... I STILL DON'T THINK THIS IS RIGHT!
REALLY? I THOUGHT SHE MADE IT SOUND CONVINC-ING.
YOU'RE EASY TO FOOL.
む—ん…
HRMMM
BUT MAYBE THIS IS FOR THE BEST ...?
IN TEN MONTHS, YOU MIGHT GET STRONG ENOUGH TO BEAT HER, RIGHT?
G-GOOD POINT !!
FIRST, I'LL LOOK FOR A WAY TO GET STRONGER USING THE OTHER 450 YEN!!
......
OH! I CAN GET THAT GUM THAT COMES WITH A WHISTLE AND USE IT TO SUMMON A DOG!
YOU'RE STILL HUNG UP ON THAT CANDY!

Tag: Dog

TRYING TO MAKE A PROJECTILE WEAPON

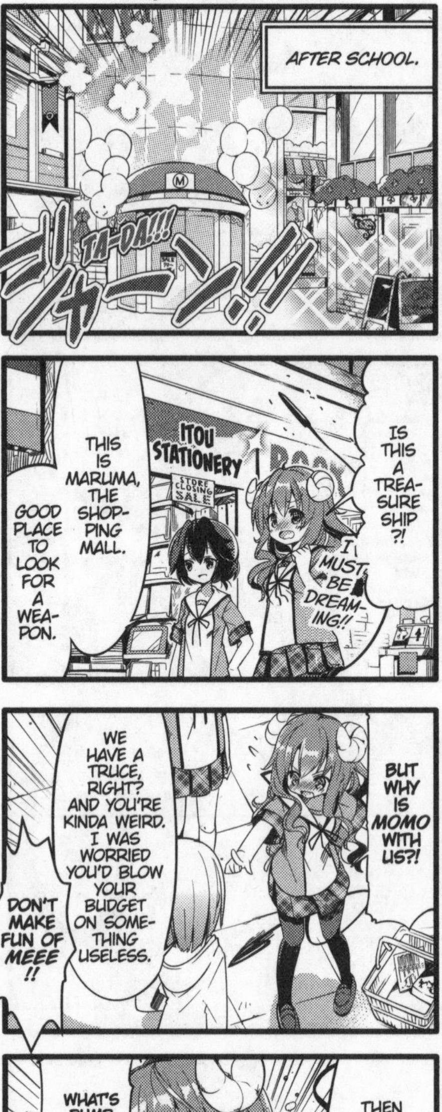
AFTER SCHOOL.
TA-DA!!!
ジャーン!!
IS THIS A TREASURE SHIP?!
I MUST BE DREAMING!!
ITOU STATIONERY
STORE CLOSING SALE
THIS IS MARUMA, THE SHOPPING MALL.
GOOD PLACE TO LOOK FOR A WEAPON.
BUT WHY IS MOMO WITH US?!
WE HAVE A TRUCE, RIGHT? AND YOU'RE KINDA WEIRD. I WAS WORRIED YOU'D BLOW YOUR BUDGET ON SOMETHING USELESS.
DON'T MAKE FUN OF MEEE!!
THEN THOSE CHOPSTICKS AND RUBBER BANDS AREN'T FOR SOME DUMB IDEA?
WHAT'S DUMB ABOUT A CHOPSTICK AND RUBBER BAND GUN?!
FINE, I'LL PUT THEM BACK!!
RUBBER BANDS

DELICIOUS SMELL

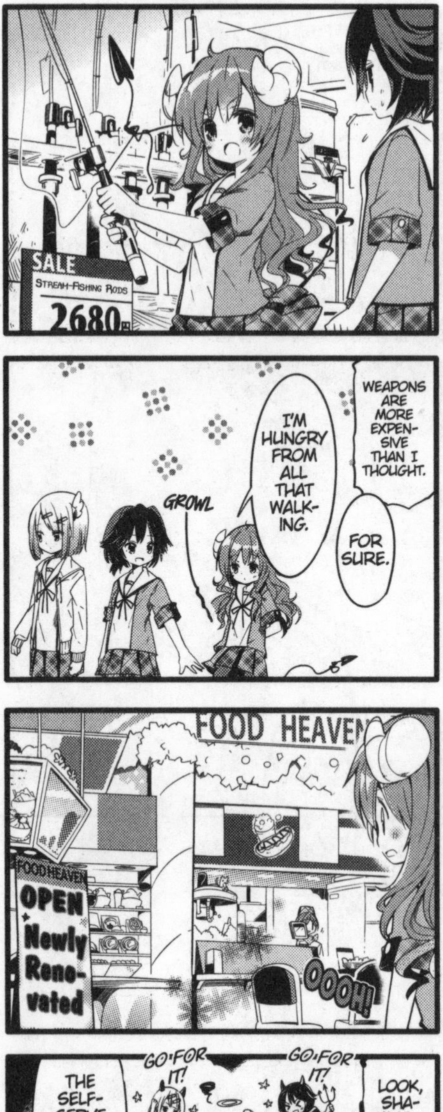
SALE
STREAM-FISHING RODS
2680円
WEAPONS ARE MORE EXPENSIVE THAN I THOUGHT.
I'M HUNGRY FROM ALL THAT WALKING.
FOR SURE.
GROWL
FOOD HEAVEN
FOOD HEAVEN
OPEN
Newly Renovated
OOOH!
LOOK, SHAMIKO--THE FOOD COURT'S BEEN RENOVATED!
GO FOR IT!
GO FOR IT!
THE SELF-SERVE UDON IS REALLY GOOD.
PLEASE STOP.
STOP IT!

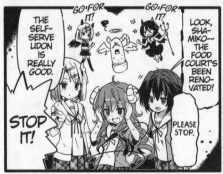

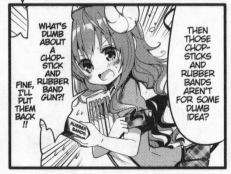

TOO MANY OPTIONS

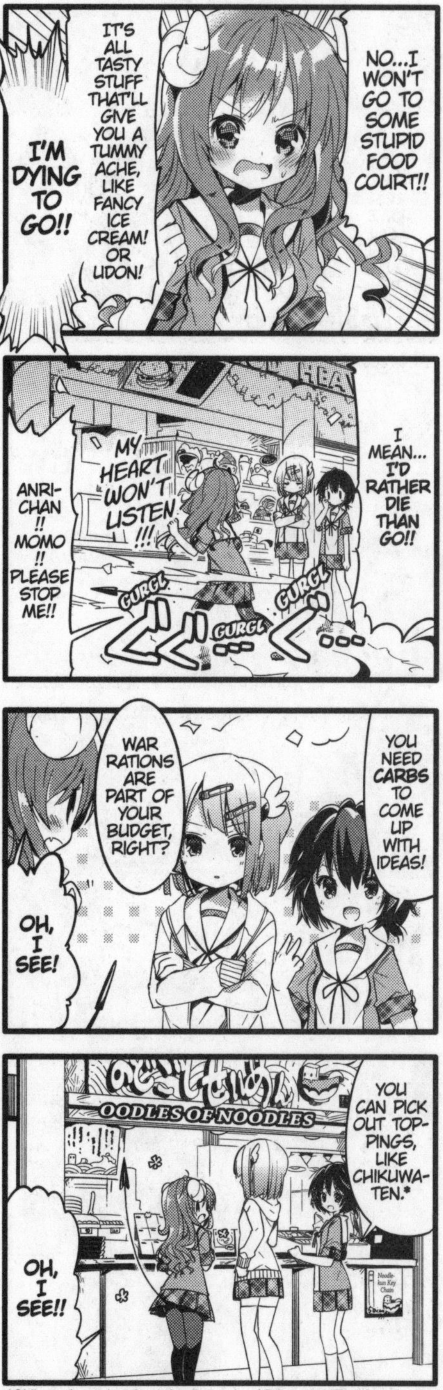

NO...I WON'T GO TO SOME STUPID FOOD COURT!!
IT'S ALL TASTY STUFF THAT'LL GIVE YOU A TUMMY ACHE, LIKE FANCY ICE CREAM! OR UDON!
I'M DYING TO GO!!
I MEAN... I'D RATHER DIE THAN GO!!
MY HEART WON'T LISTEN!!!
ANRI-CHAN!! MOMO!! PLEASE STOP ME!!
GURGL
GURGL
GURGL
YOU NEED CARBS TO COME UP WITH IDEAS!
WAR RATIONS ARE PART OF YOUR BUDGET, RIGHT?
OH, I SEE!
OODLES OF NOODLES
YOU CAN PICK OUT TOPPINGS, LIKE CHIKUWA-TEN.*
OH, I SEE!!

*Chikuwa is a tube-shaped cake made of fish paste. "Ten" here is short for "tempura" (batter-fried).

TEMPURA TEMPTATION

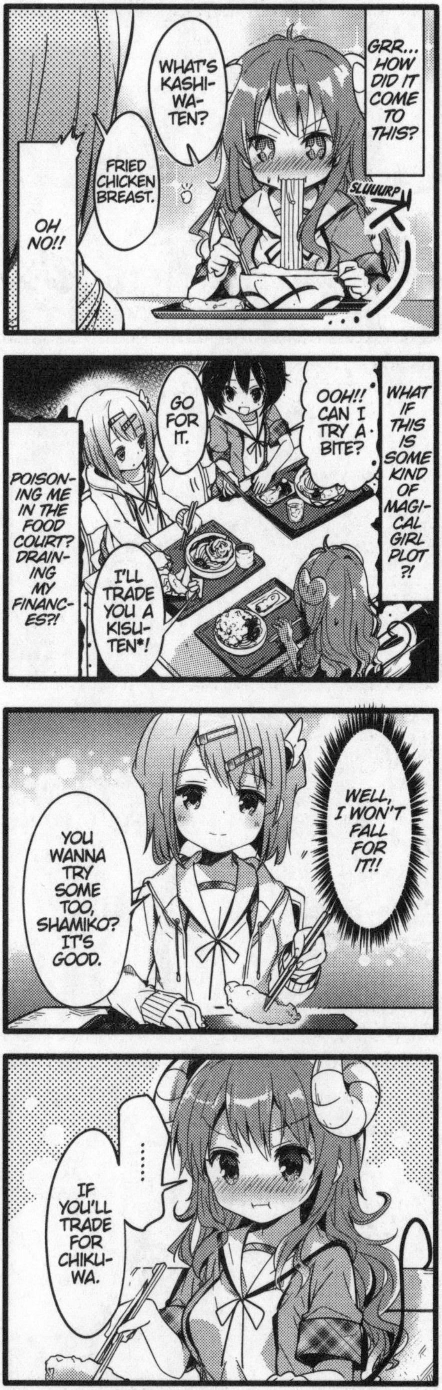

GRR... HOW DID IT COME TO THIS?
WHAT'S KASHIWA-TEN?
FRIED CHICKEN BREAST.
SLUUURP
OH NO!!
WHAT IF THIS IS SOME KIND OF MAGICAL GIRL PLOT?!
OOH!! CAN I TRY A BITE?
GO FOR IT.
I'LL TRADE YOU A KISU-TEN*!
POISONING ME IN THE FOOD COURT? DRAINING MY FINANCES?!
WELL, I WON'T FALL FOR IT!!
YOU WANNA TRY SOME TOO, SHAMIKO? IT'S GOOD.
......
IF YOU'LL TRADE FOR CHIKUWA.

*Kisu-ten is a kind of batter-fried fish.

TASTY, TASTY SALT

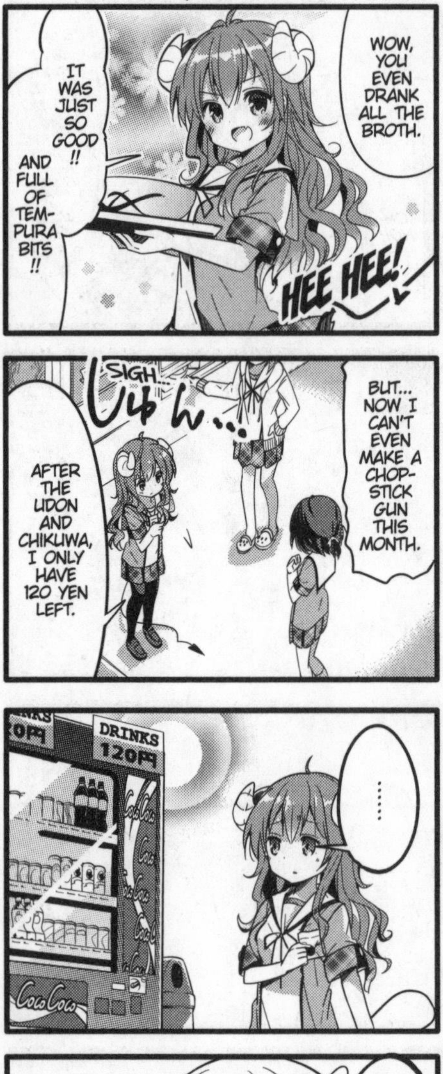
WOW, YOU EVEN DRANK ALL THE BROTH.
IT WAS JUST SO GOOD!!
AND FULL OF TEMPURA BITS!!
HEE HEE!
BUT... NOW I CAN'T EVEN MAKE A CHOPSTICK GUN THIS MONTH.
SIGH...
AFTER THE UDON AND CHIKUWA, I ONLY HAVE 120 YEN LEFT.
DRINKS 120円
......
YOU THIRSTY, SHAMIKO?
I WON'T FALL FOR THAT AGAIN!!
AFTER ALL THAT BROTH...

HALF-BAKED

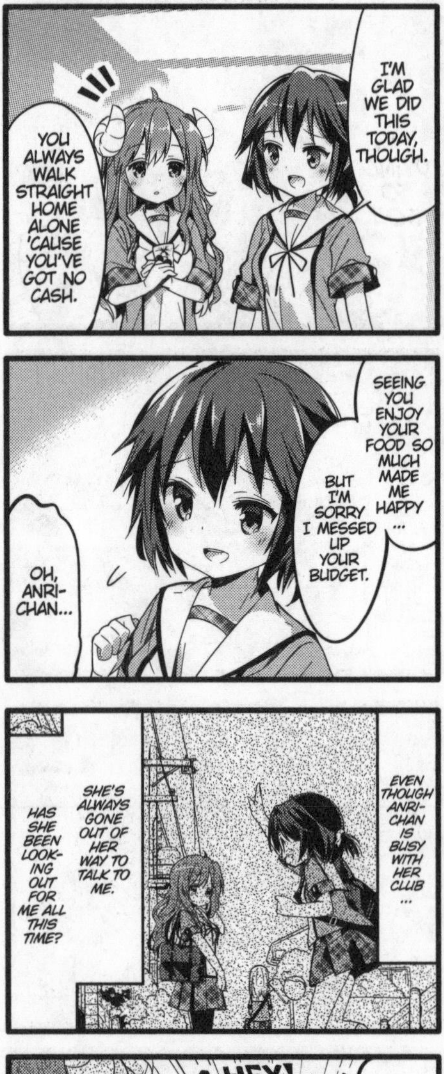
I'M GLAD WE DID THIS TODAY, THOUGH.
YOU ALWAYS WALK STRAIGHT HOME ALONE 'CAUSE YOU'VE GOT NO CASH.
SEEING YOU ENJOY YOUR FOOD SO MUCH MADE ME HAPPY...
BUT I'M SORRY I MESSED UP YOUR BUDGET.
OH, ANRI-CHAN...
EVEN THOUGH ANRI-CHAN IS BUSY WITH HER CLUB...
SHE'S ALWAYS GONE OUT OF HER WAY TO TALK TO ME.
HAS SHE BEEN LOOKING OUT FOR ME ALL THIS TIME?
HEY!
FROM NOW ON, I'M TAKING THIS SERIOUSLY!!
THEN WHAT HAVE YOU BEEN DOING BEFORE THIS?

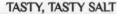

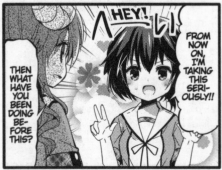

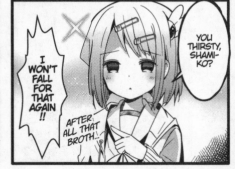

IN ONE GULP (OF THREE)

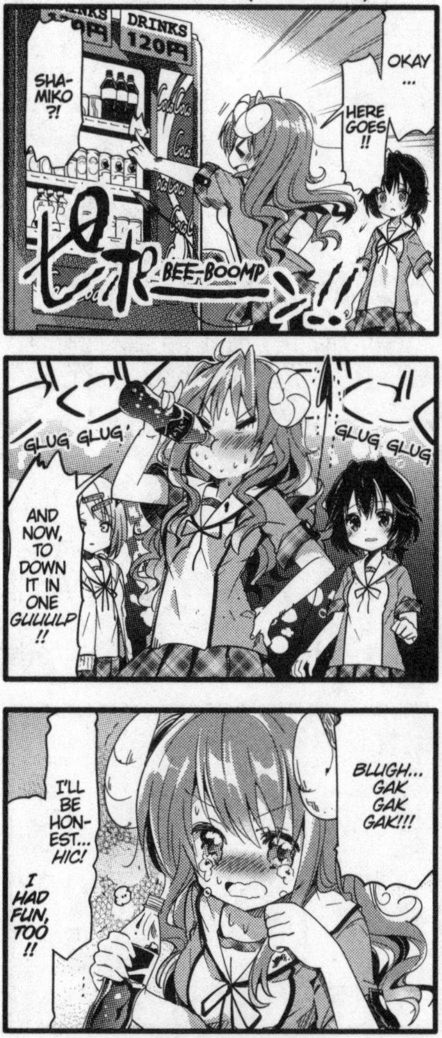
OKAY ... HERE GOES!!
SHAMIKO?!
DRINKS 120円
BEE-BOOMP
GLUG GLUG
GLUG GLUG
AND NOW, TO DOWN IT IN ONE GULULP!!
BLUGH... GAK GAK GAK!!!
I'LL BE HONEST... HIC!
I HAD FUN, TOO!!
IF YOU WANT... HIC! I'LL EVEN COME AGAIN NEXT MONTH... HIC!!
HIC...
REALLY?! THANKS! BUT, UH, DON'T PUSH YOURSELF!!
HIC...
HIC...
SHAMIKO'S REMAINING BUDGET FOR THE MONTH: ZERO YEN.

DEMON WITH BIG DREAMS

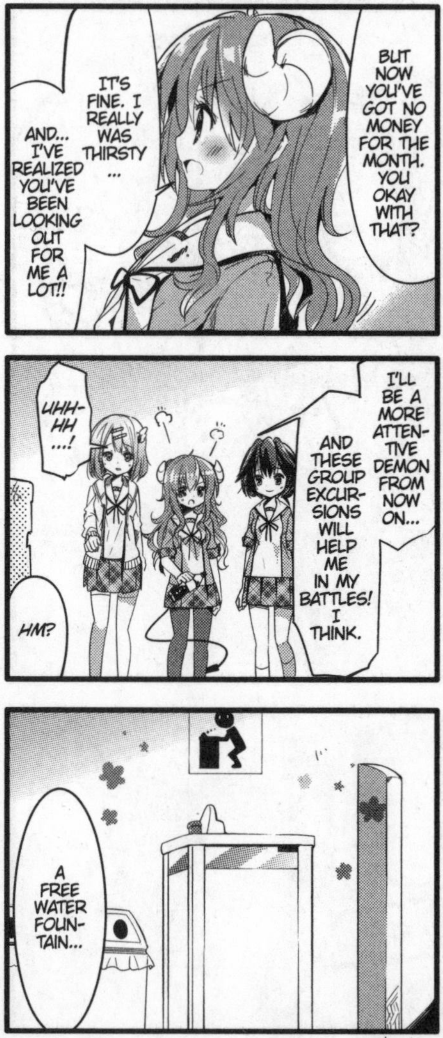
BUT NOW YOU'VE GOT NO MONEY FOR THE MONTH. YOU OKAY WITH THAT?
IT'S FINE. I REALLY WAS THIRSTY ...
AND... I'VE REALIZED YOU'VE BEEN LOOKING OUT FOR ME A LOT!!
I'LL BE A MORE ATTENTIVE DEMON FROM NOW ON...
AND THESE GROUP EXCURSIONS WILL HELP ME IN MY BATTLES! I THINK.
UHHHH...!
HM?
A FREE WATER FOUNTAIN...
I'LL GET YOU NEXT TIME, JUST YOU WAAAIT!!
HUH? WHY ME?
JAB
DON'T GIVE UP, SHAMIKO!! YOU CAN SAVE A LOT ON DRINKS IF YOU'RE CAREFUL!!

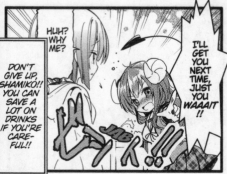

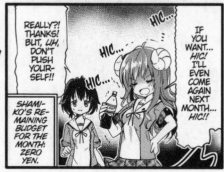

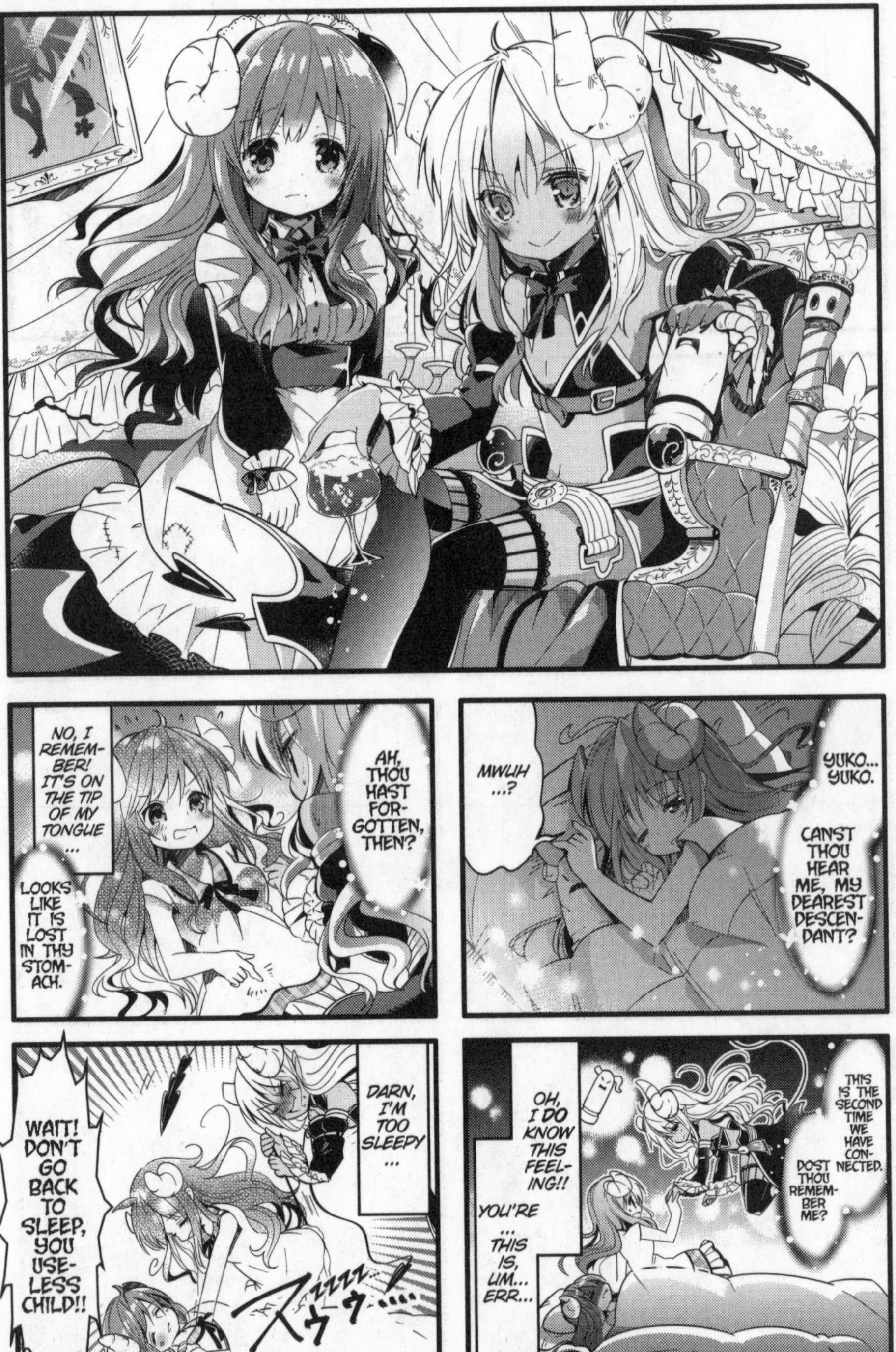
YUKO... YUKO.
CANST THOU HEAR ME, MY DEAREST DESCENDANT?
MWUH ...?
AH, THOU HAST FORGOTTEN, THEN?
NO, I REMEMBER! IT'S ON THE TIP OF MY TONGUE ...
LOOKS LIKE IT IS LOST IN THY STOMACH.
THIS IS THE SECOND TIME WE HAVE CONNECTED.
DOST THOU REMEMBER ME?
OH, I DO KNOW THIS FEELING!!
YOU'RE ... THIS IS, UM... ERR...
DARN, I'M TOO SLEEPY ...
ZZZZ....
WAIT! DON'T GO BACK TO SLEEP, YOU USELESS CHILD!!

NEVER A SINGLE VICTORY

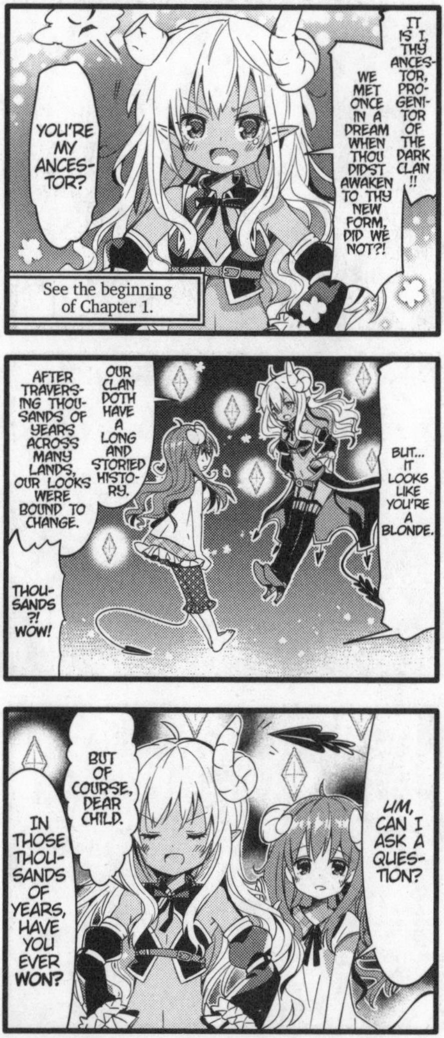
IT IS I, THY ANCESTOR, PROGENITOR OF THE DARK CLAN!!
WE MET ONCE IN A DREAM WHEN THOU DIDST AWAKEN TO THY NEW FORM, DID WE NOT?!
YOU'RE MY ANCESTOR?
See the beginning of Chapter 1.
BUT... IT LOOKS LIKE YOU'RE A BLONDE.
OUR CLAN DOTH HAVE A LONG AND STORIED HISTORY.
AFTER TRAVERSING THOUSANDS OF YEARS ACROSS MANY LANDS, OUR LOOKS WERE BOUND TO CHANGE.
THOUSANDS?! WOW!
UM, CAN I ASK A QUESTION?
BUT OF COURSE, DEAR CHILD.
IN THOSE THOUSANDS OF YEARS, HAVE YOU EVER WON?
......
DOST THOU LIKEST THE SPARKLES? IT TOOK ME HALF A DAY TO HANG THEM.
I TAKE IT, THEN, THAT YOUR TRACK RECORD ISN'T VERY GOOD!

UDON MEMORIES

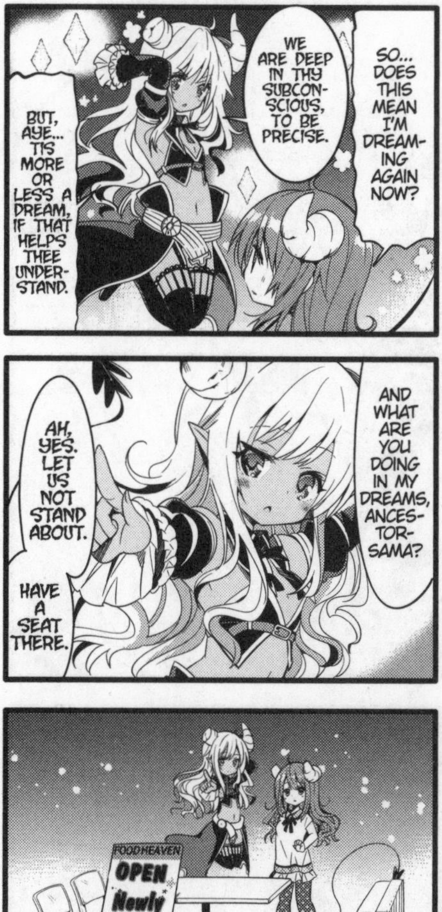
SO... DOES THIS MEAN I'M DREAMING AGAIN NOW?
WE ARE DEEP IN THY SUBCONSCIOUS, TO BE PRECISE.
BUT, AYE... TIS MORE OR LESS A DREAM, IF THAT HELPS THEE UNDERSTAND.
AND WHAT ARE YOU DOING IN MY DREAMS, ANCESTOR-SAMA?
AH, YES. LET US NOT STAND ABOUT.
HAVE A SEAT THERE.
FOOD HEAVEN
OPEN
Newly Renovated
Everything 20% OFF
WAIT, I'VE SEEN THESE SEATS BEFORE!
THE SIGN, TOO!
I DREW THEM FROM THY SUBCONSCIOUS, AFTER ALL!!
BLAME THY OWN BRAIN, NOT ME!
OPEN
Newly Renovated

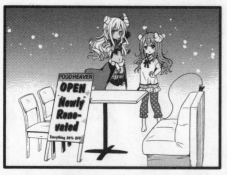

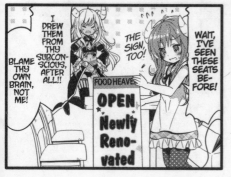

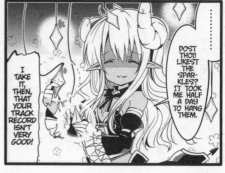

A DIFFERENT KIND OF DREAM

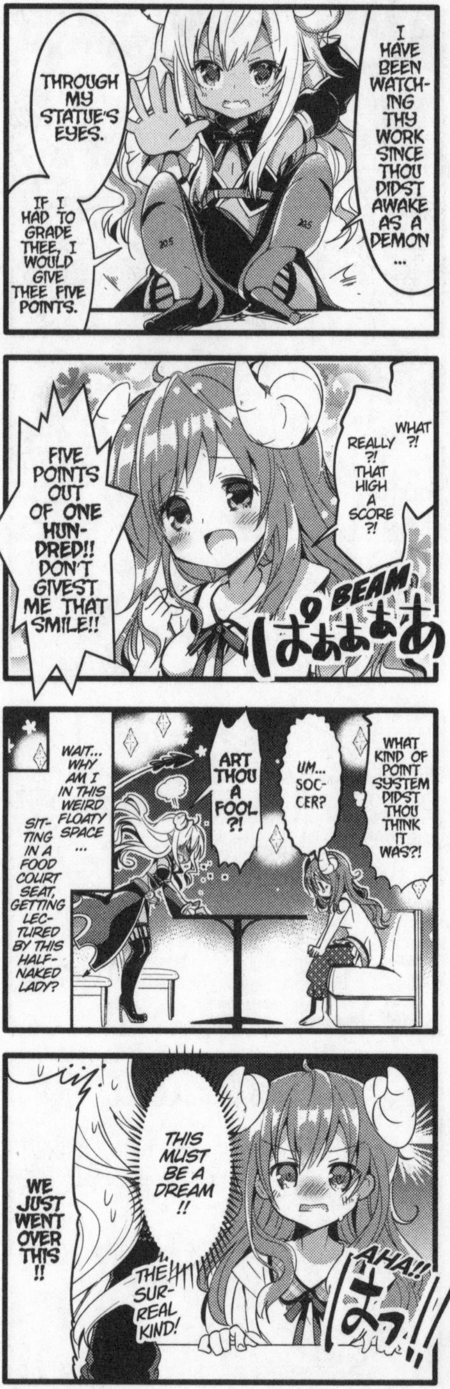
I HAVE BEEN WATCHING THY WORK SINCE THOU DIDST AWAKE AS A DEMON...
THROUGH MY STATUE'S EYES.
IF I HAD TO GRADE THEE, I WOULD GIVE THEE FIVE POINTS.
WHAT ?!
REALLY ?! THAT HIGH A SCORE ?!
FIVE POINTS OUT OF ONE HUNDRED!! DON'T GIVEST ME THAT SMILE!!
BEAM
ぱぁぁぁあ
WHAT KIND OF POINT SYSTEM DIDST THOU THINK IT WAS?!
UM... SOCCER?
ART THOU A FOOL ?!
WAIT... WHY AM I IN THIS WEIRD FLOATY SPACE... SITTING IN A FOOD COURT SEAT, GETTING LECTURED BY THIS HALF-NAKED LADY?
AHA!!
はっ!!
THIS MUST BE A DREAM!!
WE JUST WENT OVER THIS!!
THE SURREAL KIND!

THAT BUBBLY FEELING

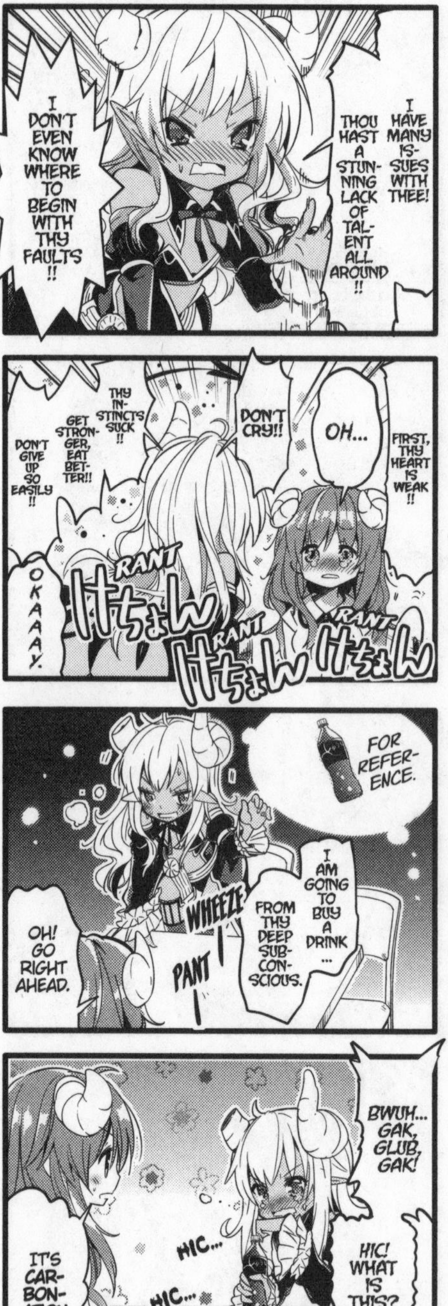
I HAVE MANY ISSUES WITH THEE!
THOU HAST A STUNNING LACK OF TALENT ALL AROUND!!
I DON'T EVEN KNOW WHERE TO BEGIN WITH THY FAULTS!!
FIRST, THY HEART IS WEAK!!
OH...
DON'T CRY!!
THY INSTINCTS SUCK!!
GET STRONGER, EAT BETTER!!
DON'T GIVE UP SO EASILY!!
RANT
けちょん
RANT
けちょん
RANT
けちょん
OKAAAAY.
FOR REFERENCE.
I AM GOING TO BUY A DRINK...
FROM THY DEEP SUBCONSCIOUS.
WHEEZE
PANT
OH! GO RIGHT AHEAD.
BWUH... GAK, GLUB, GAK!
HIC! WHAT IS THIS? HIC! POISON ?!
HIC...
HIC...
IT'S CARBONATION!!

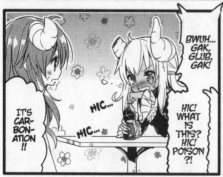

UNDERUTILIZED

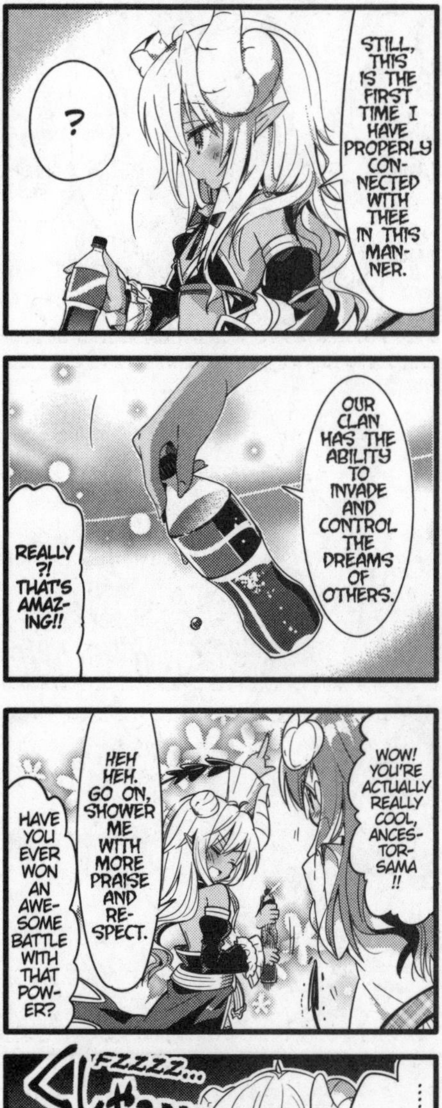
STILL, THIS IS THE FIRST TIME I HAVE PROPERLY CONNECTED WITH THEE IN THIS MANNER.
?
OUR CLAN HAS THE ABILITY TO INVADE AND CONTROL THE DREAMS OF OTHERS.
REALLY?! THAT'S AMAZING!!
WOW! YOU'RE ACTUALLY REALLY COOL, ANCESTOR-SAMA!!
HEH HEH. GO ON, SHOWER ME WITH MORE PRAISE AND RESPECT.
HAVE YOU EVER WON AN AWESOME BATTLE WITH THAT POWER?
FZZZZ...
......
I SENSE THIS DRINK COULD BE ADDICTIVE ONCE I GOT USED TO IT.
YEAH, SURE IS.

SHAMIKO SIGNAL: ONE BAR

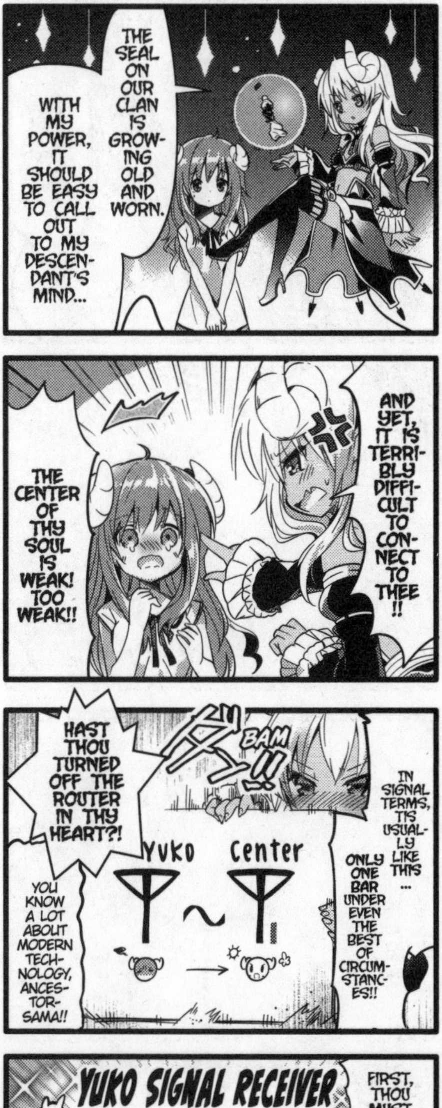
THE SEAL ON OUR CLAN IS GROWING OLD AND WORN.
WITH MY POWER, IT SHOULD BE EASY TO CALL OUT TO MY DESCENDANT'S MIND...
AND YET, IT IS TERRIBLY DIFFICULT TO CONNECT TO THEE!!
THE CENTER OF THY SOUL IS WEAK! TOO WEAK!!
BAM!!
IN SIGNAL TERMS, TIS USUALLY LIKE THIS... ONLY ONE BAR UNDER EVEN THE BEST OF CIRCUMSTANCES!!
HAST THOU TURNED OFF THE ROUTER IN THY HEART?!
Yuko
Center
YOU KNOW A LOT ABOUT MODERN TECHNOLOGY, ANCESTOR-SAMA!!
FIRST, THOU MUST BUILD AN ANTENNA NEXT TO THY PILLOW TO BETTER RECEIVE MY SIGNAL!!
YUKO SIGNAL RECEIVER
MY MOM WOULD FREAK OUT IF I DID SOMETHING LIKE THAT!!

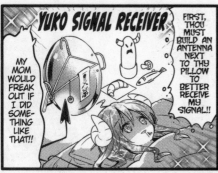

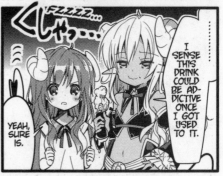

MOM'S SNOOZE BUTTON

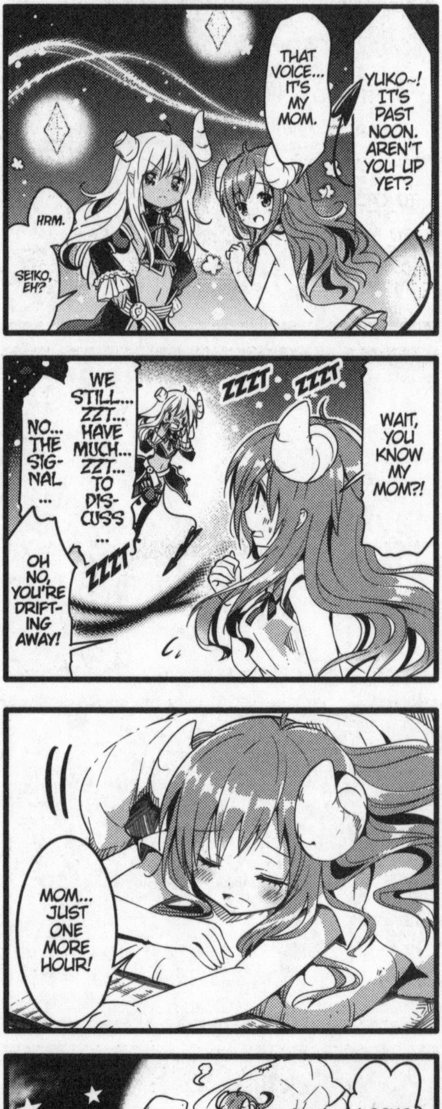
YUKO~! IT'S PAST NOON. AREN'T YOU UP YET?
THAT VOICE... IT'S MY MOM.
HRM.
SEIKO, EH?
WAIT, YOU KNOW MY MOM?!
ZZZT
ZZZT
WE STILL... ZZT... HAVE MUCH... ZZT... TO DISCUSS ...
NO... THE SIGNAL ...
ZZZT
OH NO, YOU'RE DRIFTING AWAY!
MOM... JUST ONE MORE HOUR!
LOOKS LIKE MY REAL-WORLD SELF WENT BACK TO SLEEP !!
WE'RE STILL GOOD !
TWAS PATHETIC, BUT WELL DONE!!

A BUNCH OF IMPORTANT STUFF

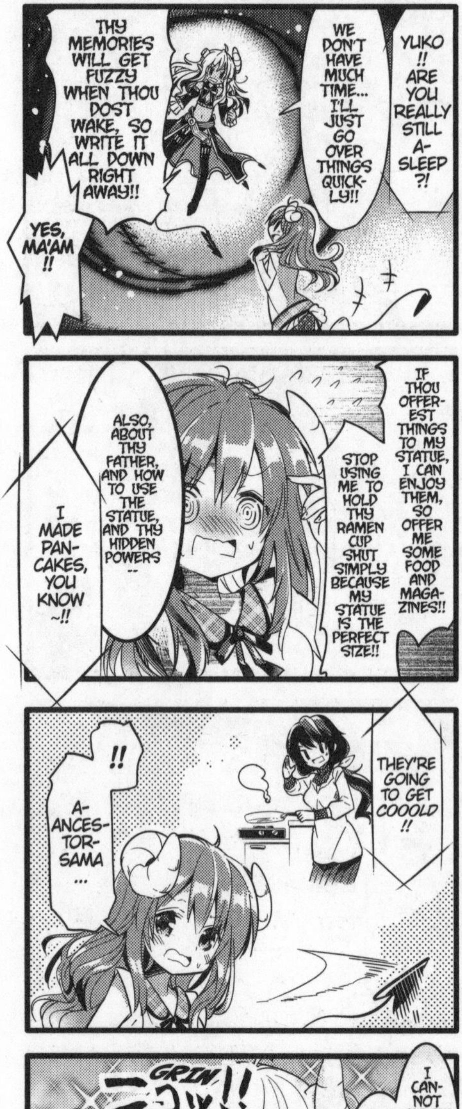
YUKO!! ARE YOU REALLY STILL ASLEEP?!
WE DON'T HAVE MUCH TIME... I'LL JUST GO OVER THINGS QUICKLY!!
THY MEMORIES WILL GET FUZZY WHEN THOU DOST WAKE, SO WRITE IT ALL DOWN RIGHT AWAY!!
YES, MA'AM!!
IF THOU OFFEREST THINGS TO MY STATUE, I CAN ENJOY THEM, SO OFFER ME SOME FOOD AND MAGAZINES!!
STOP USING ME TO HOLD THY RAMEN CUP SHUT SIMPLY BECAUSE MY STATUE IS THE PERFECT SIZE!!
ALSO, ABOUT THY FATHER, AND HOW TO USE THE STATUE, AND THY HIDDEN POWERS --
I MADE PANCAKES, YOU KNOW ~!!
THEY'RE GOING TO GET COOOLD !!
!!
A-ANCESTOR-SAMA ...
I CANNOT ALLOW THEE TO MISS PANCAKES !!
GO!! WITH THE PRIDE AND HOPE FOR OUR CLAN IN THY HEART !!
ニコッ!! GRIN
WOW! YOU TRULY ARE MY ANCESTOR!!

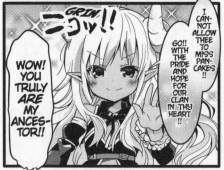

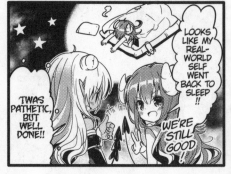

FILE OVERWRITTEN

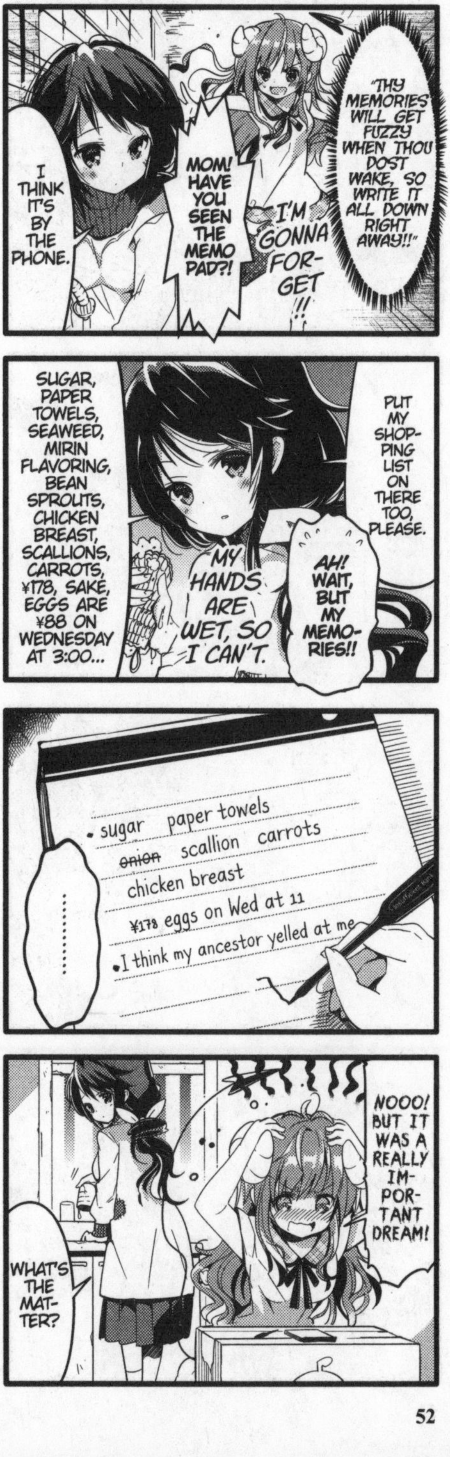
"THY MEMORIES WILL GET FUZZY WHEN THOU DOST WAKE, SO WRITE IT ALL DOWN RIGHT AWAY!!"
I'M GONNA FORGET!!
MOM! HAVE YOU SEEN THE MEMO PAD?!
I THINK IT'S BY THE PHONE.
PUT MY SHOPPING LIST ON THERE TOO, PLEASE.
AH! WAIT, BUT MY MEMORIES!!
MY HANDS ARE WET, SO I CAN'T.
SUGAR, PAPER TOWELS, SEAWEED, MIRIN FLAVORING, BEAN SPROUTS, CHICKEN BREAST, SCALLIONS, CARROTS, ¥178, SAKE, EGGS ARE ¥88 ON WEDNESDAY AT 3:00...
......
sugar paper towels
~~onion~~ scallion carrots
chicken breast
¥178 eggs on Wed at 11
I think my ancestor yelled at me
NOOO! BUT IT WAS A REALLY IMPORTANT DREAM!
WHAT'S THE MATTER?

BREAKFAST ON A BUDGET

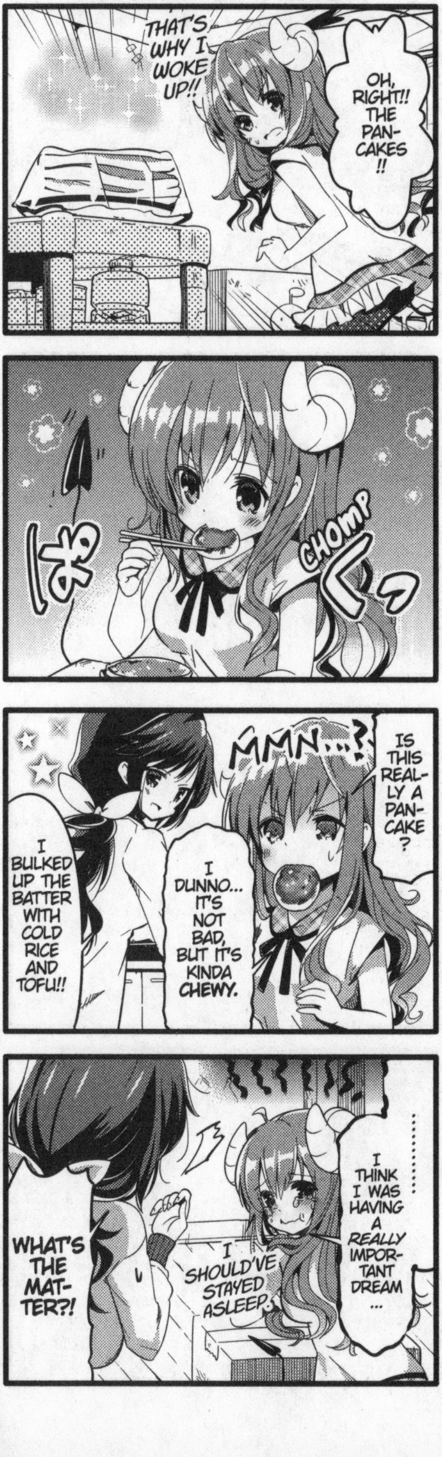
OH, RIGHT!! THE PANCAKES!!
THAT'S WHY I WOKE UP!!
CHOMP
ぱくっ
IS THIS REALLY A PANCAKE?
MMN...?
I DUNNO... IT'S NOT BAD, BUT IT'S KINDA CHEWY.
I BULKED UP THE BATTER WITH COLD RICE AND TOFU!!
......
I THINK I WAS HAVING A REALLY IMPORTANT DREAM...
I SHOULD'VE STAYED ASLEEP.
WHAT'S THE MATTER?!

A DREAM, BUT NOT A DREAM

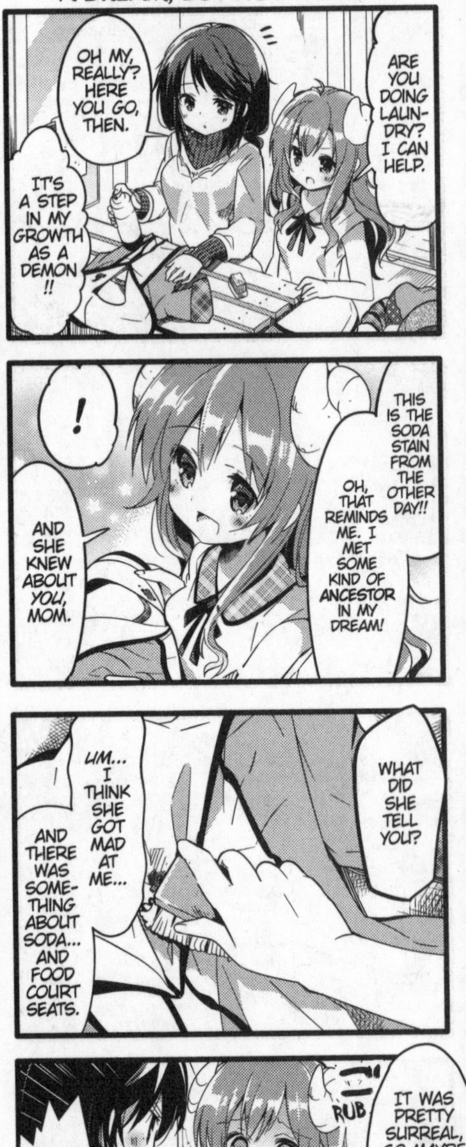
ARE YOU DOING LAUNDRY? I CAN HELP.
OH MY, REALLY? HERE YOU GO, THEN.
IT'S A STEP IN MY GROWTH AS A DEMON!!
THIS IS THE SODA STAIN FROM THE OTHER DAY!!
OH, THAT REMINDS ME. I MET SOME KIND OF ANCESTOR IN MY DREAM!
!
AND SHE KNEW ABOUT *YOU*, MOM.
WHAT DID SHE TELL YOU?
UM... I THINK SHE GOT MAD AT ME...
AND THERE WAS SOMETHING ABOUT SODA... AND FOOD COURT SEATS.
IT WAS PRETTY SURREAL, SO MAYBE IT REALLY *WAS* JUST A DREAM.
RUB
SCRUB
SCRUB
SCRUB
SCRUB
SCRUB
WAS THE DREAM JUST A DREAM?!!
I'M NOT SURE, BUT YOU *ARE* SCRUBBING THAT STAIN TOO HARD!!

HER ONLY UNIFORM

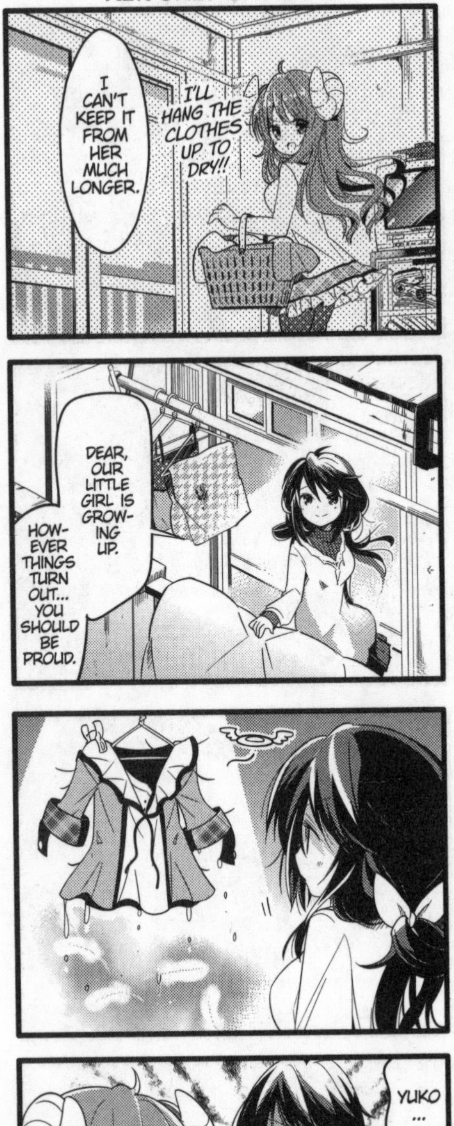
I'LL HANG THE CLOTHES UP TO DRY!!
I CAN'T KEEP IT FROM HER MUCH LONGER.
DEAR, OUR LITTLE GIRL IS GROWING UP.
HOWEVER THINGS TURN OUT... YOU SHOULD BE PROUD.
YUKO...
YOU HAVE TO WASH WOOL PROPERLY OR IT SHRINKS!!
HUH?

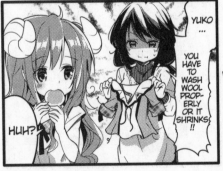

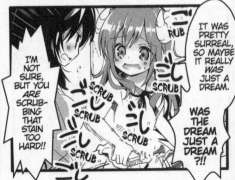

THIRD FLOOR

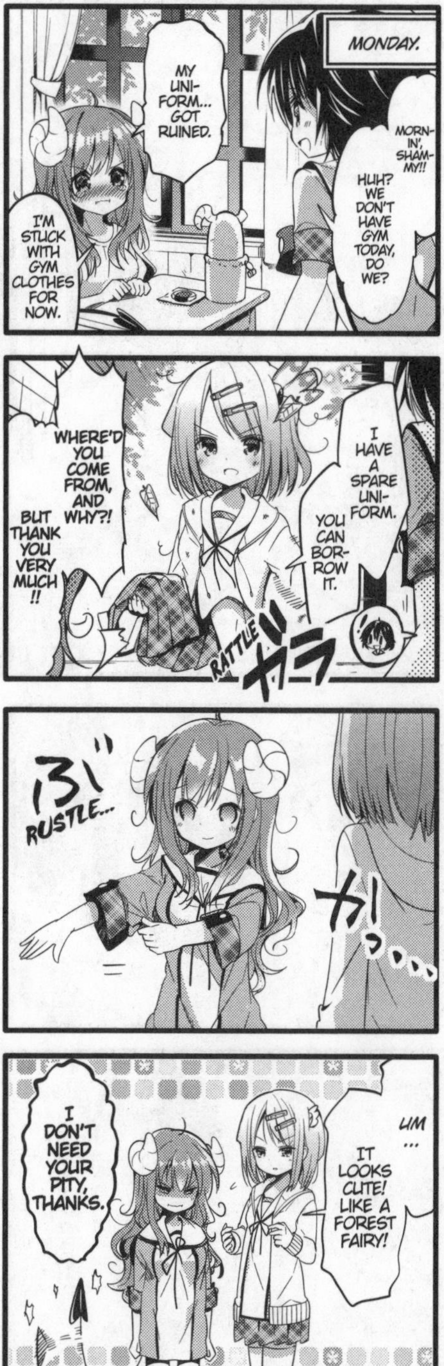

MONDAY.
MORN-IN', SHAM-MY!!
HUH? WE DON'T HAVE GYM TODAY, DO WE?
MY UNI-FORM... GOT RUINED.
I'M STUCK WITH GYM CLOTHES FOR NOW.
I HAVE A SPARE UNI-FORM.
YOU CAN BOR-ROW IT.
RATTLE
WHERE'D YOU COME FROM, AND WHY?!
BUT THANK YOU VERY MUCH!!
RUSTLE...
UM ...
IT LOOKS CUTE! LIKE A FOREST FAIRY!
I DON'T NEED YOUR PITY, THANKS.

PINK FLATTERY ATTACK

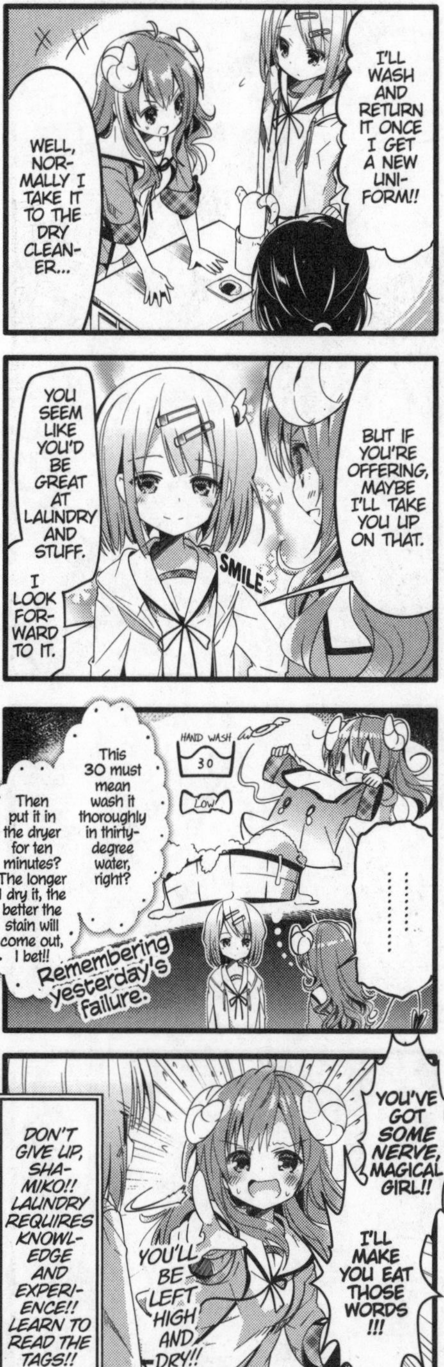

I'LL WASH AND RETURN IT ONCE I GET A NEW UNI-FORM!!
WELL, NOR-MALLY I TAKE IT TO THE DRY CLEANER...
BUT IF YOU'RE OFFERING, MAYBE I'LL TAKE YOU UP ON THAT.
SMILE
YOU SEEM LIKE YOU'D BE GREAT AT LAUNDRY AND STUFF.
I LOOK FOR-WARD TO IT.
HAND WASH
30
LOW
This 30 must mean wash it thoroughly in thirty-degree water, right?
Then put it in the dryer for ten minutes? The longer I dry it, the better the stain will come out, I bet!!
Remembering yesterday's failure.
YOU'VE GOT SOME NERVE, MAGICAL GIRL!!
I'LL MAKE YOU EAT THOSE WORDS!!!
YOU'LL BE LEFT HIGH AND DRY!!
DON'T GIVE UP, SHA-MIKO!! LAUNDRY REQUIRES KNOWL-EDGE AND EXPERI-ENCE!! LEARN TO READ THE TAGS!!

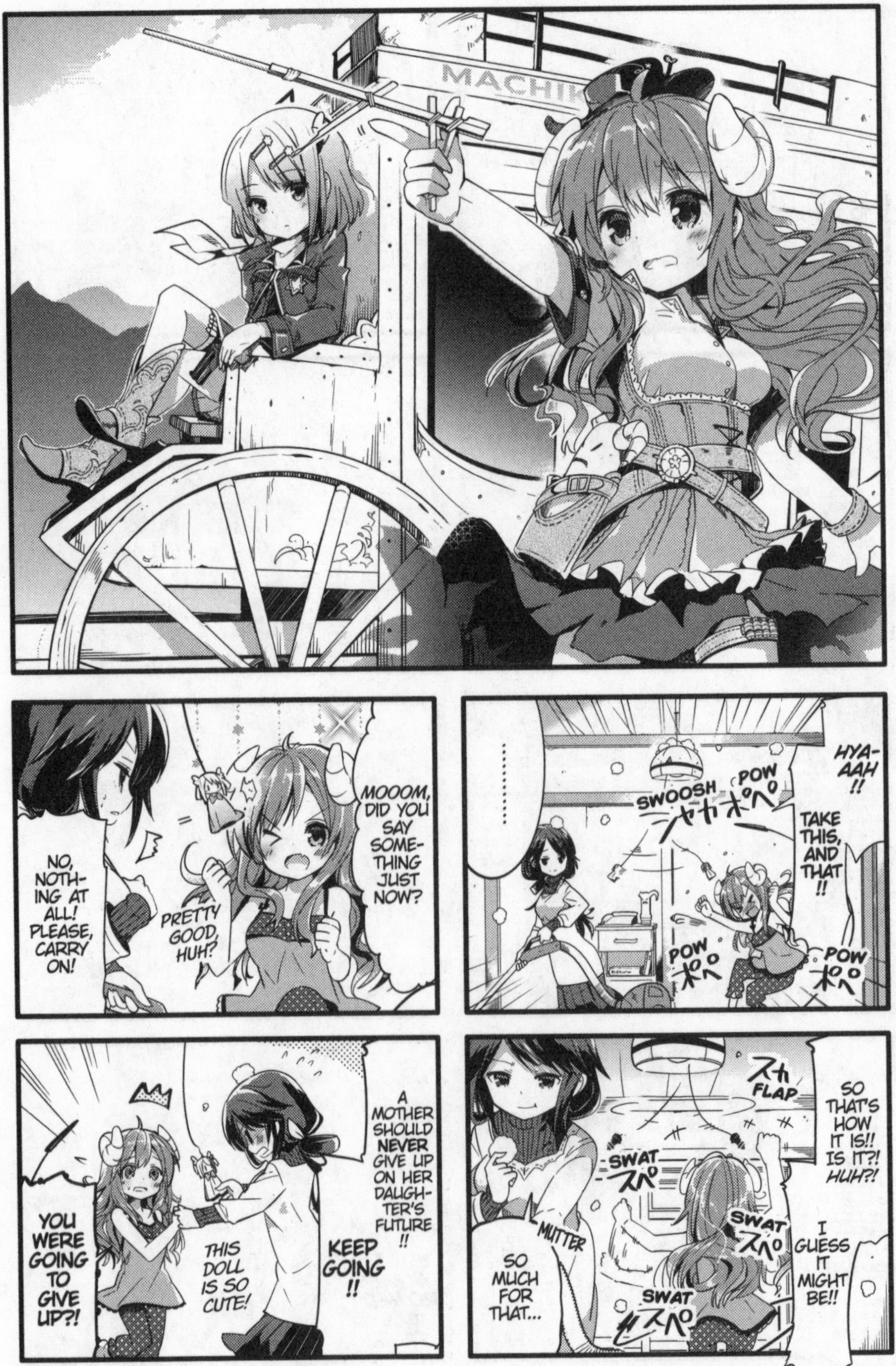
MACHIK
......
HYA-AAH!!
SWOOSH
POW
TAKE THIS, AND THAT!!
POW
POW
MOOOM, DID YOU SAY SOME-THING JUST NOW?
PRETTY GOOD, HUH?
NO, NOTH-ING AT ALL! PLEASE, CARRY ON!
SO THAT'S HOW IT IS!! IS IT?! HUH?!
FLAP
SWAT
I GUESS IT MIGHT BE!!
MUTTER
SWAT
SO MUCH FOR THAT...
SWAT
A MOTHER SHOULD NEVER GIVE UP ON HER DAUGH-TER'S FUTURE!!
KEEP GOING!!
THIS DOLL IS SO CUTE!
YOU WERE GOING TO GIVE UP?!

SEDUCTION COMPLETE

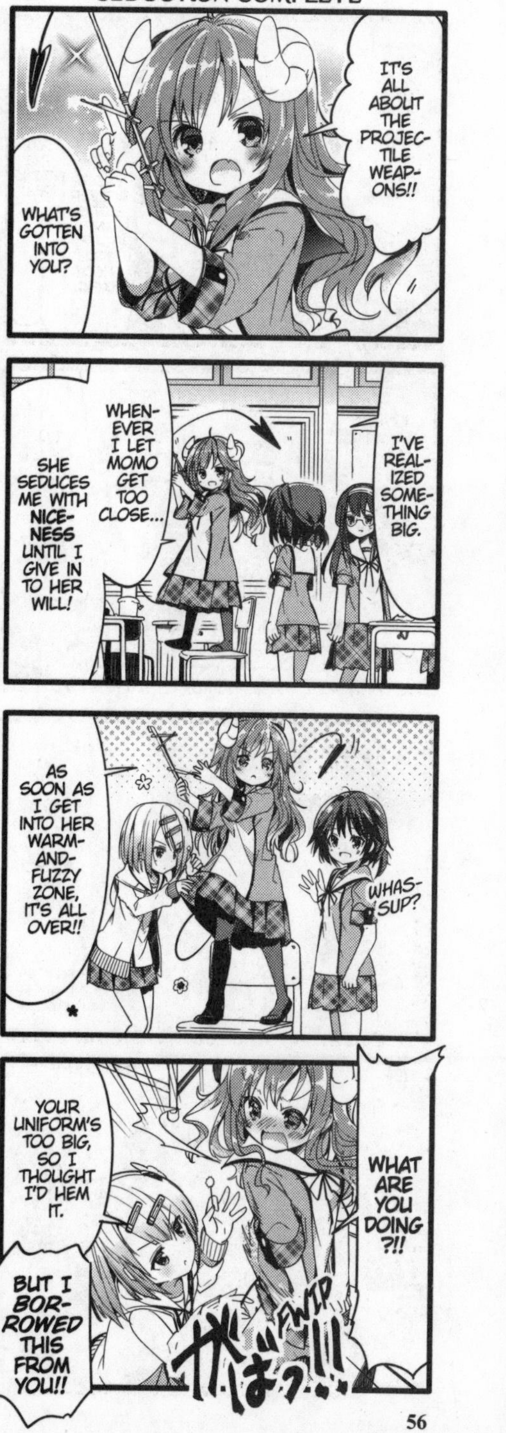
IT'S ALL ABOUT THE PROJECTILE WEAPONS!!
WHAT'S GOTTEN INTO YOU?
I'VE REALIZED SOMETHING BIG.
WHENEVER I LET MOMO GET TOO CLOSE...
SHE SEDUCES ME WITH NICENESS UNTIL I GIVE IN TO HER WILL!
WHASSUP?
AS SOON AS I GET INTO HER WARM-AND-FUZZY ZONE, IT'S ALL OVER!!
WHAT ARE YOU DOING?!!
YOUR UNIFORM'S TOO BIG, SO I THOUGHT I'D HEM IT.
BUT I BORROWED THIS FROM YOU!!
FWIP

WARM-AND-FUZZY ZONE

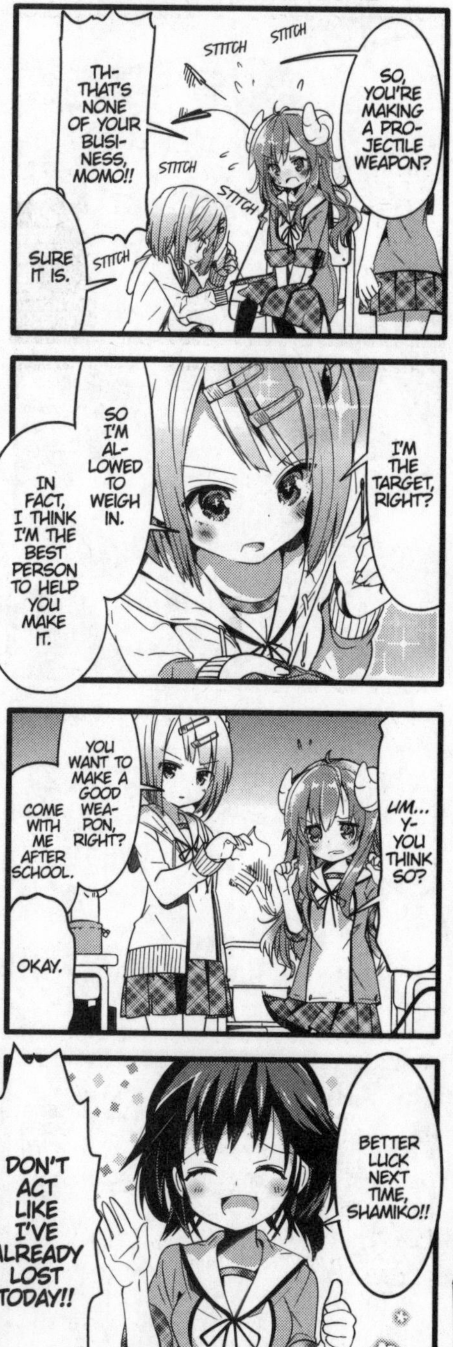
SO, YOU'RE MAKING A PROJECTILE WEAPON?
STITCH
STITCH
TH-THAT'S NONE OF YOUR BUSINESS, MOMO!!
STITCH
STITCH
SURE IT IS.
STITCH
I'M THE TARGET, RIGHT?
SO I'M ALLOWED TO WEIGH IN.
IN FACT, I THINK I'M THE BEST PERSON TO HELP YOU MAKE IT.
UM... Y-YOU THINK SO?
YOU WANT TO MAKE A GOOD WEAPON, RIGHT?
COME WITH ME AFTER SCHOOL.
OKAY.
BETTER LUCK NEXT TIME, SHAMIKO!!
DON'T ACT LIKE I'VE ALREADY LOST TODAY!!

FORMER SITE OF A LEVEL 10 PROJECTILE WEAPON

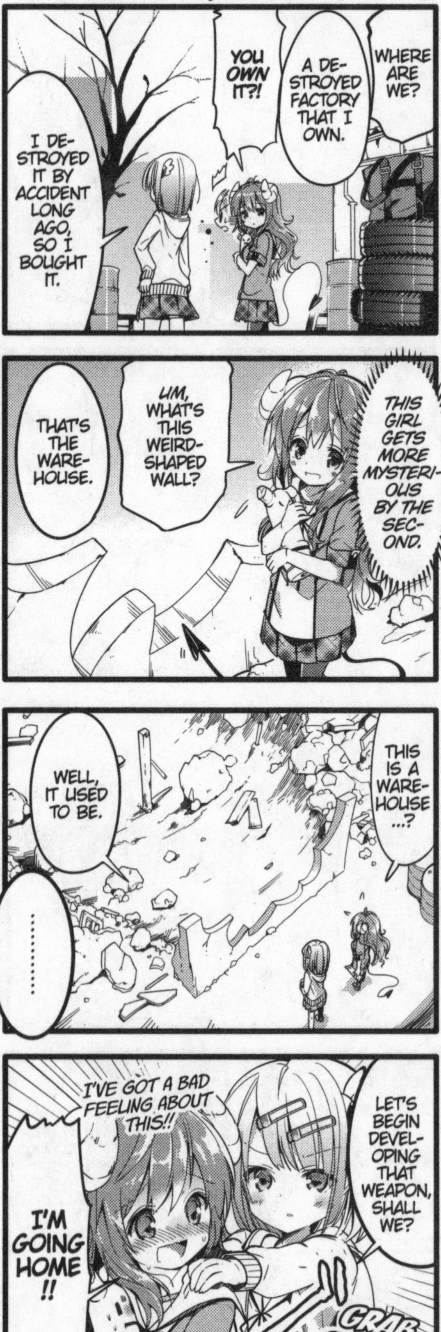

WHERE ARE WE?
A DE-STROYED FACTORY THAT I OWN.
YOU OWN IT?!
I DE-STROYED IT BY ACCIDENT LONG AGO, SO I BOUGHT IT.
THIS GIRL GETS MORE MYSTERI-OUS BY THE SEC-OND.
UM, WHAT'S THIS WEIRD-SHAPED WALL?
THAT'S THE WARE-HOUSE.
THIS IS A WARE-HOUSE ...?
WELL, IT USED TO BE.
......
LET'S BEGIN DEVEL-OPING THAT WEAPON, SHALL WE?
I'VE GOT A BAD FEELING ABOUT THIS!!
GRAB
I'M GOING HOME!!

MAGICAL GIRL LESSONS: IMAGINATION

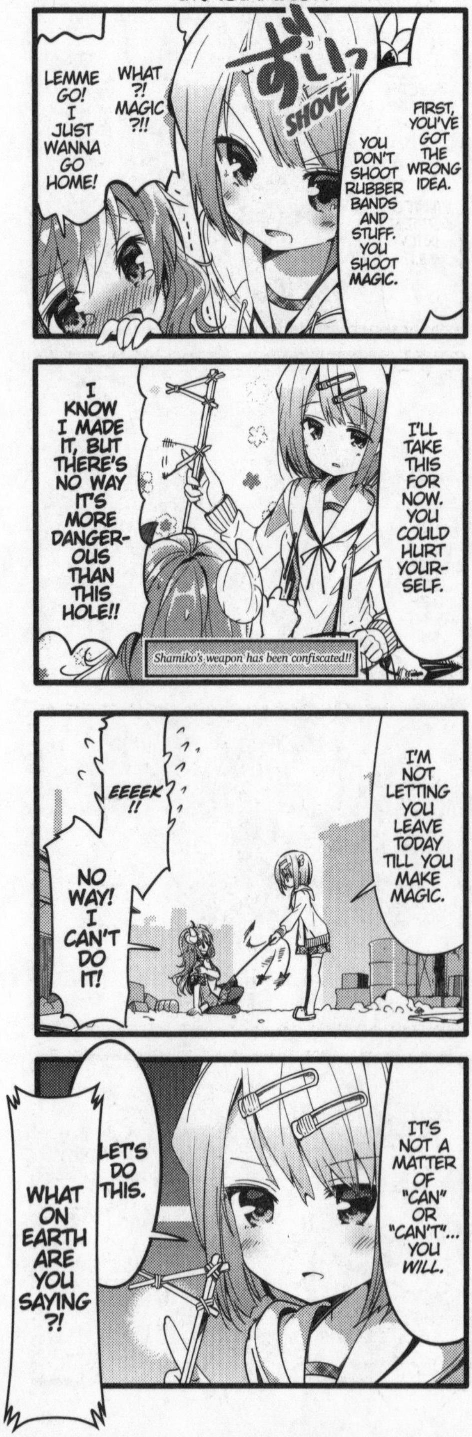

ずいっ
SHOVE
FIRST, YOU'VE GOT THE WRONG IDEA.
YOU DON'T SHOOT RUBBER BANDS AND STUFF. YOU SHOOT MAGIC.
WHAT?! MAGIC?!!
LEMME GO! I JUST WANNA GO HOME!
I'LL TAKE THIS FOR NOW. YOU COULD HURT YOURSELF.
I KNOW I MADE IT, BUT THERE'S NO WAY IT'S MORE DANGER-OUS THAN THIS HOLE!!
Shamiko's weapon has been confiscated!!
I'M NOT LETTING YOU LEAVE TODAY TILL YOU MAKE MAGIC.
EEEEK!!
NO WAY! I CAN'T DO IT!
IT'S NOT A MATTER OF "CAN" OR "CAN'T"... YOU WILL.
LET'S DO THIS.
WHAT ON EARTH ARE YOU SAYING?!

PERFECT SIZE

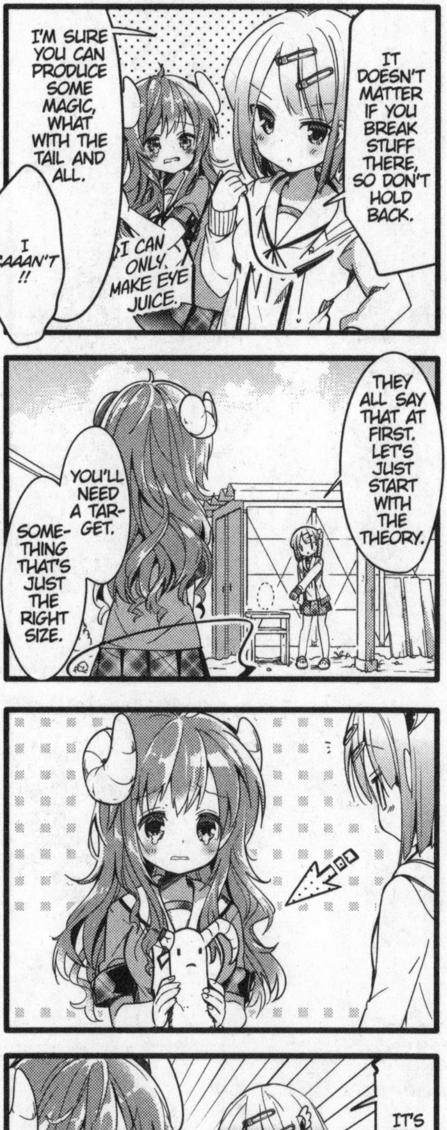
IT DOESN'T MATTER IF YOU BREAK STUFF THERE, SO DON'T HOLD BACK.
I'M SURE YOU CAN PRODUCE SOME MAGIC, WHAT WITH THE TAIL AND ALL.
I CAN ONLY MAKE EYE JUICE.
I CAAAN'T!!
THEY ALL SAY THAT AT FIRST. LET'S JUST START WITH THE THEORY.
YOU'LL NEED A TARGET.
SOMETHING THAT'S JUST THE RIGHT SIZE.
IT'S PERFECT!!
NO! THAT'S SO MEAN!!

SPECIAL STAFF

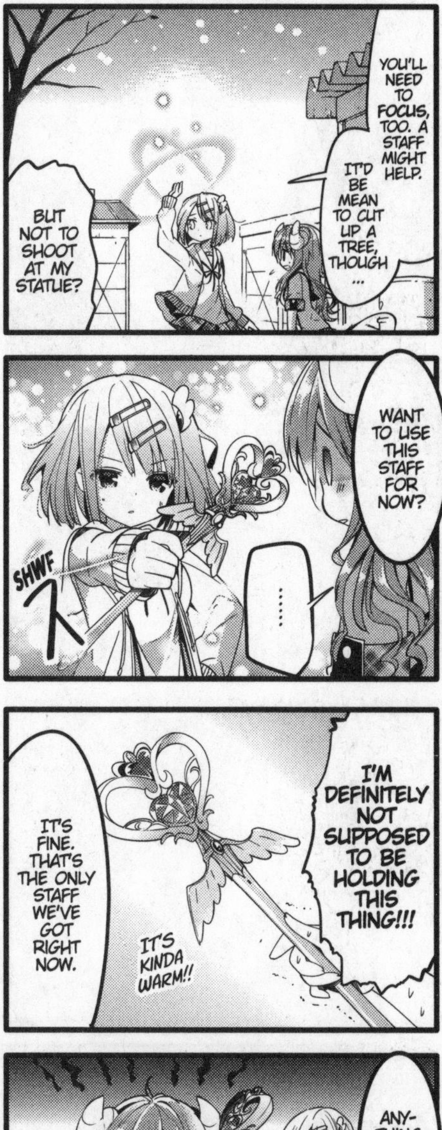
YOU'LL NEED TO FOCUS, TOO. A STAFF MIGHT HELP.
IT'D BE MEAN TO CUT UP A TREE, THOUGH...
BUT NOT TO SHOOT AT MY STATUE?
WANT TO USE THIS STAFF FOR NOW?
SHWF
......
I'M DEFINITELY NOT SUPPOSED TO BE HOLDING THIS THING!!!
IT'S KINDA WARM!!
IT'S FINE. THAT'S THE ONLY STAFF WE'VE GOT RIGHT NOW.
ANYTHING COMING OUT YET?
YEAH, A WHOLE LOTTA SWEAT.

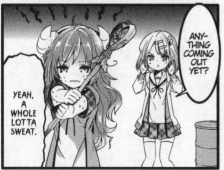

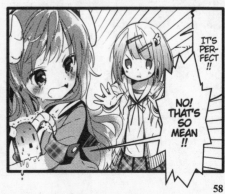

LOFTY GOALS

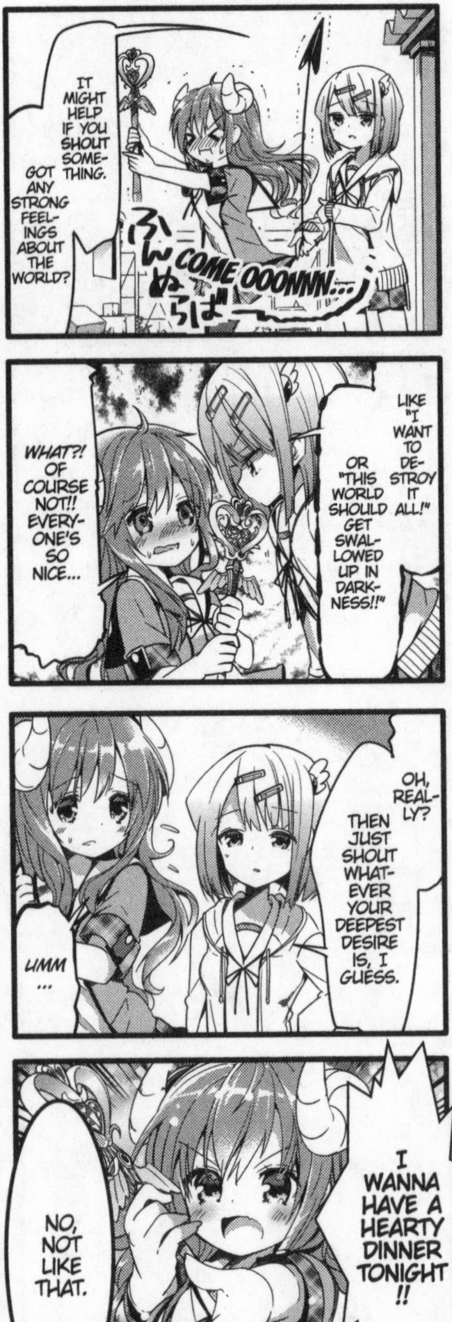
IT MIGHT HELP IF YOU SHOUT SOMETHING.
GOT ANY STRONG FEELINGS ABOUT THE WORLD?
ふんぬらば
COME OOONNN...
LIKE "I WANT TO DESTROY IT ALL!"
OR "THIS WORLD SHOULD GET SWALLOWED UP IN DARKNESS!!"
WHAT?! OF COURSE NOT!! EVERYONE'S SO NICE...
OH, REALLY?
THEN JUST SHOUT WHATEVER YOUR DEEPEST DESIRE IS, I GUESS.
UMM...
I WANNA HAVE A HEARTY DINNER TONIGHT!!
NO, NOT LIKE THAT.

MOMO'S SPECIAL ATTACK (WITH ECHO)

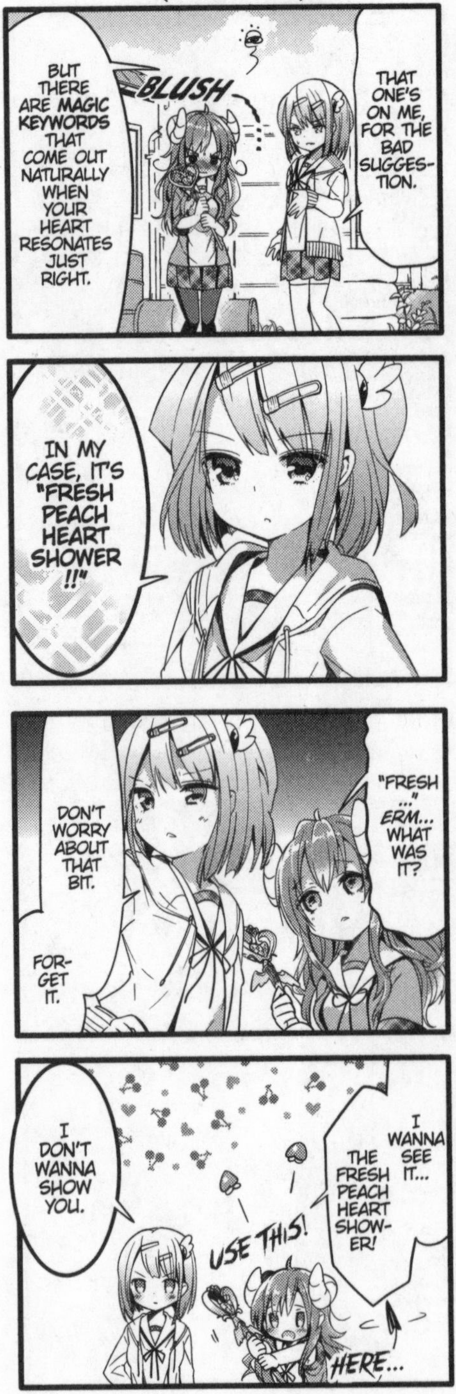
THAT ONE'S ON ME, FOR THE BAD SUGGESTION.
BLUSH
BUT THERE ARE MAGIC KEYWORDS THAT COME OUT NATURALLY WHEN YOUR HEART RESONATES JUST RIGHT.
IN MY CASE, IT'S "FRESH PEACH HEART SHOWER!!"
"FRESH..." ERM... WHAT WAS IT?
DON'T WORRY ABOUT THAT BIT.
FORGET IT.
I WANNA SEE IT... THE FRESH PEACH HEART SHOWER!
HERE...
USE THIS!
I DON'T WANNA SHOW YOU.

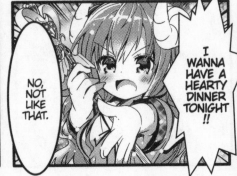

HOW HUNGRY ARE YOU?

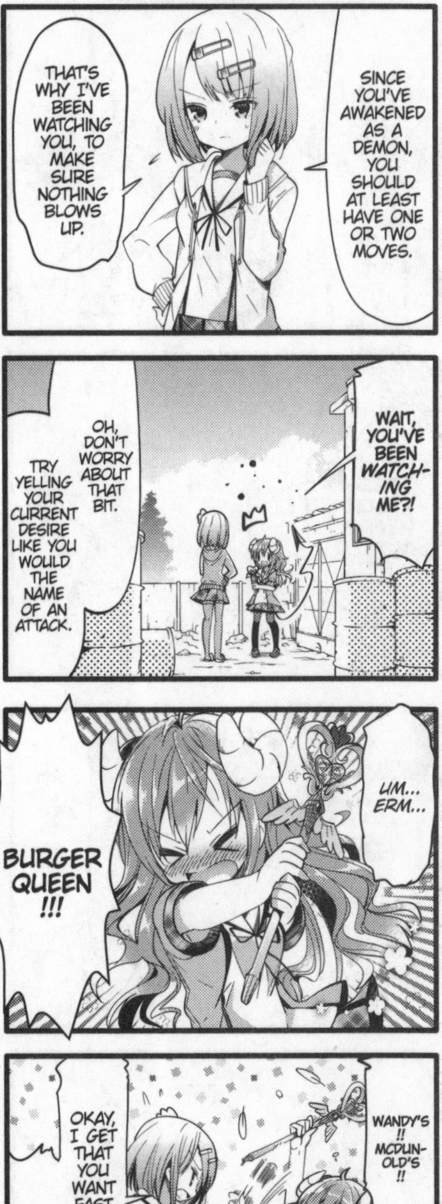

SINCE YOU'VE AWAKENED AS A DEMON, YOU SHOULD AT LEAST HAVE ONE OR TWO MOVES.
THAT'S WHY I'VE BEEN WATCHING YOU, TO MAKE SURE NOTHING BLOWS UP.
WAIT, YOU'VE BEEN WATCHING ME?!
OH, DON'T WORRY ABOUT THAT BIT.
TRY YELLING YOUR CURRENT DESIRE LIKE YOU WOULD THE NAME OF AN ATTACK.
UM... ERM...
BURGER QUEEN!!!
WANDY'S!! MCDUNOLD'S!!
OKAY, I GET THAT YOU WANT FAST FOOD.
BUT THOSE AREN'T ATTACK NAMES!!
HOW ABOUT... DONNY'S!!

READ IT AGAIN--
SHE NEVER SAID THAT

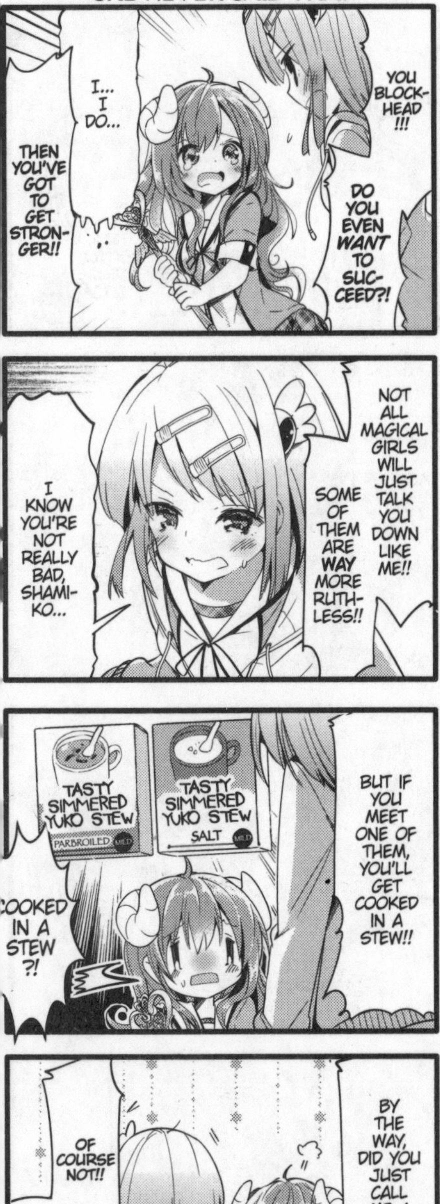

YOU BLOCKHEAD!!!
DO YOU EVEN WANT TO SUCCEED?!
I... I DO...
THEN YOU'VE GOT TO GET STRONGER!!
NOT ALL MAGICAL GIRLS WILL JUST TALK YOU DOWN LIKE ME!!
SOME OF THEM ARE WAY MORE RUTHLESS!!
I KNOW YOU'RE NOT REALLY BAD, SHAMIKO...
BUT IF YOU MEET ONE OF THEM, YOU'LL GET COOKED IN A STEW!!
TASTY SIMMERED YUKO STEW
SALT
MILD
TASTY SIMMERED YUKO STEW
PARBROILED
MILD
COOKED IN A STEW?!
BY THE WAY, DID YOU JUST CALL ME A BLOCKHEAD?!
OF COURSE NOT!!
YOU BLOCKHEAD!!

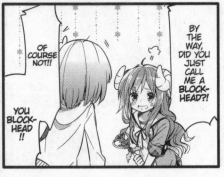

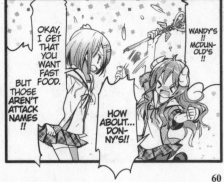

THE LEGENDARY 100% BEEF

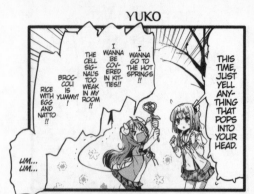

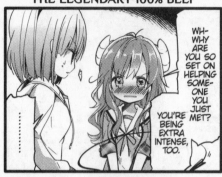

WH-WHY ARE YOU SO SET ON HELPING SOMEONE YOU JUST MET?
YOU'RE BEING EXTRA INTENSE, TOO.
......
DON'T WORRY ABOUT THAT BIT, EITHER.
HOW CAN I *NOT* WORRY ABOUT THAT BIT?!
THE SUN'S STARTING TO SET, SHAMIKO.
IF YOU CAN PRODUCE MAGIC, I'LL MAKE YOU A 100% BEEF HAMBURG STEAK.
I'LL EVEN MAKE A DEMI-GLACE SAUCE WITH A RED WINE REDUCTION.
SO, 100% BEEF REALLY DOES EXIST?!!
IT DOES! SO LET'S TRY AGAIN!!
WHAT ABOUT 120%?!
YES, MA'AM!!
100

YUKO

THIS TIME, JUST YELL ANYTHING THAT POPS INTO YOUR HEAD.
I WANNA GO TO THE HOT SPRINGS!!
I WANNA BE COVERED IN KITTIES!!
THE CELL SIGNAL'S TOO WEAK IN MY ROOM!!
BROCCOLI IS YUMMY!!
RICE WITH EGG AND NATTO!!
UM... UM...
I JUST!! WANT EVERYONE!! TO GET ALOOONG!!!
POOF!!
WOW!!
LOOK, I DID IT!!
IT'S SUPER SLOW, BUT I MADE IT~!!
SO TINY AND CUTE!!
WHY DID *THAT* LINE WORK...?

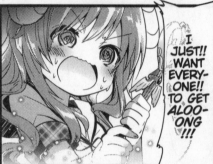

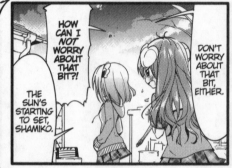

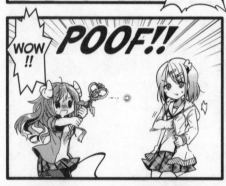

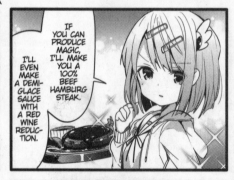

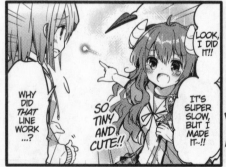

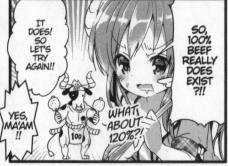

THAT KINDA HURTS

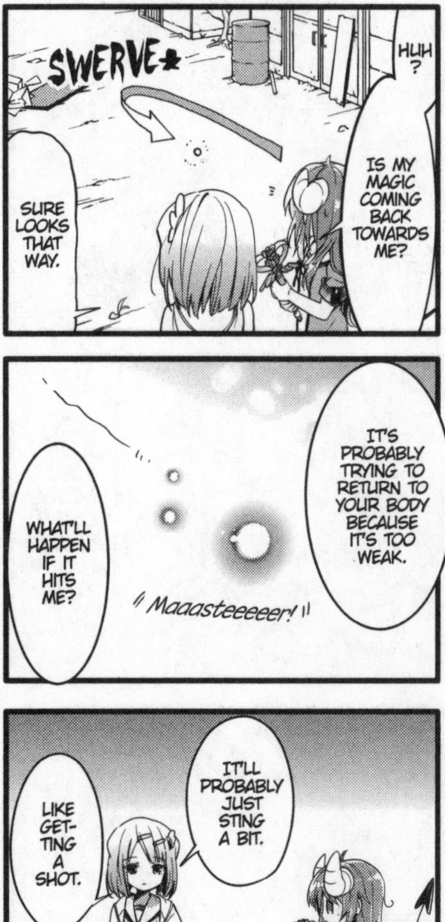
HUH?
SWERVE
IS MY MAGIC COMING BACK TOWARDS ME?
SURE LOOKS THAT WAY.
IT'S PROBABLY TRYING TO RETURN TO YOUR BODY BECAUSE IT'S TOO WEAK.
Maaasteeeeeer!
WHAT'LL HAPPEN IF IT HITS ME?
IT'LL PROBABLY JUST STING A BIT.
LIKE GETTING A SHOT.
......
DARN YOU, MAGICAL GIRL!!!
IT SHOULD FADE OUT IF YOU RUN FOR TWO TO THIRTY MINUTES.
DASH!!

SIX KILOMETERS PER HOUR

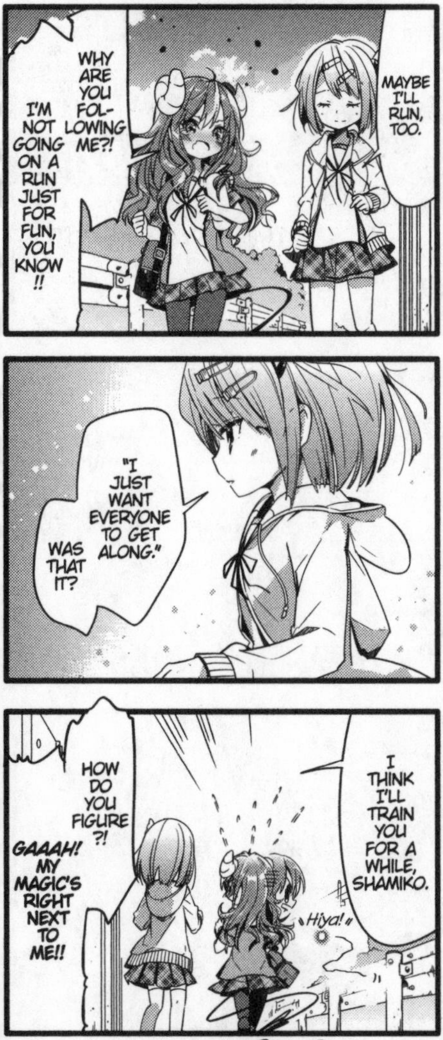
MAYBE I'LL RUN, TOO.
WHY ARE YOU FOLLOWING ME?!
I'M NOT GOING ON A RUN JUST FOR FUN, YOU KNOW!!
"I JUST WANT EVERYONE TO GET ALONG."
WAS THAT IT?
I THINK I'LL TRAIN YOU FOR A WHILE, SHAMIKO.
Hiya!
HOW DO YOU FIGURE?!
GAAAH! MY MAGIC'S RIGHT NEXT TO ME!!
ZAP!!
I'LL GET YOU NEXT T--
OOOOOOWW!!
DON'T GIVE UP, SHAMIKO! KEEP RUNNING, EVEN IF YOU GET ZAPPED!!

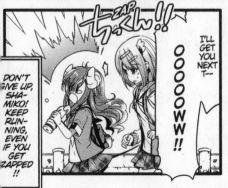

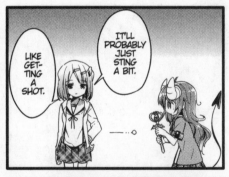

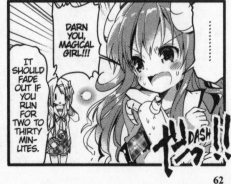

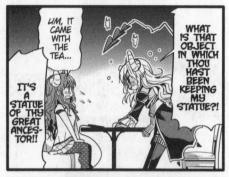

SECONDS!! DEMON GIRL NEXT DOO

(CHAPTER 5)

~ THE ANCESTOR'S VISIT ~

YOU WILL LIVE LONGER IF YOUR LOWER BODY STAYS NICE AND WARM ALL DAY.

BY ANCESTOR STATUE

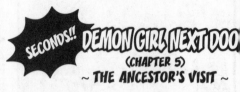

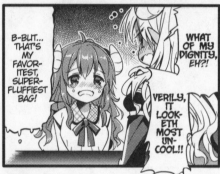

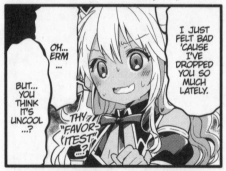

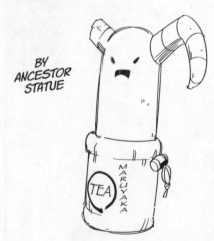

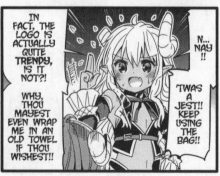

TEA
MARUYAKA

WHAT IS THAT OBJECT IN WHICH THOU HAST BEEN KEEPING MY STATUE?!
UM, IT CAME WITH THE TEA...
IT'S A STATUE OF THY GREAT ANCESTOR!!
WHAT OF MY DIGNITY, EH?!
B-BUT... THAT'S MY FAVORITEST, SUPER-FLUFFIEST BAG!
VERILY, IT LOOKETH MOST UNCOOL!!
I JUST FELT BAD 'CAUSE I'VE DROPPED YOU SO MUCH LATELY.
OH... ERM ...
BUT... YOU THINK IT'S UNCOOL ...?
THY "FAVORITEST" ...?
N... NAY!!
IN FACT, THE LOGO IS ACTUALLY QUITE TRENDY, IS IT NOT?!
'TWAS A JEST!! KEEP USING THE BAG!!
WHY, THOU MAYEST EVEN WRAP ME IN AN OLD TOWEL IF THOU WISHEST!!

SECONDS!! **DEMON GIRL NEXT DOOR**

(CHAPTER 6)

~ MOMO'S UNEXPECTED POWER ~

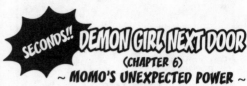

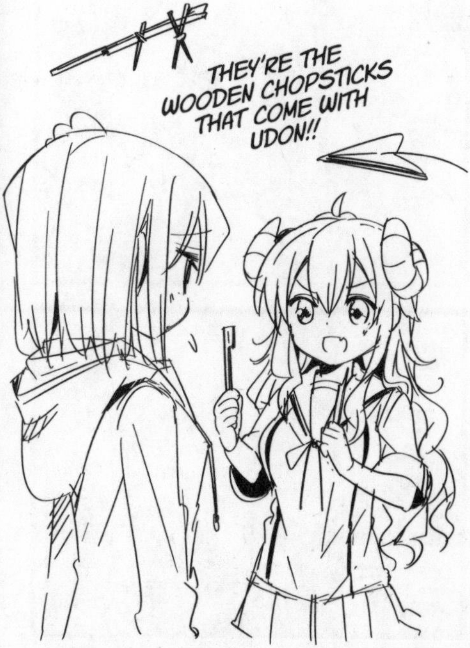
THEY'RE THE WOODEN CHOPSTICKS THAT COME WITH UDON!!

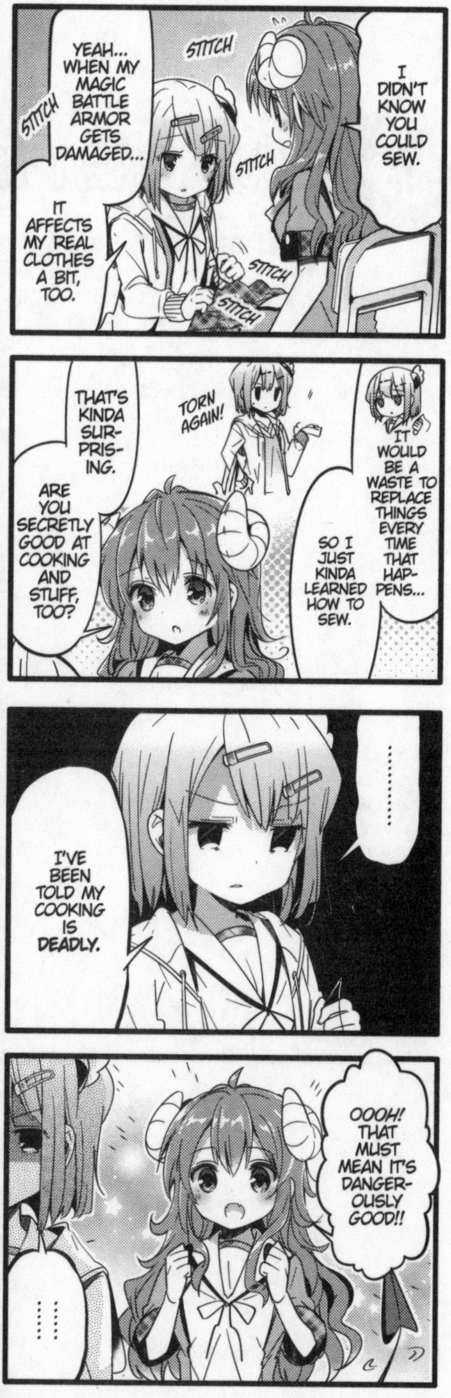
I DIDN'T KNOW YOU COULD SEW.
YEAH... WHEN MY MAGIC BATTLE ARMOR GETS DAMAGED...
IT AFFECTS MY REAL CLOTHES A BIT, TOO.
STITCH
STITCH
STITCH
STITCH
STITCH
TORN AGAIN!
IT WOULD BE A WASTE TO REPLACE THINGS EVERY TIME THAT HAP-PENS...
SO I JUST KINDA LEARNED HOW TO SEW.
THAT'S KINDA SUR-PRIS-ING.
ARE YOU SECRETLY GOOD AT COOKING AND STUFF, TOO?
....
I'VE BEEN TOLD MY COOKING IS DEADLY.
OOOH! THAT MUST MEAN IT'S DANGER-OUSLY GOOD!!
......

The Demon Girl Next Door

The Demon Girl Next Door

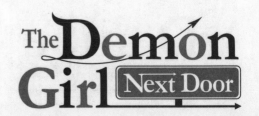

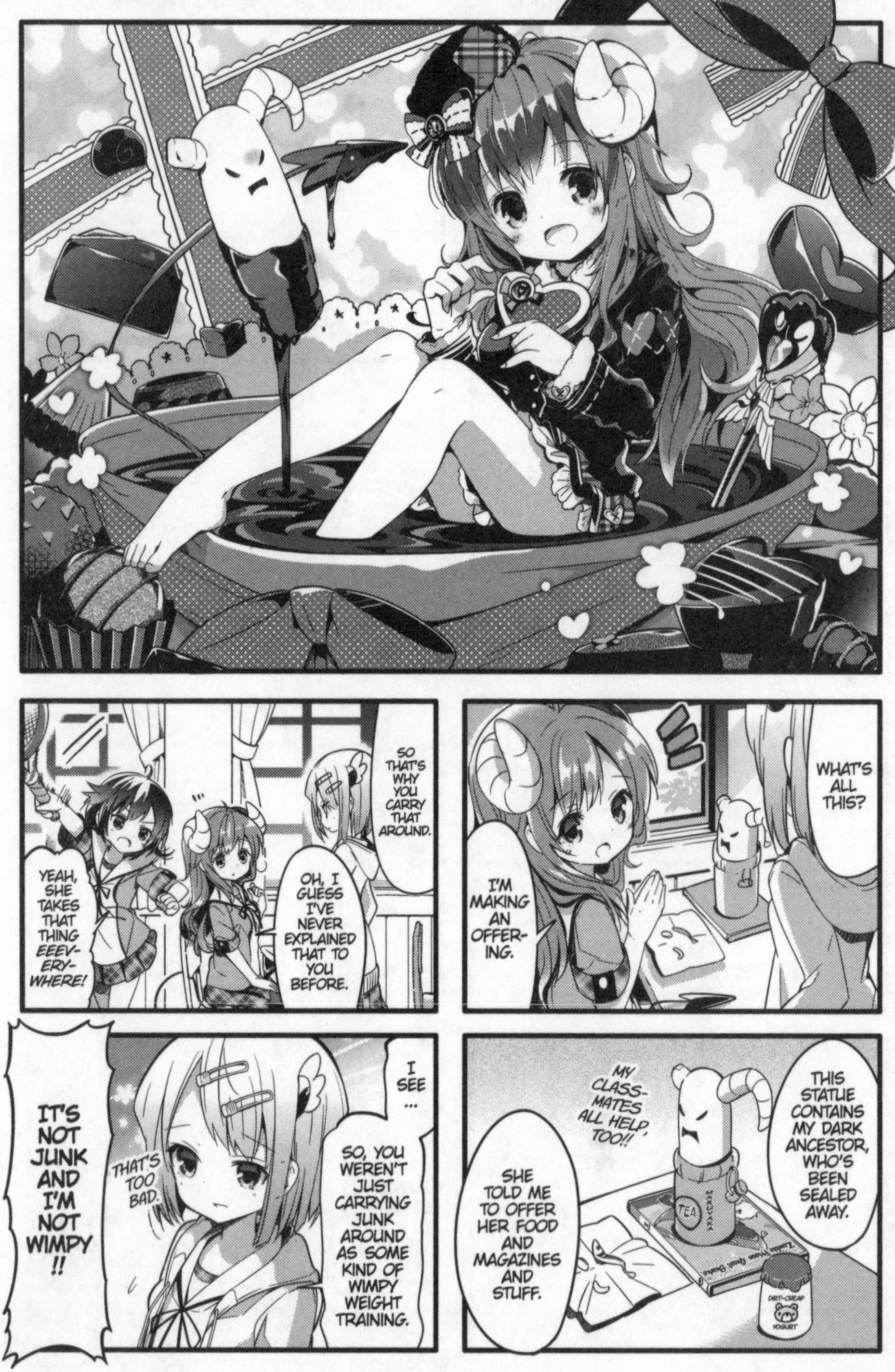
WHAT'S ALL THIS?
I'M MAKING AN OFFERING.
SO THAT'S WHY YOU CARRY THAT AROUND.
OH, I GUESS I'VE NEVER EXPLAINED THAT TO YOU BEFORE.
YEAH, SHE TAKES THAT THING EEEVERYWHERE!
THIS STATUE CONTAINS MY DARK ANCESTOR, WHO'S BEEN SEALED AWAY.
MY CLASSMATES ALL HELP, TOO!!
SHE TOLD ME TO OFFER HER FOOD AND MAGAZINES AND STUFF.
TEA
DIRT-CHEAP YOGURT
I SEE ...
SO, YOU WEREN'T JUST CARRYING JUNK AROUND AS SOME KIND OF WIMPY WEIGHT TRAINING.
THAT'S TOO BAD.
IT'S NOT JUNK AND I'M NOT WIMPY!!

THE SECRET BENEATH THE BAG

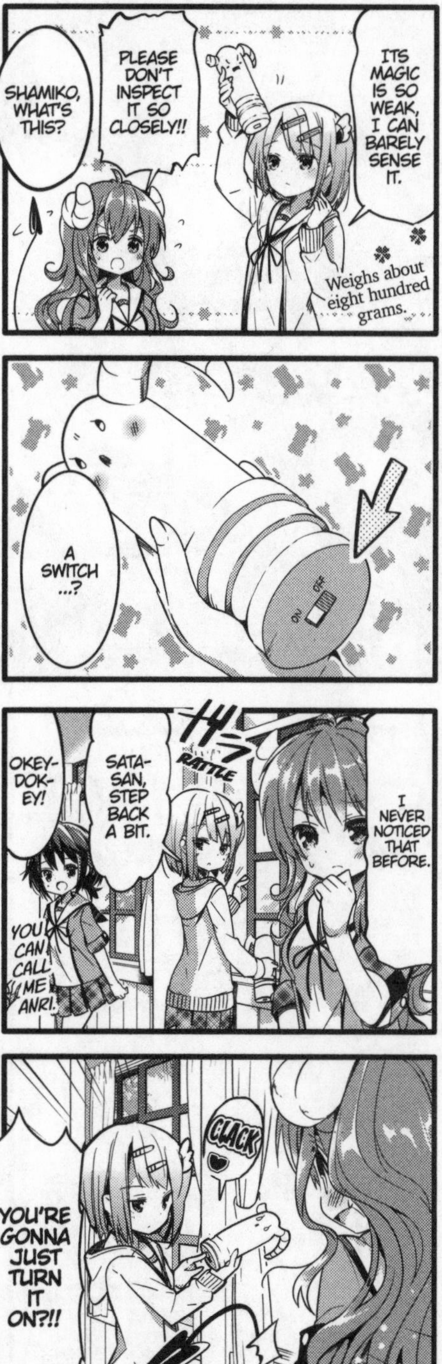
ITS MAGIC IS SO WEAK, I CAN BARELY SENSE IT.
PLEASE DON'T INSPECT IT SO CLOSELY!!
SHAMIKO, WHAT'S THIS?
Weighs about eight hundred grams.
A SWITCH ...?
I NEVER NOTICED THAT BEFORE.
RATTLE
SATA-SAN, STEP BACK A BIT.
OKEY-DOKEY!
YOU CAN CALL ME ANRI.
CLACK
YOU'RE GONNA JUST TURN IT ON?!!

A MAGICAL GIRL IS PREPARED

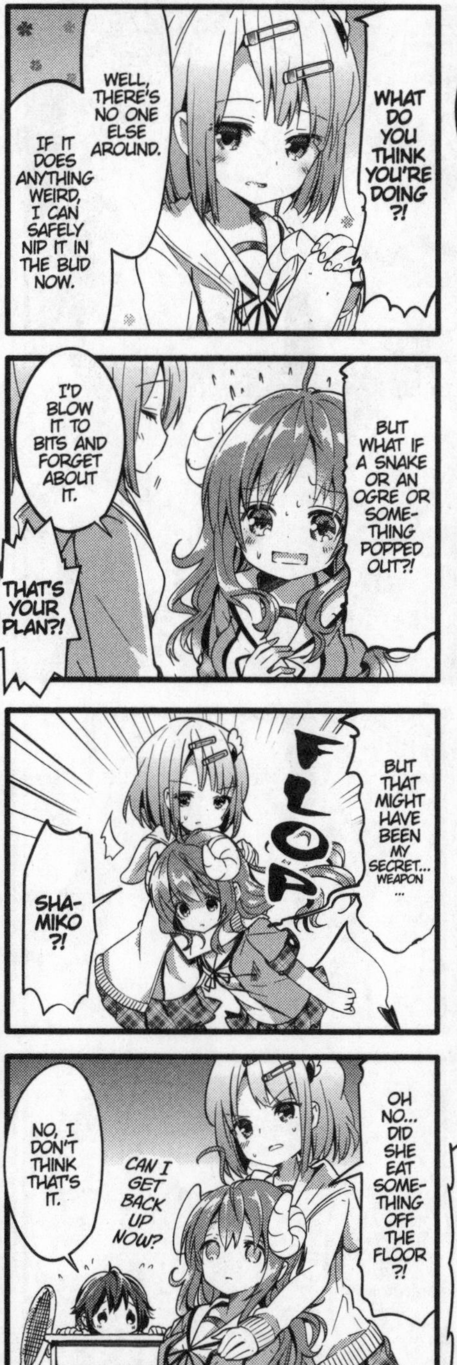
WHAT DO YOU THINK YOU'RE DOING?!
WELL, THERE'S NO ONE ELSE AROUND.
IF IT DOES ANYTHING WEIRD, I CAN SAFELY NIP IT IN THE BUD NOW.
BUT WHAT IF A SNAKE OR AN OGRE OR SOMETHING POPPED OUT?!
I'D BLOW IT TO BITS AND FORGET ABOUT IT.
THAT'S YOUR PLAN?!
BUT THAT MIGHT HAVE BEEN MY SECRET... WEAPON ...
FLOP
SHAMIKO?!
OH NO... DID SHE EAT SOMETHING OFF THE FLOOR?!
CAN I GET BACK UP NOW?
NO, I DON'T THINK THAT'S IT.

RETURN OF THE ANCESTOR

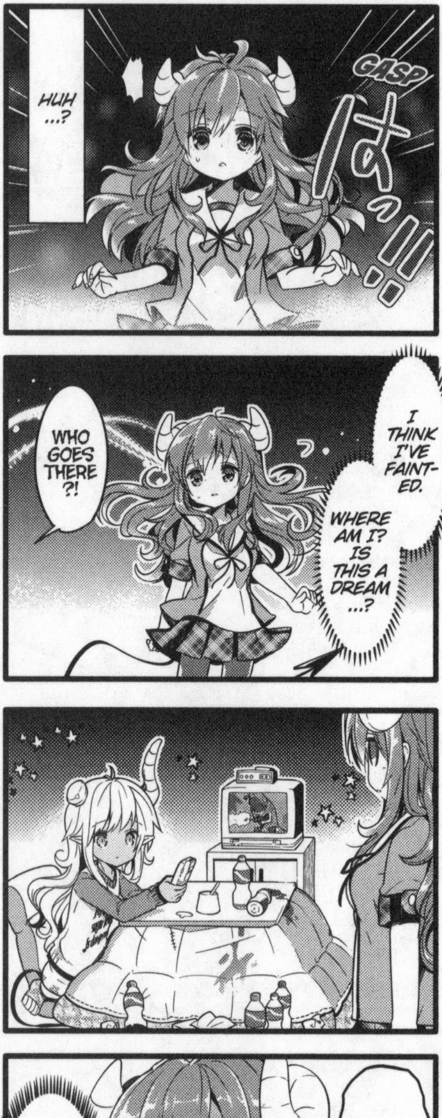
GASP
はっ!!
HUH ...?
I THINK I'VE FAINT-ED.
WHERE AM I? IS THIS A DREAM ...?
WHO GOES THERE?!
OH... UM, HELLO AGAIN...
ANCES-TOR-SAMA IN "OFF MODE"?!

SOME ASSEMBLY REQUIRED

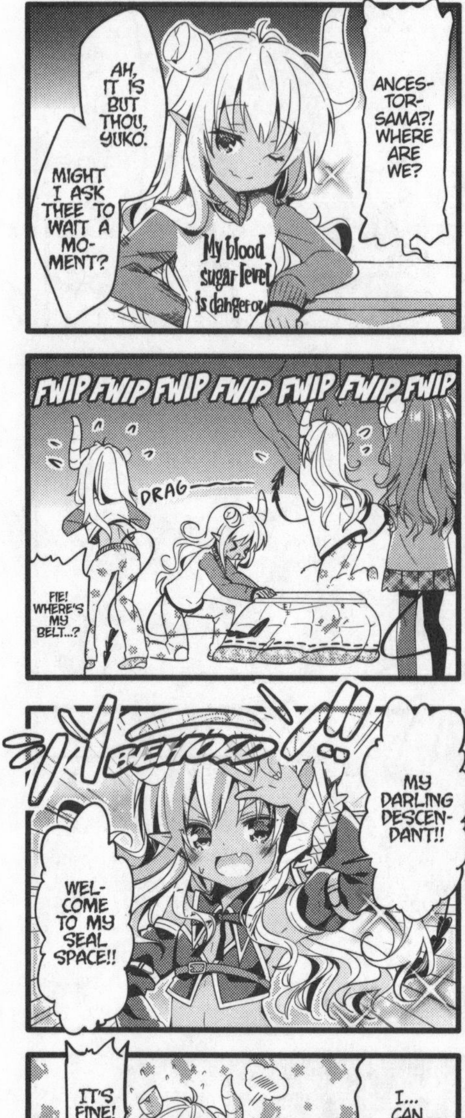
ANCES-TOR-SAMA?! WHERE ARE WE?
AH, IT IS BUT THOU, YUKO.
MIGHT I ASK THEE TO WAIT A MO-MENT?
My blood sugar-level is dangerou
FWIP FWIP FWIP FWIP FWIP FWIP FWIP
DRAG
FIE! WHERE'S MY BELT...?
BEHOLD
MY DARLING DESCEN-DANT!!
WEL-COME TO MY SEAL SPACE!!
I... CAN HELP YOU FIND YOUR CLOTHES.
IT'S FINE!
THIS IS WHAT THEY CALLETH "A LOOK"!

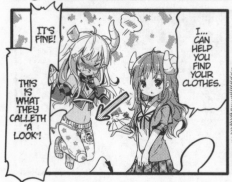

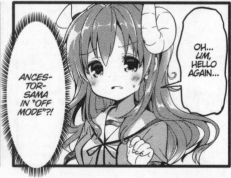

AN ANCESTOR ENTERS THE FRAY

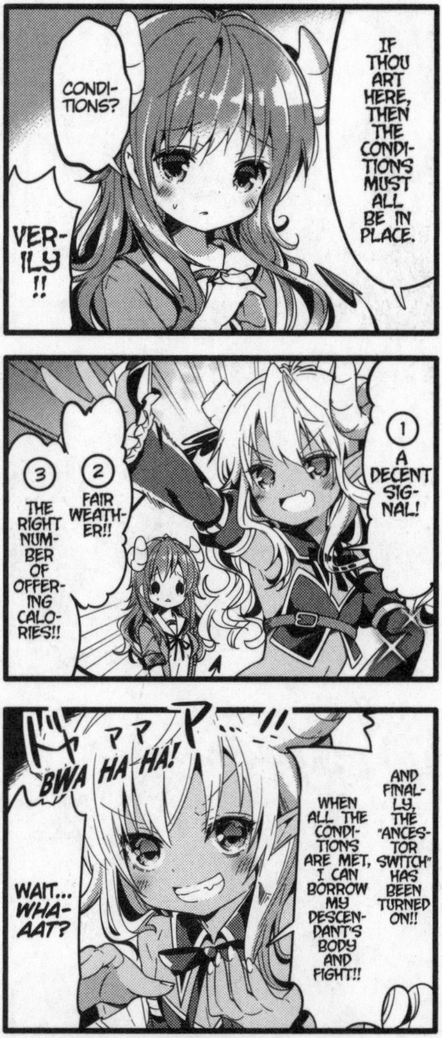
IF THOU ART HERE, THEN THE CONDITIONS MUST ALL BE IN PLACE.
CONDITIONS?
VERILY!!
① A DECENT SIGNAL!
② FAIR WEATHER!!
③ THE RIGHT NUMBER OF OFFERING CALORIES!!
ドァァァア…!!
AND FINALLY, THE "ANCESTOR SWITCH" HAS BEEN TURNED ON!!
WHEN ALL THE CONDITIONS ARE MET, I CAN BORROW MY DESCENDANT'S BODY AND FIGHT!!
BWA HA HA!
WAIT... WHA-AAT?
I GET TO GO OUTSIDE AT LAA-AST!!
BUT WHAT AM I SUPPOSED TO DO?!
JUST RELAX!! SIT AT THE KOTATSU!!

MOMO'S FLASH OF GENIUS

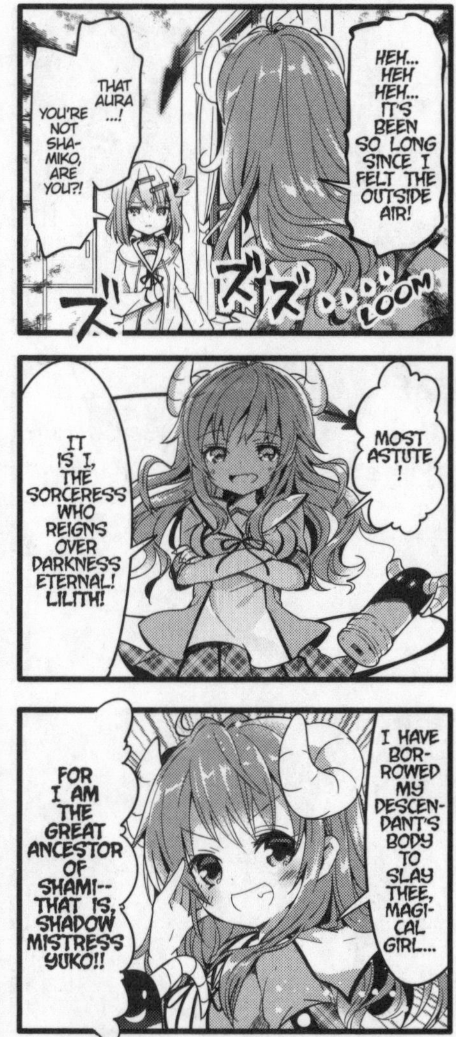
HEH... HEH HEH... IT'S BEEN SO LONG SINCE I FELT THE OUTSIDE AIR!
THAT AURA...!
YOU'RE NOT SHAMIKO, ARE YOU?!
ズズ
LOOM
ズ
MOST ASTUTE!
IT IS I, THE SORCERESS WHO REIGNS OVER DARKNESS ETERNAL! LILITH!
I HAVE BORROWED MY DESCENDANT'S BODY TO SLAY THEE, MAGICAL GIRL...
FOR I AM THE GREAT ANCESTOR OF SHAMI--THAT IS, SHADOW MISTRESS YUKO!!
!
SO, YOU'RE SHAMIKO SENIOR...
SHAMISEN*!!
HOW DAREST THOU, FOOLISH FOOL!!
HEH!

*Momo is comparing Lilith's name (Shamiko Senior or ShamiSen), to a samisen, a traditional Japanese stringed instrument.

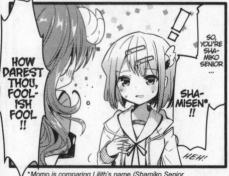

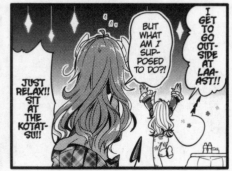

DEMONS HAVE FEELINGS, TOO

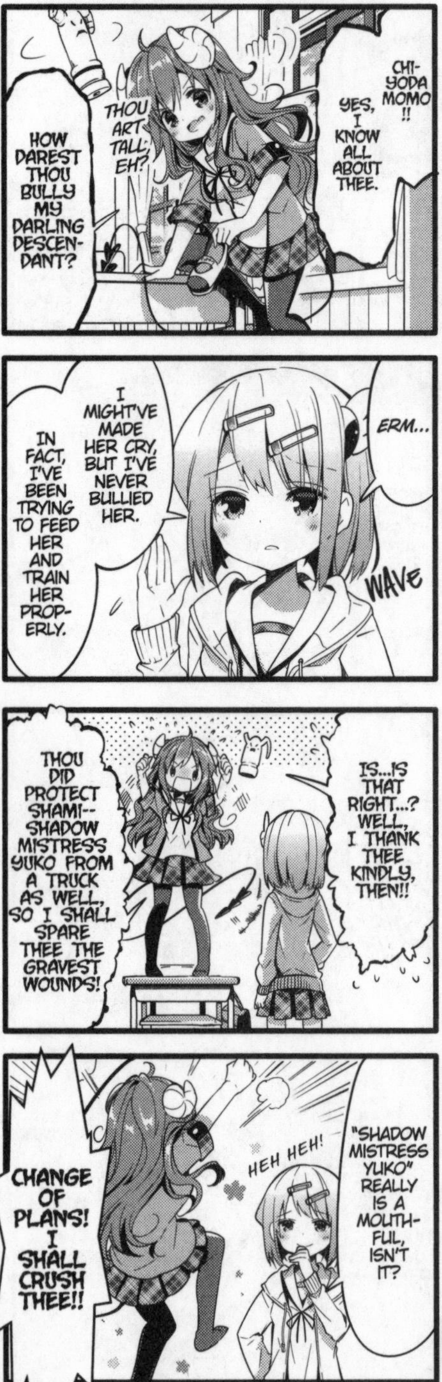
CHI-YODA MOMO !!
YES, I KNOW ALL ABOUT THEE.
THOU ART TALL, EH?
HOW DAREST THOU BULLY MY DARLING DESCEN-DANT?
ERM...
I MIGHT'VE MADE HER CRY, BUT I'VE NEVER BULLIED HER.
IN FACT, I'VE BEEN TRYING TO FEED HER AND TRAIN HER PROP-ERLY.
WAVE
IS...IS THAT RIGHT...? WELL, I THANK THEE KINDLY, THEN!!
THOU DID PROTECT SHAMI-- SHADOW MISTRESS YUKO FROM A TRUCK AS WELL, SO I SHALL SPARE THEE THE GRAVEST WOUNDS!
"SHADOW MISTRESS YUKO" REALLY IS A MOUTH-FUL, ISN'T IT?
HEH HEH!
CHANGE OF PLANS! I SHALL CRUSH THEE!!

SHAMIKO'S CRANIUM PROTECTION SQUAD

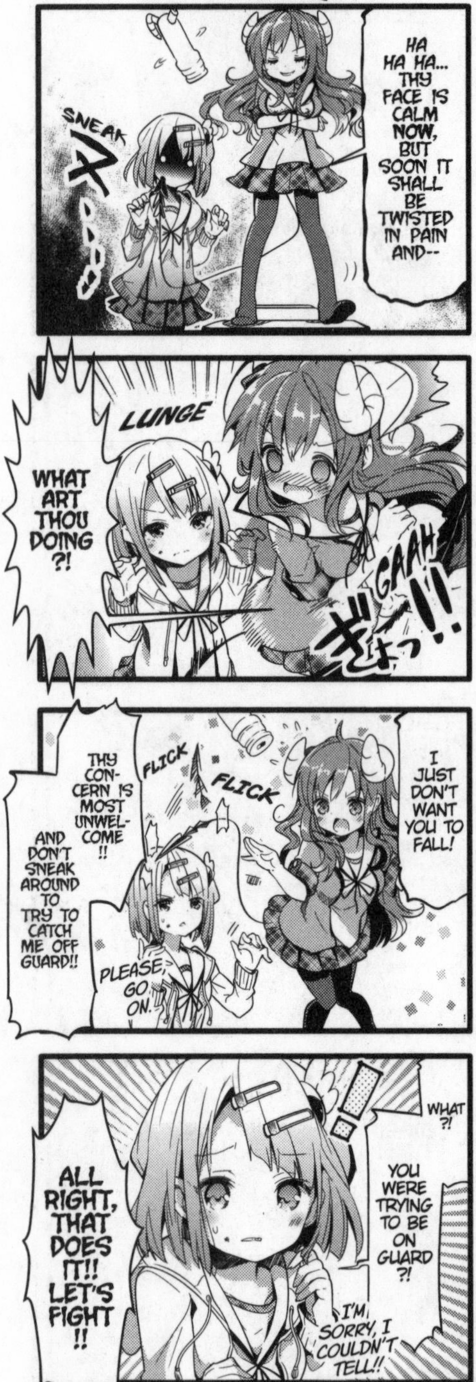
HA HA HA... THY FACE IS CALM NOW, BUT SOON IT SHALL BE TWISTED IN PAIN AND--
SNEAK
LUNGE
GAAH
ぎょっ!!
WHAT ART THOU DOING ?!
I JUST DON'T WANT YOU TO FALL!
FLICK
FLICK
THY CON-CERN IS MOST UNWEL-COME !!
AND DON'T SNEAK AROUND TO TRY TO CATCH ME OFF GUARD!!
PLEASE, GO ON.
WHAT ?!
YOU WERE TRYING TO BE ON GUARD ?!
I'M SORRY, I COULDN'T TELL!!
ALL RIGHT, THAT DOES IT!! LET'S FIGHT !!

THE OLD HEAVE-HO

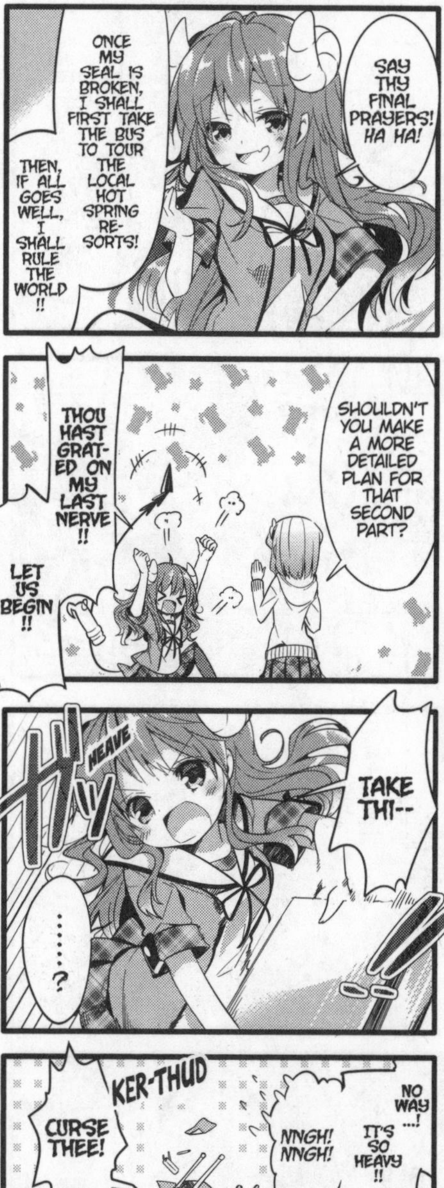
SAY THY FINAL PRAYERS! HA HA!
ONCE MY SEAL IS BROKEN, I SHALL FIRST TAKE THE BUS TO TOUR THE LOCAL HOT SPRING RESORTS!
THEN, IF ALL GOES WELL, I SHALL RULE THE WORLD!!
SHOULDN'T YOU MAKE A MORE DETAILED PLAN FOR THAT SECOND PART?
THOU HAST GRATED ON MY LAST NERVE!!
LET US BEGIN!!
HEAVE
TAKE THI--
......?
KER-THUD
NO WAY...! IT'S SO HEAVY!!
NNGH! NNGH!
CURSE THEE!
FWSH

MOMO SOFTENS THE BLOW

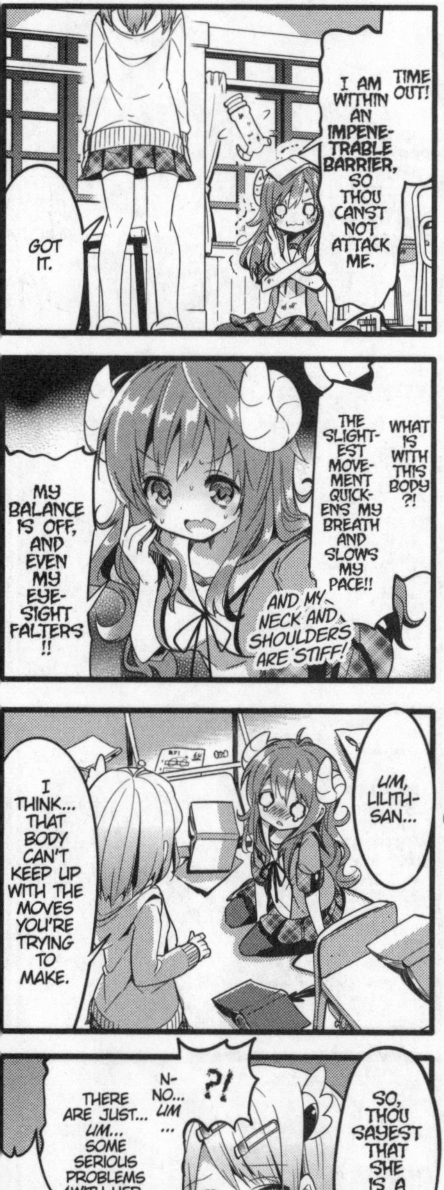
TIME OUT!
I AM WITHIN AN IMPENETRABLE BARRIER, SO THOU CANST NOT ATTACK ME.
GOT IT.
WHAT IS WITH THIS BODY?!
THE SLIGHTEST MOVEMENT QUICKENS MY BREATH AND SLOWS MY PACE!!
MY BALANCE IS OFF, AND EVEN MY EYESIGHT FALTERS!!
AND MY NECK AND SHOULDERS ARE STIFF!
UM, LILITH-SAN...
I THINK... THAT BODY CAN'T KEEP UP WITH THE MOVES YOU'RE TRYING TO MAKE.
SO, THOU SAYEST THAT SHE IS A WIMPY KLUTZ?
?!
N-NO... UM...
THERE ARE JUST... UM... SOME SERIOUS PROBLEMS WITH HER REFLEXES... AND EVERYTHING ELSE.
I HAVE SOME SERIOUS PROBLEMS WITH THY ACT!!

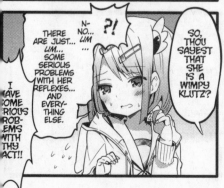

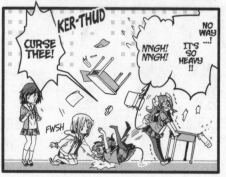

THE ZAP TRAP RETURNS

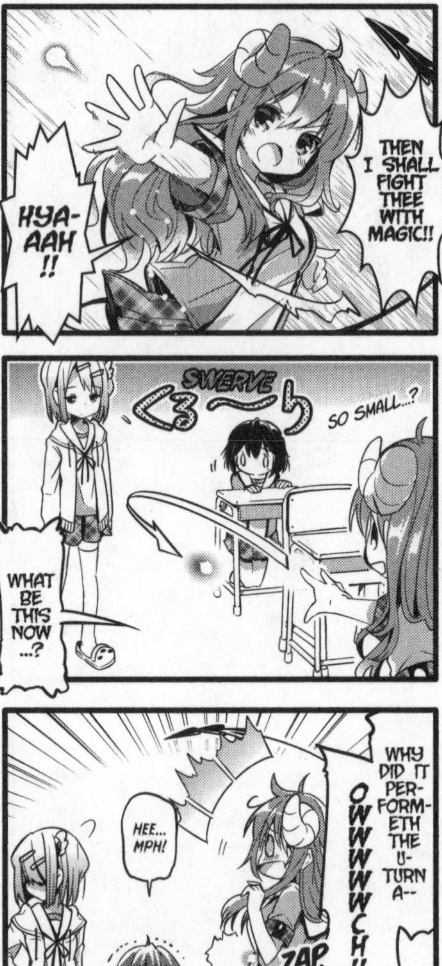
THEN I SHALL FIGHT THEE WITH MAGIC!!
HYA-AAH!!
SWERVE
くる〜り
SO SMALL...?
WHAT BE THIS NOW...?
WHY DID IT PERFORMETH THE U-TURN A--
OWWWWWCH!!
HEE... MPH!
ZAP
ちっくん!!
HOW DARE THOU LAUGH, LOWLY HUMAN?!
I'M NOT... SNRK... L-LAUGHING... MPH...AT ALL.
THOU ART A POOR LIAR!!

KNOWS WHEN SHE'S BEATEN

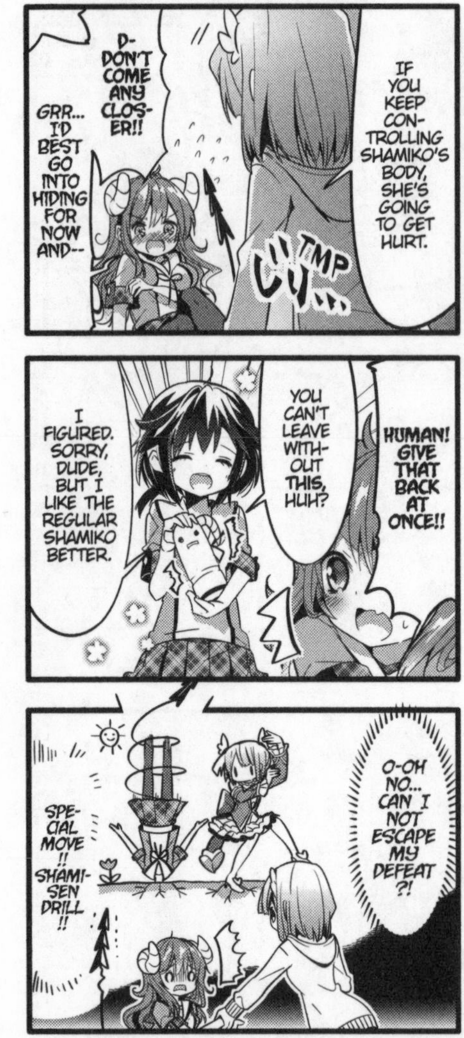
IF YOU KEEP CON-TROLLING SHAMIKO'S BODY, SHE'S GOING TO GET HURT.
D-DON'T COME ANY CLOS-ER!!
TMP
じり...
GRR... I'D BEST GO INTO HIDING FOR NOW AND--
HUMAN! GIVE THAT BACK AT ONCE!!
YOU CAN'T LEAVE WITH-OUT THIS, HUH?
I FIGURED. SORRY, DUDE, BUT I LIKE THE REGULAR SHAMIKO BETTER.
O-OH NO... CAN I NOT ESCAPE MY DEFEAT?!
SPE-CIAL MOVE!! SHAMI-SEN DRILL!!
MAY I AT LEAST GET...
A LAST SOUVENIR TO TAKE TO HELL?
BLUBBER
BLUBBER
SOB!
SOB!
SOB!
WOW, YOU GIVE UP FAST!!

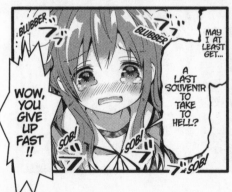

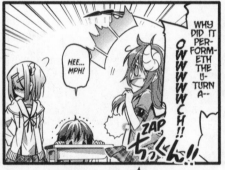

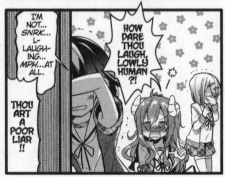

SHOULDER MASSAGE

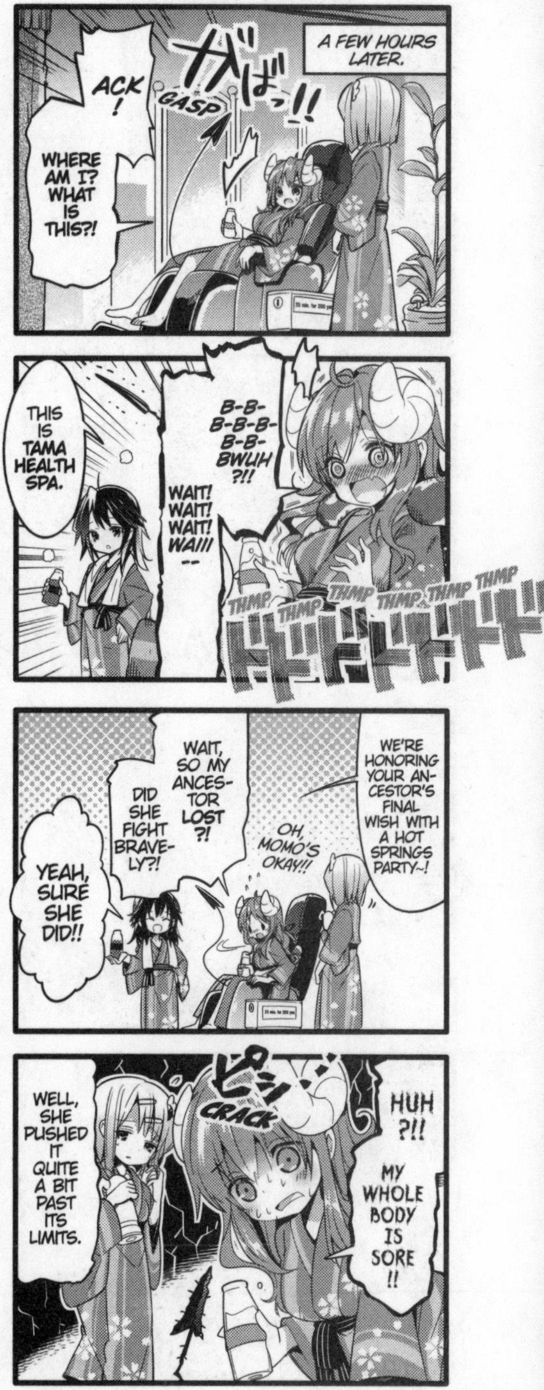

A FEW HOURS LATER.
がばっ!!
GASP
ACK!
WHERE AM I? WHAT IS THIS?!
B-B-B-B-B-B-B-BWUH?!!
WAIT! WAIT! WAIT! WAI!!--
THIS IS TAMA HEALTH SPA.
THMP THMP THMP THMP THMP THMP
ドドドドドド
WE'RE HONORING YOUR ANCESTOR'S FINAL WISH WITH A HOT SPRINGS PARTY~!
WAIT, SO MY ANCESTOR LOST?!
OH, MOMO'S OKAY!!
DID SHE FIGHT BRAVELY?!
YEAH, SURE SHE DID!!
HUH?!! MY WHOLE BODY IS SORE!!
ピシッ
CRACK
WELL, SHE PUSHED IT QUITE A BIT PAST ITS LIMITS.

MIGHT AS WELL ENJOY IT

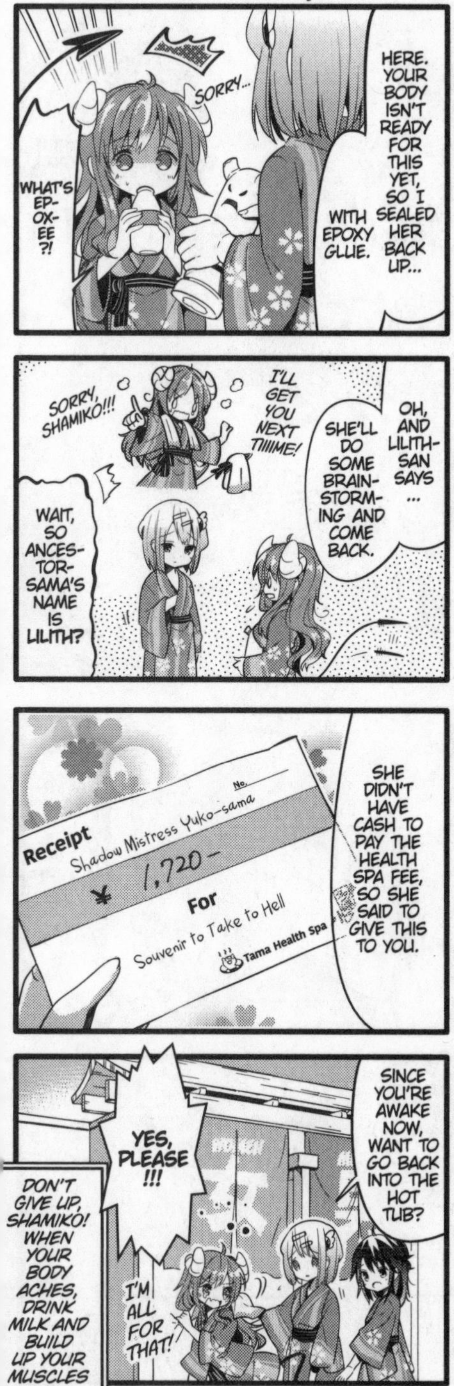

HERE. YOUR BODY ISN'T READY FOR THIS YET, SO I SEALED HER BACK UP...
WITH EPOXY GLUE.
SORRY...
WHAT'S EP-OX-EE?!
OH, AND LILITH-SAN SAYS...
SHE'LL DO SOME BRAINSTORMING AND COME BACK.
I'LL GET YOU NEXT TIIIIME!
SORRY, SHAMIKO!!!
WAIT, SO ANCESTOR-SAMA'S NAME IS LILITH?
SHE DIDN'T HAVE CASH TO PAY THE HEALTH SPA FEE, SO SHE SAID TO GIVE THIS TO YOU.
No.
Receipt
Shadow Mistress Yuko-sama
¥ 1,720-
For
Souvenir to Take to Hell
Tama Health Spa
SINCE YOU'RE AWAKE NOW, WANT TO GO BACK INTO THE HOT TUB?
YES, PLEASE!!!
I'M ALL FOR THAT!
DON'T GIVE UP, SHAMIKO! WHEN YOUR BODY ACHES, DRINK MILK AND BUILD UP YOUR MUSCLES!!

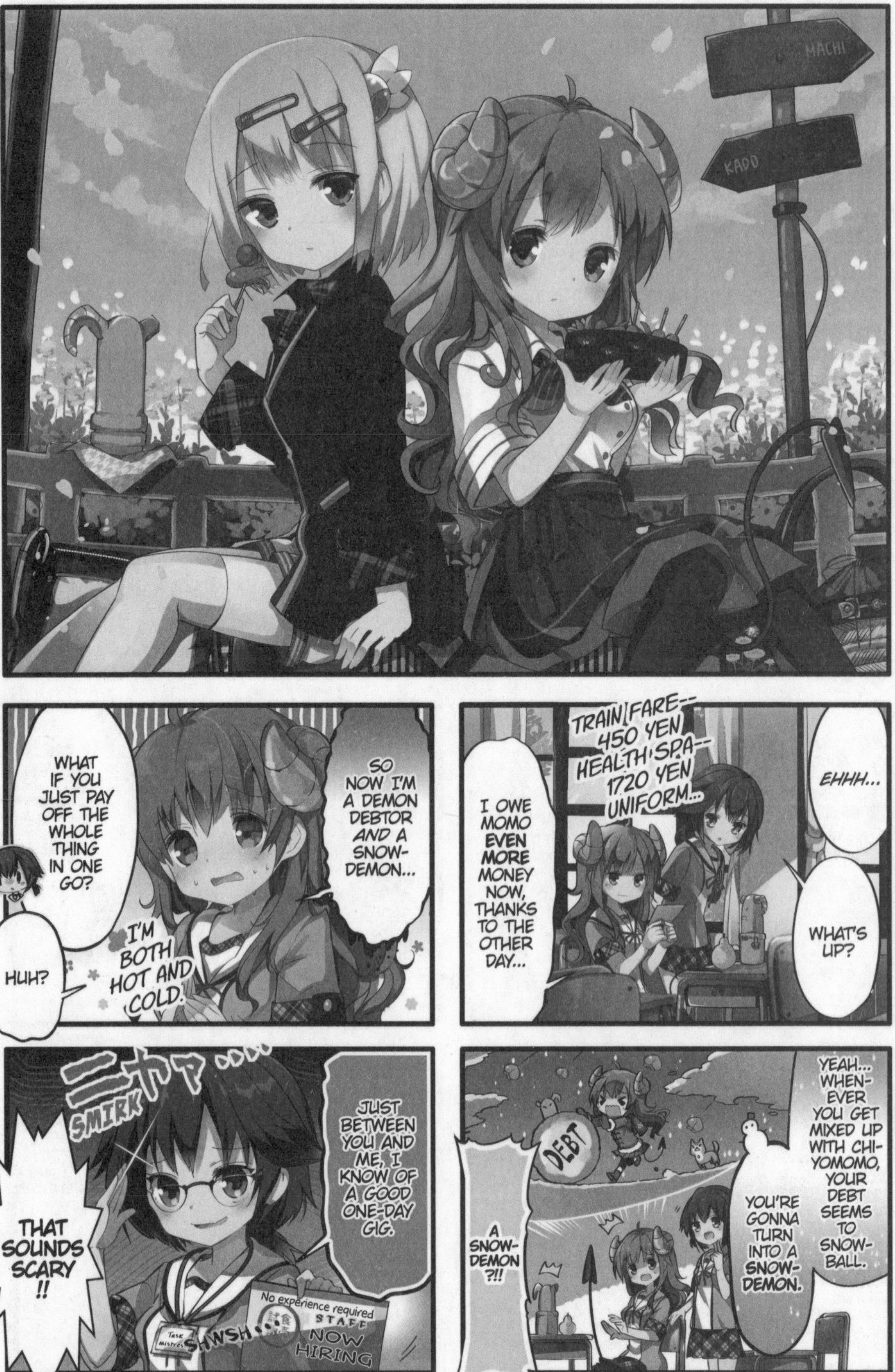
MACHI
KADO
EHHH...
WHAT'S UP?
TRAIN FARE-- 450 YEN HEALTH SPA-- 1720 YEN UNIFORM...
I OWE MOMO EVEN MORE MONEY NOW, THANKS TO THE OTHER DAY...
SO NOW I'M A DEMON DEBTOR AND A SNOW-DEMON...
I'M BOTH HOT AND COLD.
WHAT IF YOU JUST PAY OFF THE WHOLE THING IN ONE GO?
HUH?
YEAH... WHEN-EVER YOU GET MIXED UP WITH CHI-YOMOMO, YOUR DEBT SEEMS TO SNOW-BALL.
YOU'RE GONNA TURN INTO A SNOW-DEMON.
DEBT
A SNOW-DEMON?!!
JUST BETWEEN YOU AND ME, I KNOW OF A GOOD ONE-DAY GIG.
ニヤァ...
SMIRK
THAT SOUNDS SCARY!!
No experience required
STAFF
NOW HIRING
Task Mistress
SHWSH...

THREE SKETCHY HOURS

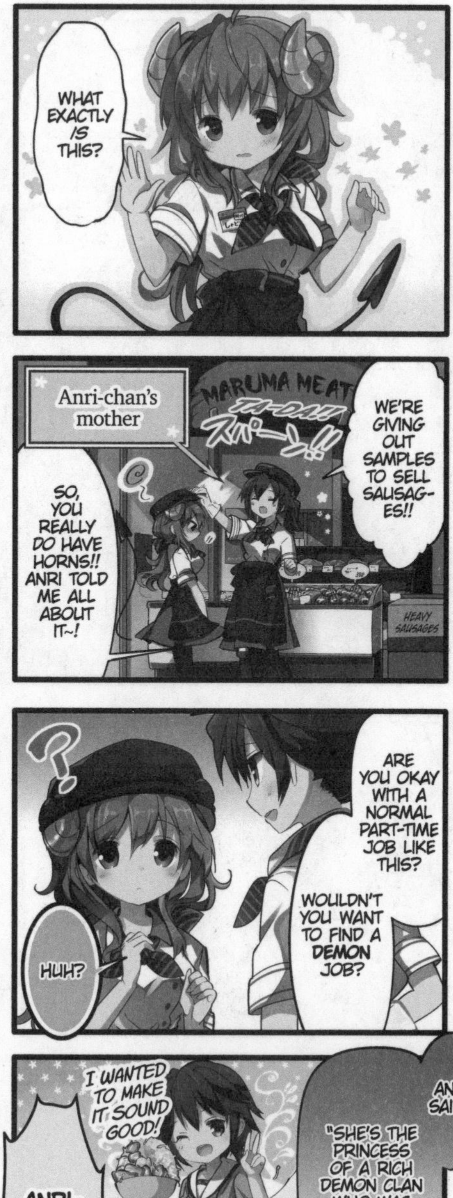
WHAT EXACTLY IS THIS?
WE'RE GIVING OUT SAMPLES TO SELL SAUSAG-ES!!
MARUMA MEAT
TA-DA!! スパーン!!
Anri-chan's mother
SO, YOU REALLY DO HAVE HORNS!! ANRI TOLD ME ALL ABOUT IT~!
HEAVY SAUSAGES
ARE YOU OKAY WITH A NORMAL PART-TIME JOB LIKE THIS?
WOULDN'T YOU WANT TO FIND A DEMON JOB?
HUH?
ANRI SAID...
"SHE'S THE PRINCESS OF A RICH DEMON CLAN WHO WAS TRICKED INTO A MASSIVE LIFE DEBT BY AN EVIL ENEMY."
WILL YOU BE ALL RIGHT?
I WANTED TO MAKE IT SOUND GOOD!
ANRI-CHAN REALLY LAID IT ON THICK!!
NO, WE'RE JUST POOR.

ENCOUNTER WITH THE UNKNOWN

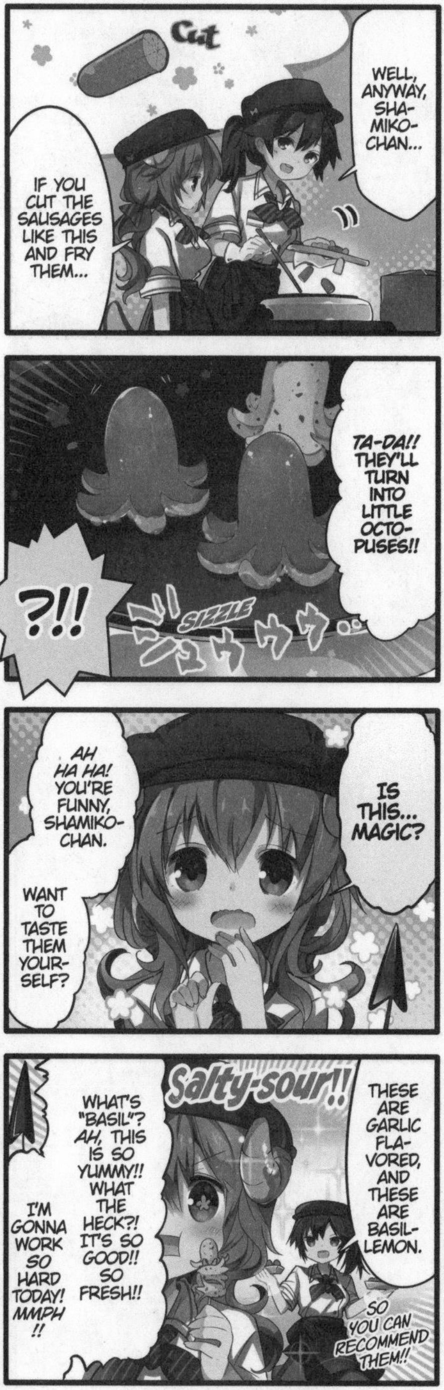
Cut
WELL, ANYWAY, SHAMIKO-CHAN...
IF YOU CUT THE SAUSAGES LIKE THIS AND FRY THEM...
TA-DA!! THEY'LL TURN INTO LITTLE OCTOPUSES!!
SIZZLE ジュウウウ..
?!!
IS THIS... MAGIC?
AH HA HA! YOU'RE FUNNY, SHAMIKO-CHAN.
WANT TO TASTE THEM YOURSELF?
THESE ARE GARLIC FLAVORED, AND THESE ARE BASIL-LEMON.
SO YOU CAN RECOMMEND THEM!!
Salty-sour!!
WHAT'S "BASIL"? AH, THIS IS SO YUMMY!! WHAT THE HECK?! IT'S SO GOOD!! SO FRESH!!
I'M GONNA WORK SO HARD TODAY! MMPH!!

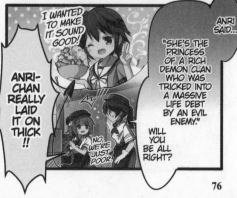

KEEP IT UNDER 40K

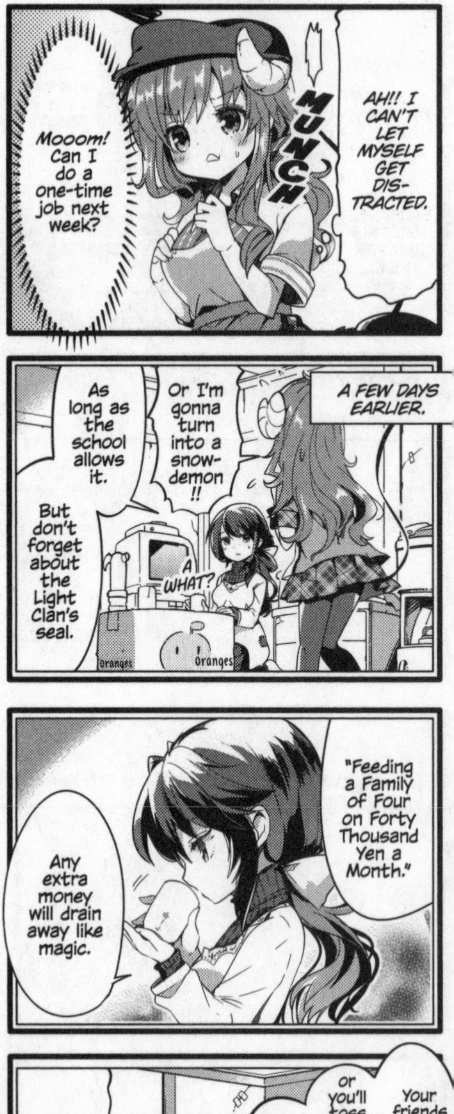
AH!! I CAN'T LET MYSELF GET DISTRACTED.
MUNCH
Mooom! Can I do a one-time job next week?
A FEW DAYS EARLIER.
Or I'm gonna turn into a snow-demon!!
As long as the school allows it.
But don't forget about the Light Clan's seal.
A WHAT?
Oranges
Oranges
"Feeding a Family of Four on Forty Thousand Yen a Month."
Any extra money will drain away like magic.
Your friends will get married out of the blue...
or you'll toss your whole coin purse into the shrine's offering box...
or lose your wallet in a gutter.
Aren't those last two just you being klutzy?
AH-CHOO!!

MYSTERIOUS KINDNESS

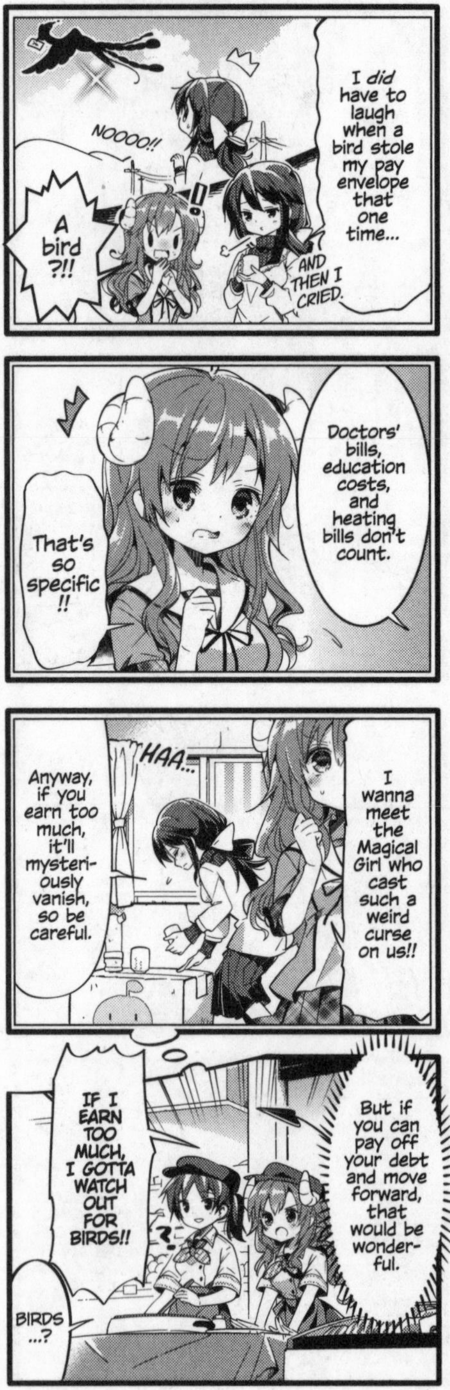
I *did* have to laugh when a bird stole my pay envelope that one time...
AND THEN I CRIED.
NOOOO!!
!
A bird?!!
Doctors' bills, education costs, and heating bills don't count.
That's so specific!!
I wanna meet the Magical Girl who cast such a weird curse on us!!
HAA...
Anyway, if you earn too much, it'll mysteriously vanish, so be careful.
But if you can pay off your debt and move forward, that would be wonderful.
IF I EARN TOO MUCH, I GOTTA WATCH OUT FOR BIRDS!!
?
BIRDS...?

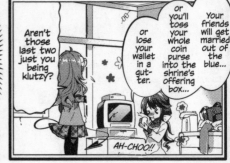

PUTTING THE CART BEFORE THE DEMON

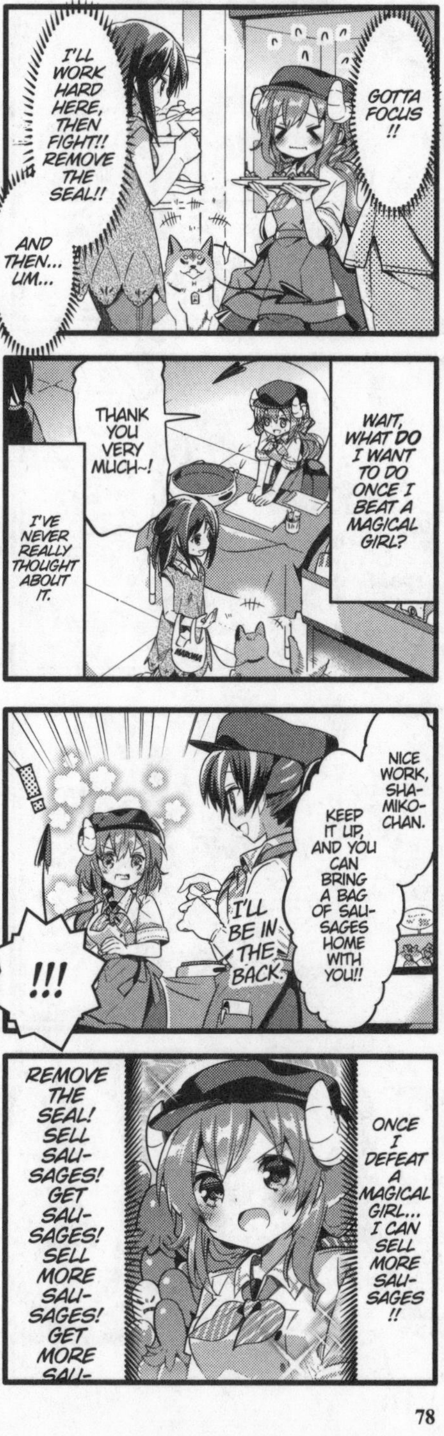
GOTTA FOCUS !!
I'LL WORK HARD HERE, THEN FIGHT!! REMOVE THE SEAL!!
AND THEN... UM...
WAIT, WHAT DO I WANT TO DO ONCE I BEAT A MAGICAL GIRL?
THANK YOU VERY MUCH~!
I'VE NEVER REALLY THOUGHT ABOUT IT.
NICE WORK, SHAMIKO-CHAN.
KEEP IT UP, AND YOU CAN BRING A BAG OF SAUSAGES HOME WITH YOU!!
I'LL BE IN THE BACK.
!!!
ONCE I DEFEAT A MAGICAL GIRL... I CAN SELL MORE SAUSAGES !!
REMOVE THE SEAL! SELL SAUSAGES! GET SAUSAGES! SELL MORE SAUSAGES! GET MORE SAU-

SAY, "AHH!"

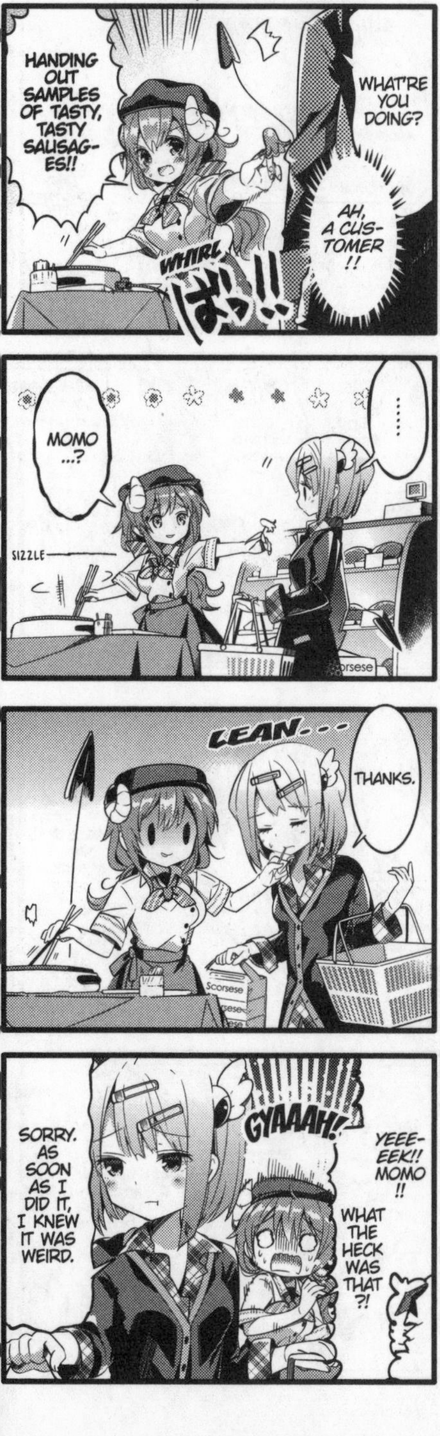
WHAT'RE YOU DOING?
AH, A CUSTOMER !!
HANDING OUT SAMPLES OF TASTY, TASTY SAUSAGES!!
WHIRL
ばっ!!
......
MOMO ...?
SIZZLE
THANKS.
LEAN...
YEEEEEK!! MOMO !!
WHAT THE HECK WAS THAT ?!
GYAAAH!
SORRY. AS SOON AS I DID IT, I KNEW IT WAS WEIRD.

YOU'RE NOT WRONG

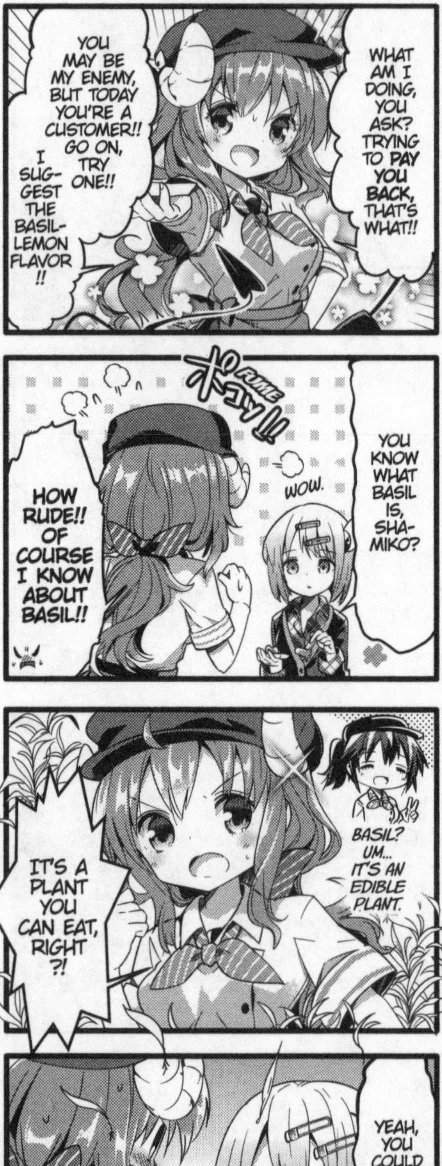
WHAT AM I DOING, YOU ASK? TRYING TO PAY YOU BACK, THAT'S WHAT!!
YOU MAY BE MY ENEMY, BUT TODAY YOU'RE A CUSTOMER!! GO ON, TRY ONE!!
I SUGGEST THE BASIL-LEMON FLAVOR!!
YOU KNOW WHAT BASIL IS, SHAMIKO?
FUME
WOW.
HOW RUDE!! OF COURSE I KNOW ABOUT BASIL!!
BASIL? UM... IT'S AN EDIBLE PLANT.
IT'S A PLANT YOU CAN EAT, RIGHT?!
YEAH, YOU COULD SAY THAT.
WHAT'S WITH THE FACE?!

SALTY, SOUR SAUSAGES

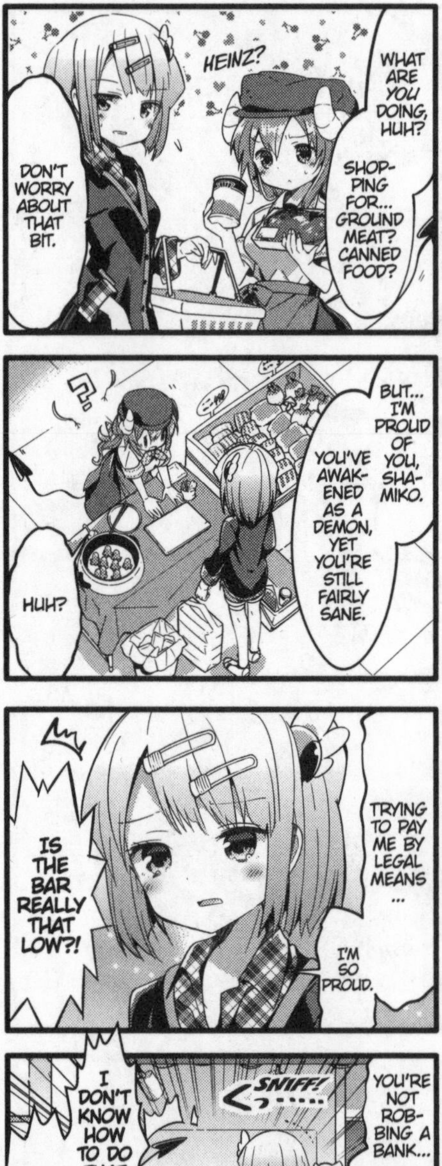
WHAT ARE YOU DOING, HUH?
HEINZ?
SHOPPING FOR... GROUND MEAT? CANNED FOOD?
DON'T WORRY ABOUT THAT BIT.
BUT... I'M PROUD OF YOU, SHAMIKO.
YOU'VE AWAKENED AS A DEMON, YET YOU'RE STILL FAIRLY SANE.
HUH?
TRYING TO PAY ME BY LEGAL MEANS...
I'M SO PROUD.
IS THE BAR REALLY THAT LOW?!
YOU'RE NOT ROBBING A BANK...
OR TRYING TO HYPNOTIZE SOME RICH FAMILY.
SNIFF!
I DON'T KNOW HOW TO DO THAT!!
WHAT KIND OF CRAZINESS HAVE YOU DEALT WITH?!

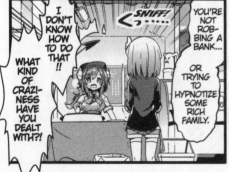

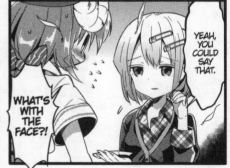

FRESH PEACH CONCENTRATION

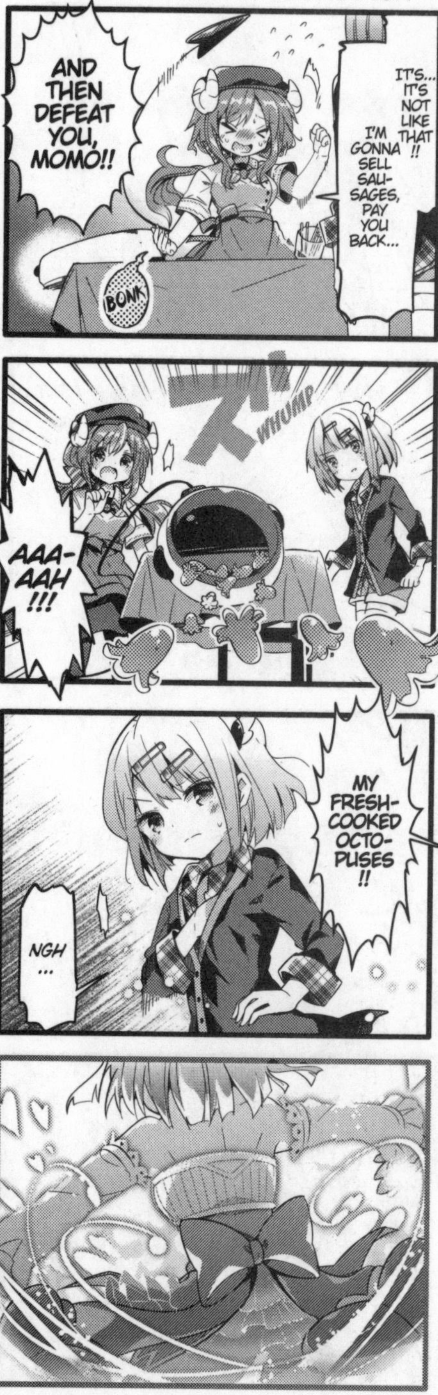
IT'S... IT'S NOT LIKE THAT!!
I'M GONNA SELL SAUSAGES, PAY YOU BACK...
AND THEN DEFEAT YOU, MOMO!!
BONK
WHUMP
AAA-AAH!!!
MY FRESH-COOKED OCTOPUSES!!
NGH...

TRIUMPHANT RETURN

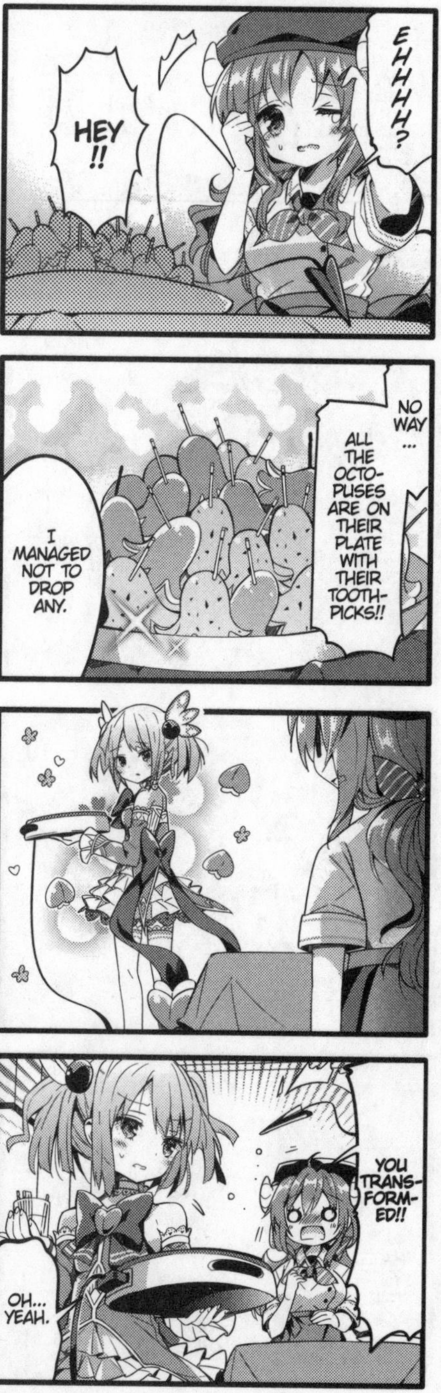
EHHHHH?
HEY!!
NO WAY...
ALL THE OCTOPUSES ARE ON THEIR PLATE WITH THEIR TOOTHPICKS!!
I MANAGED NOT TO DROP ANY.
YOU TRANSFORMED!!
OH... YEAH.

SHAMIKO'S POWER PUNCHES

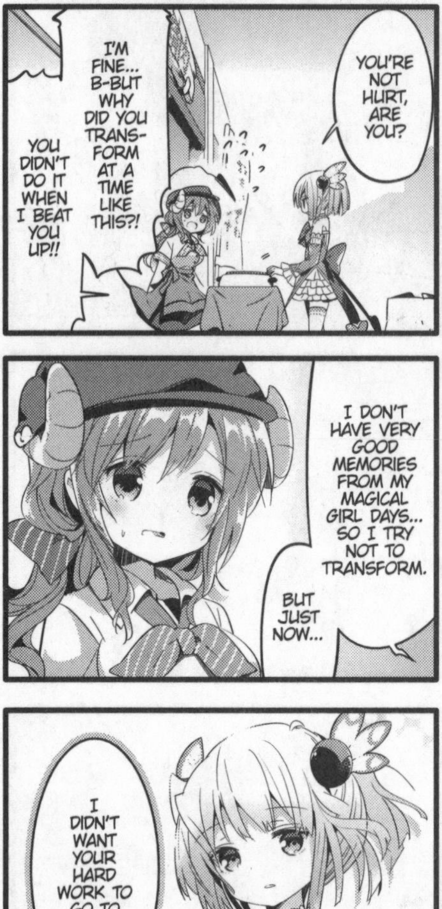
YOU'RE NOT HURT, ARE YOU?
I'M FINE... B-BUT WHY DID YOU TRANSFORM AT A TIME LIKE THIS?!
YOU DIDN'T DO IT WHEN I BEAT YOU UP!!
I DON'T HAVE VERY GOOD MEMORIES FROM MY MAGICAL GIRL DAYS... SO I TRY NOT TO TRANSFORM.
BUT JUST NOW...
I DIDN'T WANT YOUR HARD WORK TO GO TO WASTE.
シャモン
SHOOM
AS I AM NOW...
I CAN HANDLE YOUR WIMPY PUNCHES, BUT I HAD TO TRANSFORM TO SAVE ALL THE OCTOPUSES.
HM?
DID YOU SAY SOMETHING REALLY INSULTING JUST NOW?

PINK BARRIER

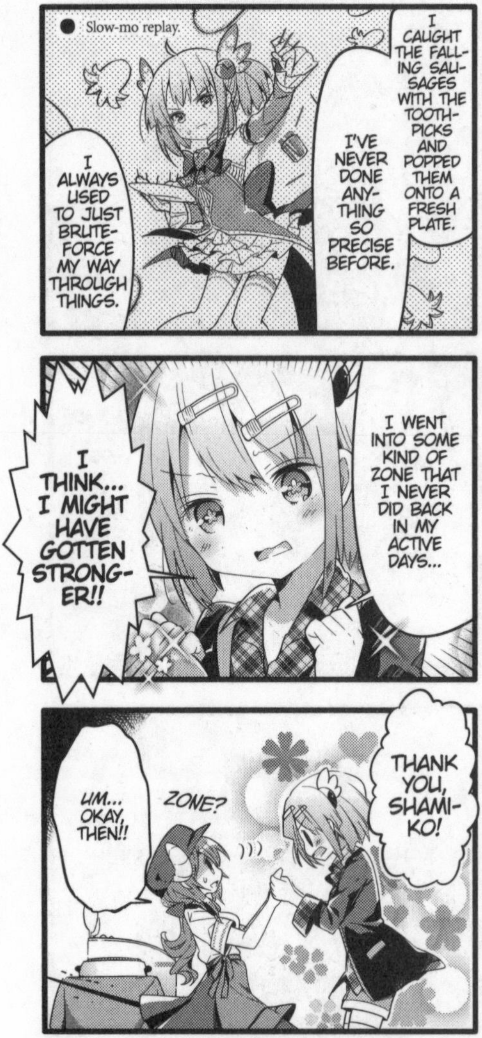
Slow-mo replay.
I CAUGHT THE FALLING SAUSAGES WITH THE TOOTHPICKS AND POPPED THEM ONTO A FRESH PLATE.
I'VE NEVER DONE ANYTHING SO PRECISE BEFORE.
I ALWAYS USED TO JUST BRUTE-FORCE MY WAY THROUGH THINGS.
I WENT INTO SOME KIND OF ZONE THAT I NEVER DID BACK IN MY ACTIVE DAYS...
I THINK... I MIGHT HAVE GOTTEN STRONGER!!
THANK YOU, SHAMIKO!
ZONE?
UM... OKAY, THEN!!
ARGH!
SQUEEZE...
NOW SHE'LL BE EVEN HARDER TO BEAT!

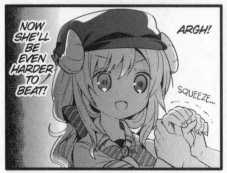

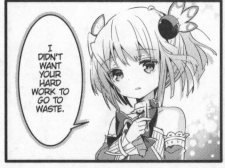

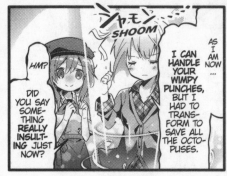

A DEMON WHO CAN SAY "THANK YOU"

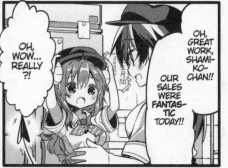

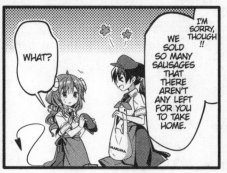

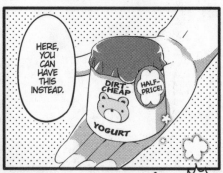

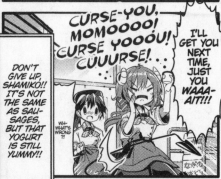

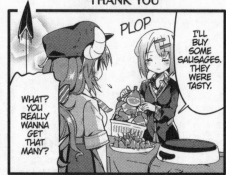

I'LL BUY SOME SAUSAGES. THEY WERE TASTY.
PLOP
WHAT? YOU REALLY WANNA GET THAT MANY?
TMP TMP TMP
MOMO! I'LL GET YOU NEXT TIME, JUST...
NO... WAIT, THAT'S NOT WHAT I MEAN.
THANK YOU VERY MUCH.
SAME TO YOU.

RETURN OF THE DIRT-CHEAP YOGURT

OH, GREAT WORK, SHAMIKO-CHAN!! OUR SALES WERE FANTASTIC TODAY!!
OH, WOW... REALLY?!
I'M SORRY, THOUGH!! WE SOLD SO MANY SAUSAGES THAT THERE AREN'T ANY LEFT FOR YOU TO TAKE HOME.
WHAT?
MARUMA
HERE, YOU CAN HAVE THIS INSTEAD.
HALF-PRICE!
DIRT-CHEAP
YOGURT
I'LL GET YOU NEXT TIME, JUST YOU WAAA-AIT!!!
CURSE-YOU, MOMOOOO! CURSE YOOOU! CUUURSE!...
WH-WHAT'S WRONG?!
DON'T GIVE UP, SHAMIKO!! IT'S NOT THE SAME AS SAUSAGES, BUT THAT YOGURT IS STILL YUMMY!!

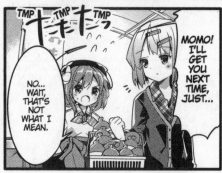

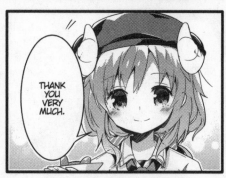

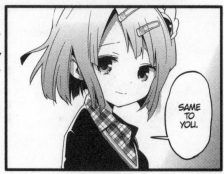

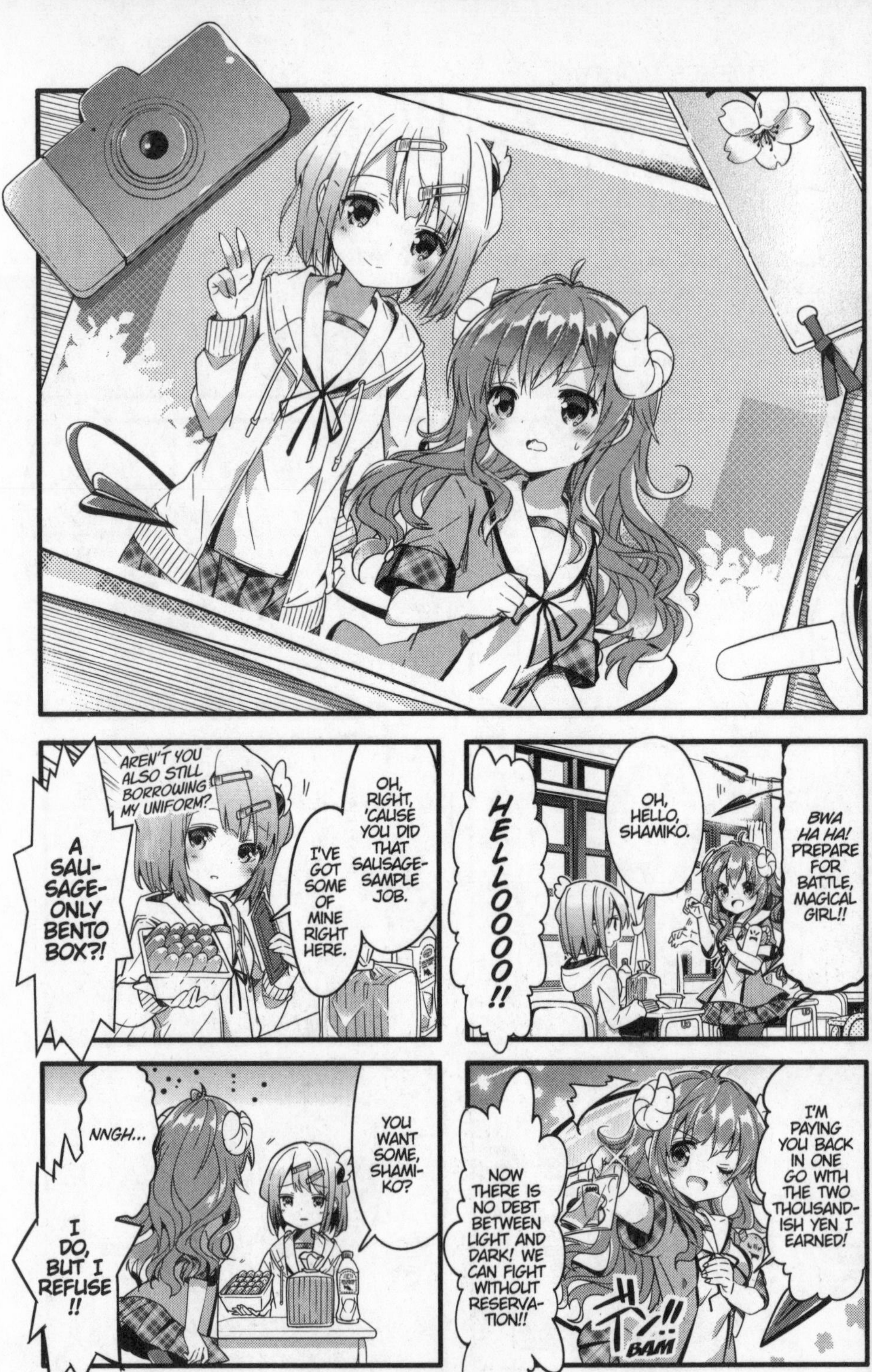
BWA HA HA! PREPARE FOR BATTLE, MAGICAL GIRL!!
OH, HELLO, SHAMIKO.
HELLOOOOO!!
OH, RIGHT, 'CAUSE YOU DID THAT SAUSAGE-SAMPLE JOB.
I'VE GOT SOME OF MINE RIGHT HERE.
AREN'T YOU ALSO STILL BORROWING MY UNIFORM?
A SAUSAGE-ONLY BENTO BOX?!
I'M PAYING YOU BACK IN ONE GO WITH THE TWO THOUSAND-ISH YEN I EARNED!
NOW THERE IS NO DEBT BETWEEN LIGHT AND DARK! WE CAN FIGHT WITHOUT RESERVATION!!
BAM
YOU WANT SOME, SHAMIKO?
NNGH...
I DO, BUT I REFUSE!!

NO TOOLS

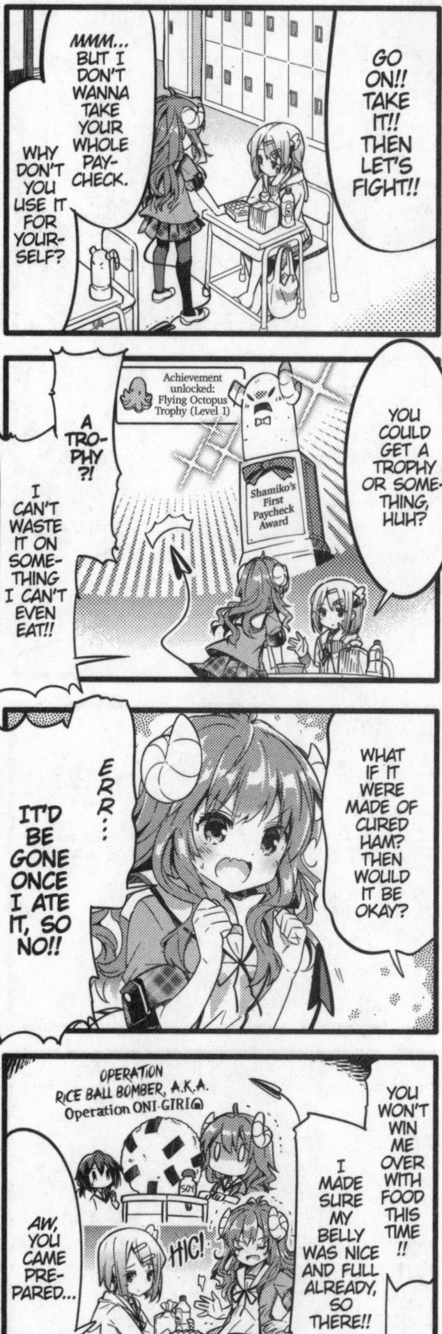
GO ON!! TAKE IT!! THEN LET'S FIGHT!!
MMM... BUT I DON'T WANNA TAKE YOUR WHOLE PAY-CHECK.
WHY DON'T YOU USE IT FOR YOUR-SELF?
YOU COULD GET A TROPHY OR SOME-THING, HUH?
Achievement unlocked: Flying Octopus Trophy (Level 1)
Shamiko's First Paycheck Award
A TRO-PHY?!
I CAN'T WASTE IT ON SOME-THING I CAN'T EVEN EAT!!
WHAT IF IT WERE MADE OF CURED HAM? THEN WOULD IT BE OKAY?
ERR...
IT'D BE GONE ONCE I ATE IT, SO NO!!
YOU WON'T WIN ME OVER WITH FOOD THIS TIME!!
I MADE SURE MY BELLY WAS NICE AND FULL ALREADY, SO THERE!!
OPERATION RICE BALL BOMBER, A.K.A. Operation ONI-GIRI
SOY
HIC!
AW, YOU CAME PRE-PARED...

FREE ICE TROPHY

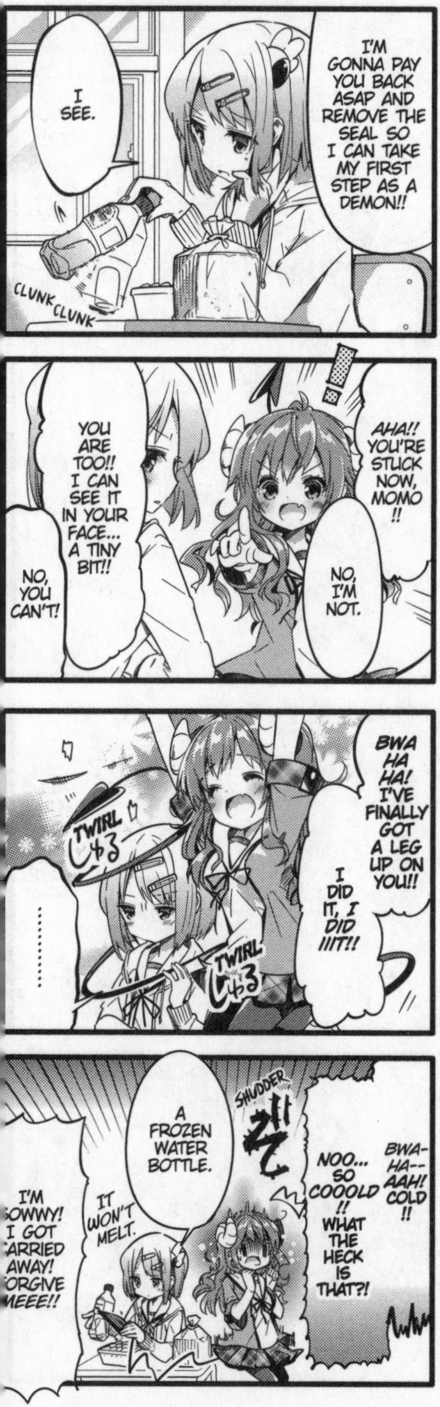
I'M GONNA PAY YOU BACK ASAP AND REMOVE THE SEAL SO I CAN TAKE MY FIRST STEP AS A DEMON!!
I SEE.
CLUNK CLUNK
!
AHA!! YOU'RE STUCK NOW, MOMO!!
NO, I'M NOT.
YOU ARE TOO!! I CAN SEE IT IN YOUR FACE... A TINY BIT!!
NO, YOU CAN'T!
BWA HA HA! I'VE FINALLY GOT A LEG UP ON YOU!!
I DID IT, I DID IIIT!!
TWIRL しゅる
TWIRL しゅる
......
BWA-HA--AAH! COLD!!
NOO... SO COOOLD!! WHAT THE HECK IS THAT?!
SHUDDER ぞぞ
A FROZEN WATER BOTTLE.
IT WON'T MELT.
I'M SOWWY! I GOT CARRIED AWAY! FORGIVE MEEE!!

THE YOSHIDA FAMILY REVEALED!

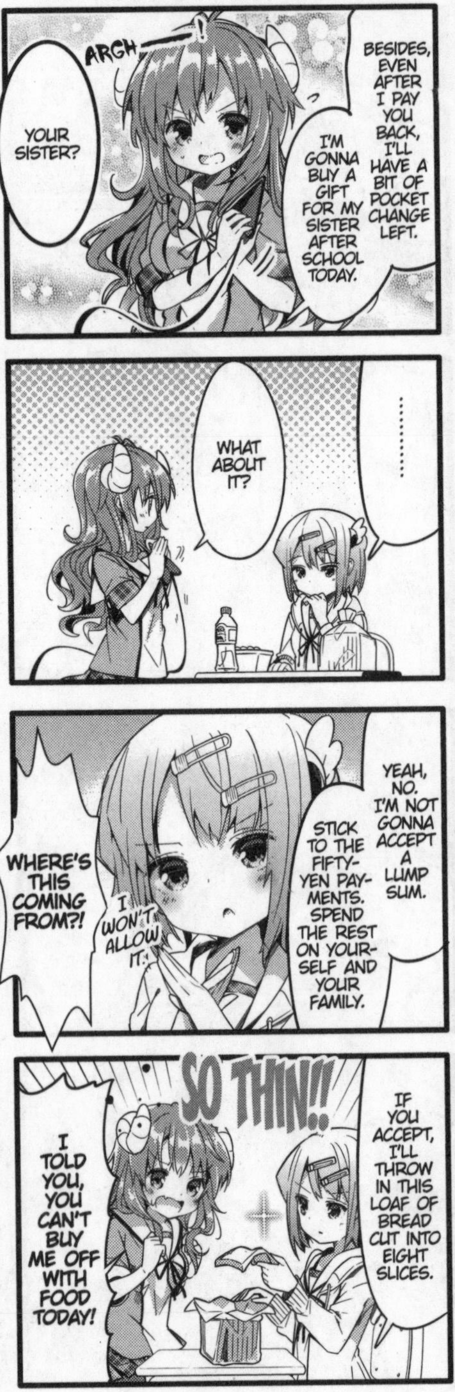
BESIDES, EVEN AFTER I PAY YOU BACK, I'LL HAVE A BIT OF POCKET CHANGE LEFT.
I'M GONNA BUY A GIFT FOR MY SISTER AFTER SCHOOL TODAY.
ARGH
YOUR SISTER?
......
WHAT ABOUT IT?
YEAH, NO. I'M NOT GONNA ACCEPT A LUMP SUM.
STICK TO THE FIFTY-YEN PAYMENTS. SPEND THE REST ON YOURSELF AND YOUR FAMILY.
I WON'T ALLOW IT.
WHERE'S THIS COMING FROM?!
SO THIN!!
IF YOU ACCEPT, I'LL THROW IN THIS LOAF OF BREAD CUT INTO EIGHT SLICES.
I TOLD YOU, YOU CAN'T BUY ME OFF WITH FOOD TODAY!

IT'S PRETTY TASTY LIKE THIS

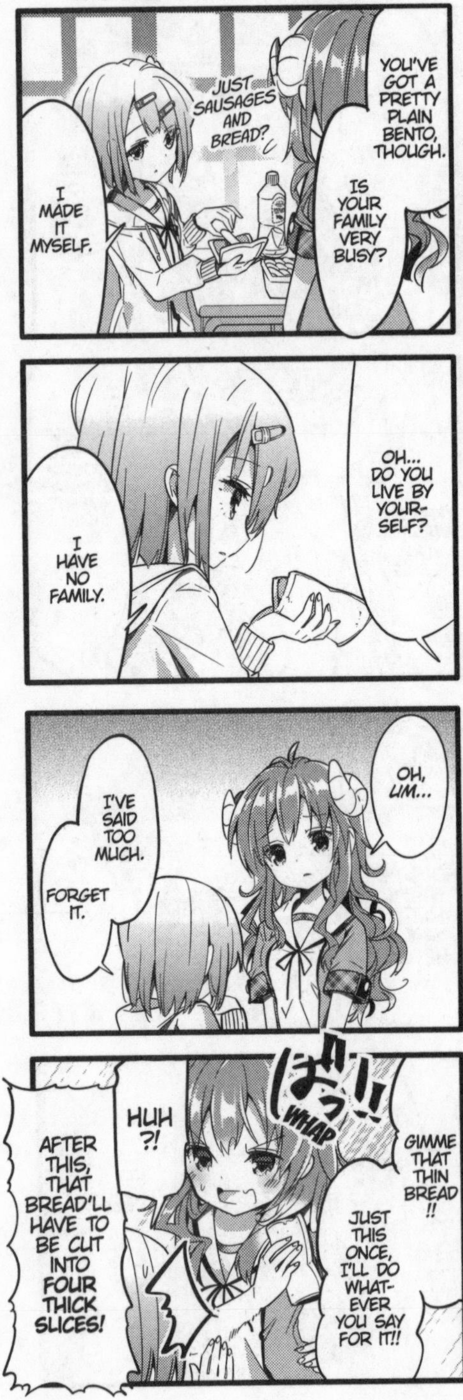
YOU'VE GOT A PRETTY PLAIN BENTO, THOUGH.
IS YOUR FAMILY VERY BUSY?
JUST SAUSAGES AND BREAD?
I MADE IT MYSELF.
OH... DO YOU LIVE BY YOURSELF?
I HAVE NO FAMILY.
OH, UM...
I'VE SAID TOO MUCH.
FORGET IT.
GIMME THAT THIN BREAD!!
JUST THIS ONCE, I'LL DO WHATEVER YOU SAY FOR IT!!
ぱっ!!
WHAP
HUH?!
AFTER THIS, THAT BREAD'LL HAVE TO BE CUT INTO FOUR THICK SLICES!

A BIG SISTER'S PRIDE

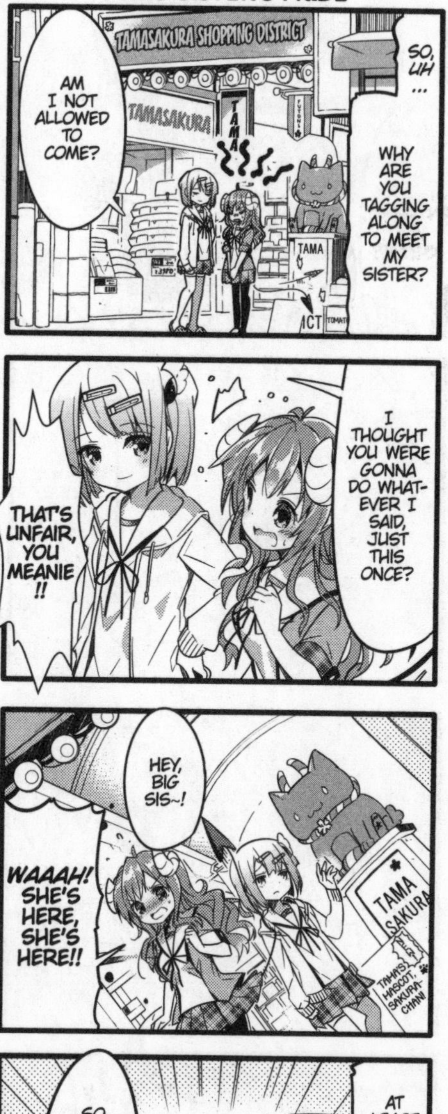
TAMASAKURA SHOPPING DISTRICT
TAMASAKURA
TAMA
SO, UH ...
WHY ARE YOU TAGGING ALONG TO MEET MY SISTER?
AM I NOT ALLOWED TO COME?
I THOUGHT YOU WERE GONNA DO WHATEVER I SAID, JUST THIS ONCE?
THAT'S UNFAIR, YOU MEANIE!!
HEY, BIG SIS~!
WAAAH! SHE'S HERE, SHE'S HERE!!
TAMA SAKURA
TAMA'S MASCOT, SAKURA-CHAN
AT LEAST HIDE YOUR IDENTITY!!
I'VE TOLD MY SISTER THAT WE'RE LOCKED IN AN EPIC BATTLE!!
PLEASE!!
SO, YOU LAID IT ON THICK, HUH?
NO, I DIDN'T! I LAID IT ON THIN!!

AN INTENSE COVER STORY

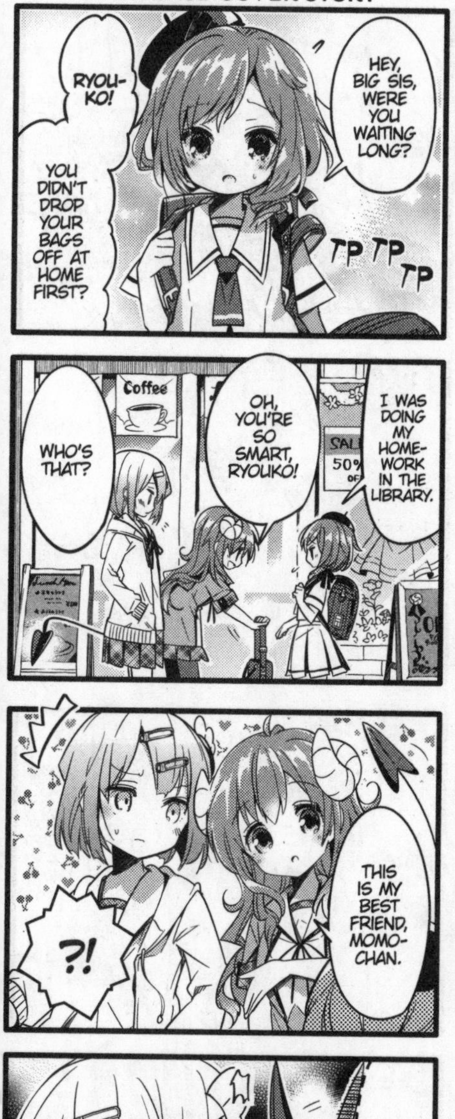
HEY, BIG SIS, WERE YOU WAITING LONG?
RYOUKO!
YOU DIDN'T DROP YOUR BAGS OFF AT HOME FIRST?
TP TP TP
I WAS DOING MY HOMEWORK IN THE LIBRARY.
OH, YOU'RE SO SMART, RYOUKO!
WHO'S THAT?
Coffee
SALE 50% OFF
THIS IS MY BEST FRIEND, MOMO-CHAN.
?!
Don't make that freaked-out face!!
PSST! こっち
PSST! こっち
Work with me here!!
GOT IT.

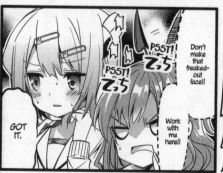

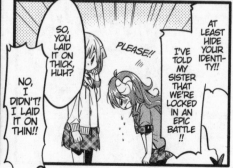

JUST ASSUME SHE'LL GET HURT

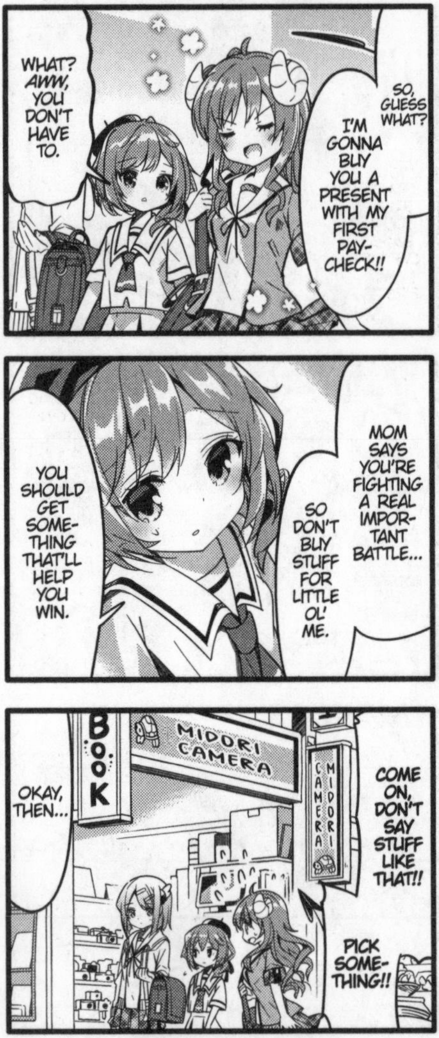
SO, GUESS WHAT?
I'M GONNA BUY YOU A PRESENT WITH MY FIRST PAY-CHECK!!
WHAT? AWW, YOU DON'T HAVE TO.
MOM SAYS YOU'RE FIGHTING A REAL IMPORTANT BATTLE...
SO DON'T BUY STUFF FOR LITTLE OL' ME.
YOU SHOULD GET SOMETHING THAT'LL HELP YOU WIN.
MIDORI CAMERA
BOOK
COME ON, DON'T SAY STUFF LIKE THAT!!
PICK SOMETHING!!
OKAY, THEN...
BANDAGES AND A FIRST-AID KIT.
I'M NOT GONNA GET HURT!!
YOU DON'T NEED TO BE A COMBAT MEDIC!!

THE WONDERS OF SEAWEED

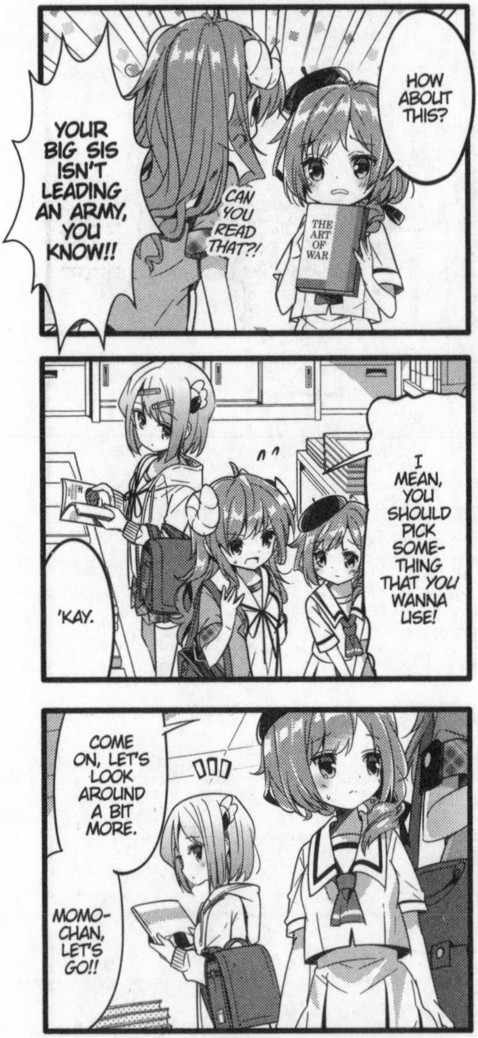
HOW ABOUT THIS?
THE ART OF WAR
CAN YOU READ THAT?!
YOUR BIG SIS ISN'T LEADING AN ARMY, YOU KNOW!!
I MEAN, YOU SHOULD PICK SOMETHING THAT YOU WANNA USE!
'KAY.
COME ON, LET'S LOOK AROUND A BIT MORE.
MOMO-CHAN, LET'S GO!!
BIG SIS...
IT'S GOOD FOR YOU.
I WANT THE FAMILY-SIZED PACK OF SEAWEED.
YOU'RE TOO YOUNG TO WORRY ABOUT OUR DIET!!

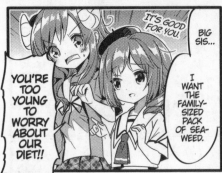

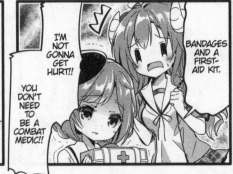

EASY-TO-READ SISTERS

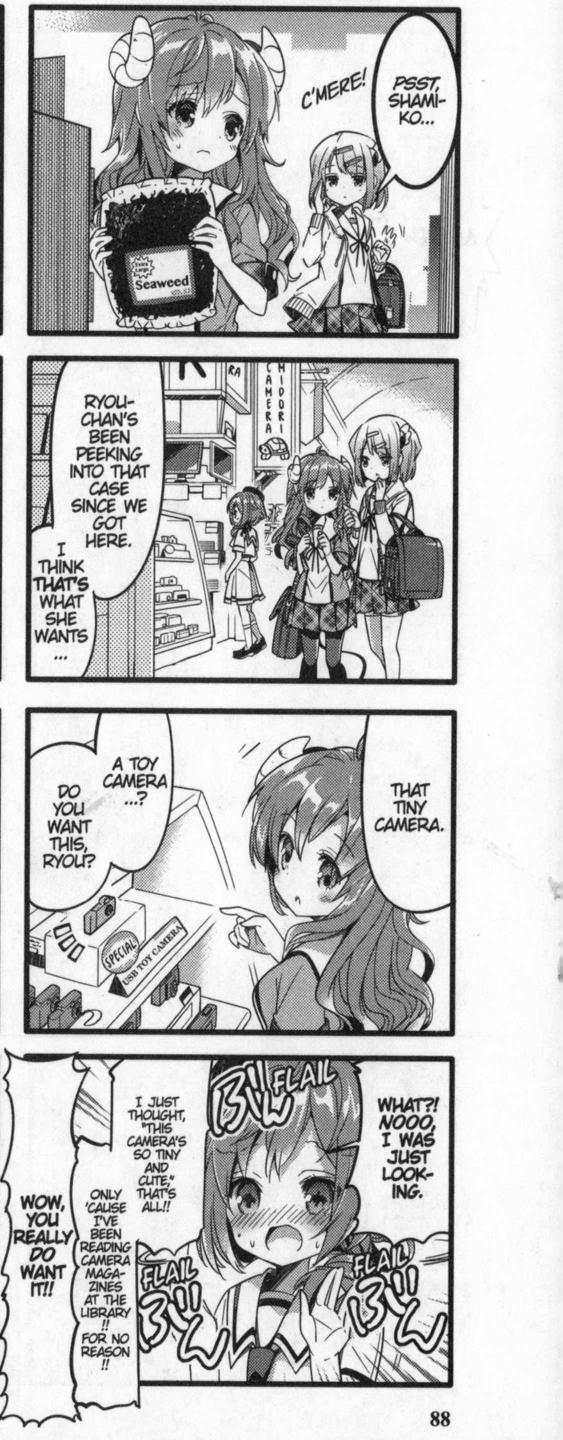
PSST, SHAMIKO...
C'MERE!
Extra Large Seaweed
RYOU-CHAN'S BEEN PEEKING INTO THAT CASE SINCE WE GOT HERE.
I THINK THAT'S WHAT SHE WANTS...
CAMERA MIDORI
THAT TINY CAMERA.
A TOY CAMERA...?
DO YOU WANT THIS, RYOU?
SPECIAL
USB TOY CAMERA
WHAT?! NOOO, I WAS JUST LOOKING.
FLAIL
I JUST THOUGHT, "THIS CAMERA'S SO TINY AND CUTE," THAT'S ALL!!
ONLY 'CAUSE I'VE BEEN READING CAMERA MAGAZINES AT THE LIBRARY FOR NO REASON!!
FLAIL
FLAIL
WOW, YOU REALLY DO WANT IT!!

THE SHOCKING TRUTH REVEALED!!

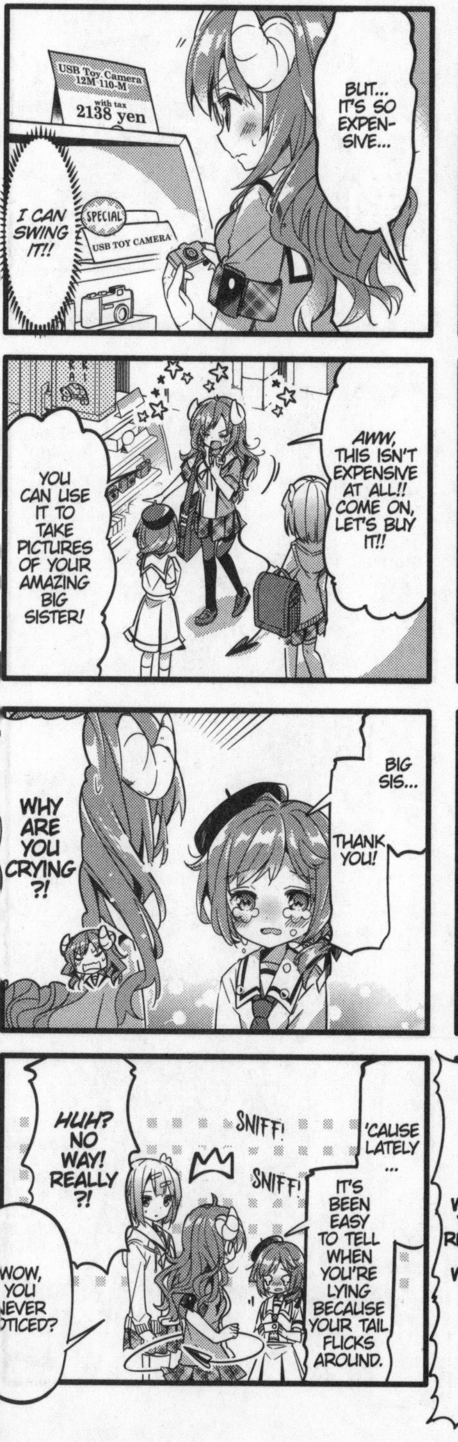
BUT... IT'S SO EXPENSIVE...
USB Toy Camera 12M 110-M with tax 2138 yen
I CAN SWING IT!!
SPECIAL
USB TOY CAMERA
AWW, THIS ISN'T EXPENSIVE AT ALL!! COME ON, LET'S BUY IT!!
YOU CAN USE IT TO TAKE PICTURES OF YOUR AMAZING BIG SISTER!
BIG SIS...
THANK YOU!
WHY ARE YOU CRYING?!
'CAUSE LATELY...
IT'S BEEN EASY TO TELL WHEN YOU'RE LYING BECAUSE YOUR TAIL FLICKS AROUND.
SNIFF!
SNIFF!
HUH? NO WAY! REALLY?!
WOW, YOU EVER OTICED?

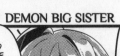

YOU HAVEN'T FORGOTTEN, HUH?

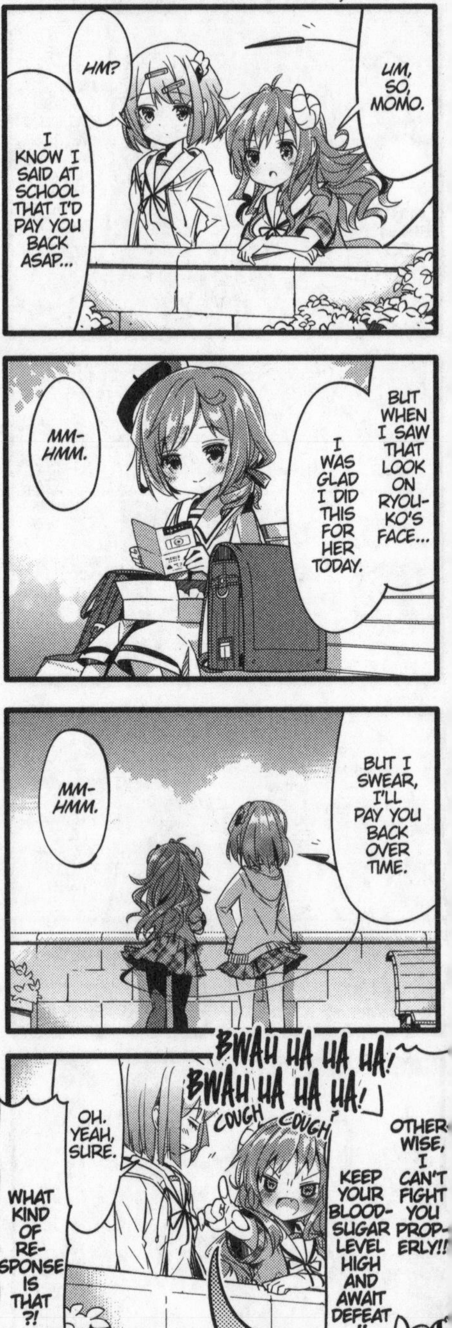
UM, SO, MOMO.
HM?
I KNOW I SAID AT SCHOOL THAT I'D PAY YOU BACK ASAP...
BUT WHEN I SAW THAT LOOK ON RYOUKO'S FACE...
I WAS GLAD I DID THIS FOR HER TODAY.
MM-HMM.
BUT I SWEAR, I'LL PAY YOU BACK OVER TIME.
MM-HMM.
BWAH HA HA HA!
BWAH HA HA HA!
COUGH COUGH
OTHERWISE, I CAN'T FIGHT YOU PROPERLY!!
KEEP YOUR BLOOD-SUGAR LEVEL HIGH AND AWAIT DEFEAT!!
OH. YEAH, SURE.
WHAT KIND OF RESPONSE IS THAT?!

DEMON BIG SISTER

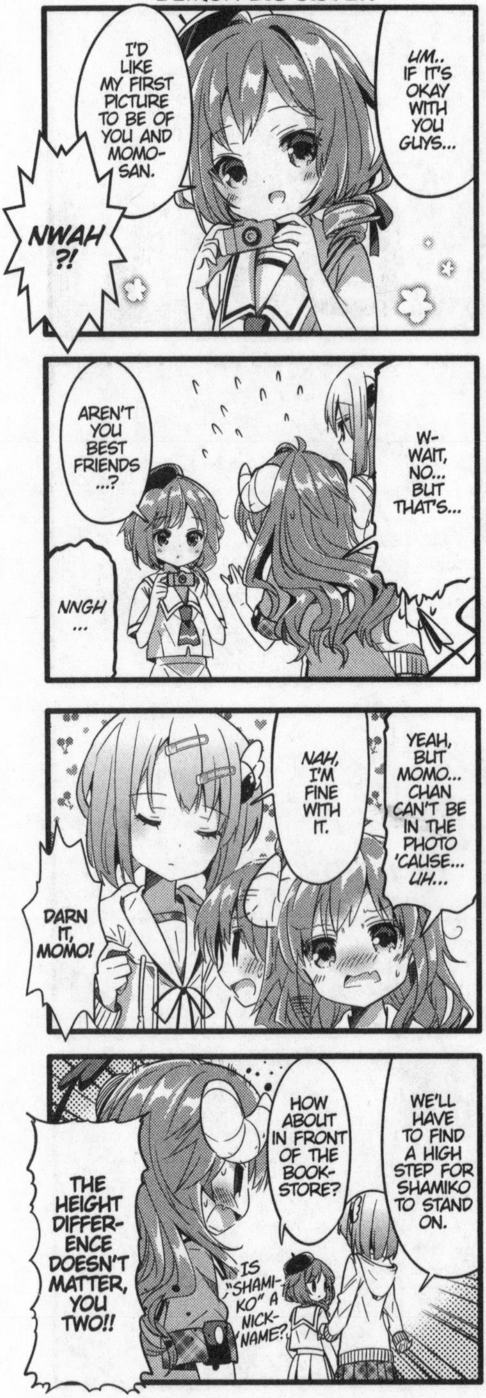
UM.. IF IT'S OKAY WITH YOU GUYS...
I'D LIKE MY FIRST PICTURE TO BE OF YOU AND MOMO-SAN.
NWAH?!
W-WAIT, NO... BUT THAT'S...
AREN'T YOU BEST FRIENDS...?
NNGH...
YEAH, BUT MOMO... CHAN CAN'T BE IN THE PHOTO 'CAUSE... UH...
NAH, I'M FINE WITH IT.
DARN IT, MOMO!
WE'LL HAVE TO FIND A HIGH STEP FOR SHAMIKO TO STAND ON.
HOW ABOUT IN FRONT OF THE BOOKSTORE?
IS "SHAMIKO" A NICKNAME?
THE HEIGHT DIFFERENCE DOESN'T MATTER, YOU TWO!!

UNITED STATES OF...

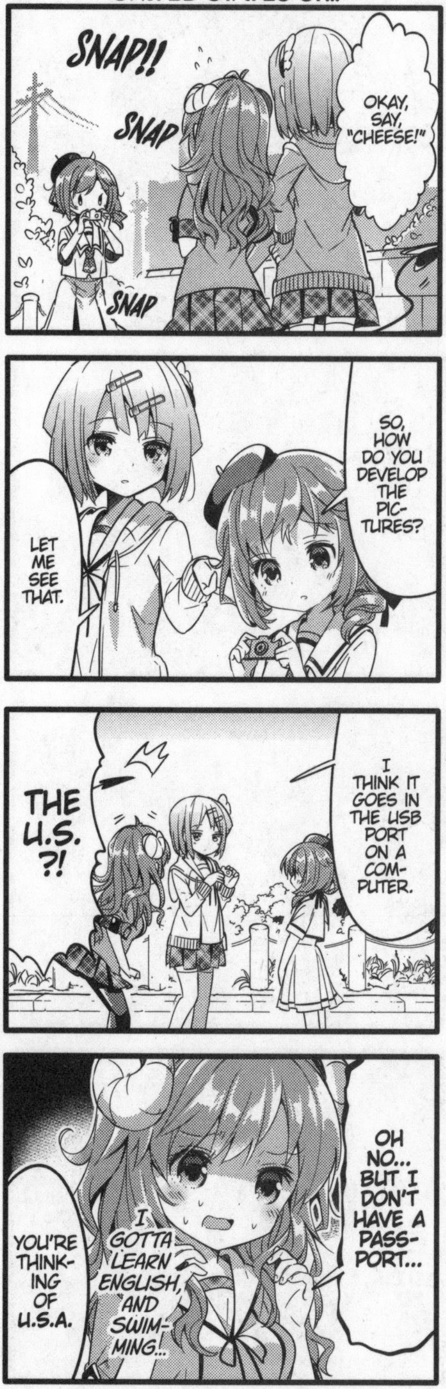
OKAY, SAY, "CHEESE!"
SNAP!!
SNAP
SNAP
SO, HOW DO YOU DEVELOP THE PICTURES?
LET ME SEE THAT.
I THINK IT GOES IN THE USB PORT ON A COMPUTER.
THE U.S.?!
OH NO... BUT I DON'T HAVE A PASSPORT...
I GOTTA LEARN ENGLISH, AND SWIMMING...
YOU'RE THINKING OF U.S.A.

DIGNITY IN DANGER

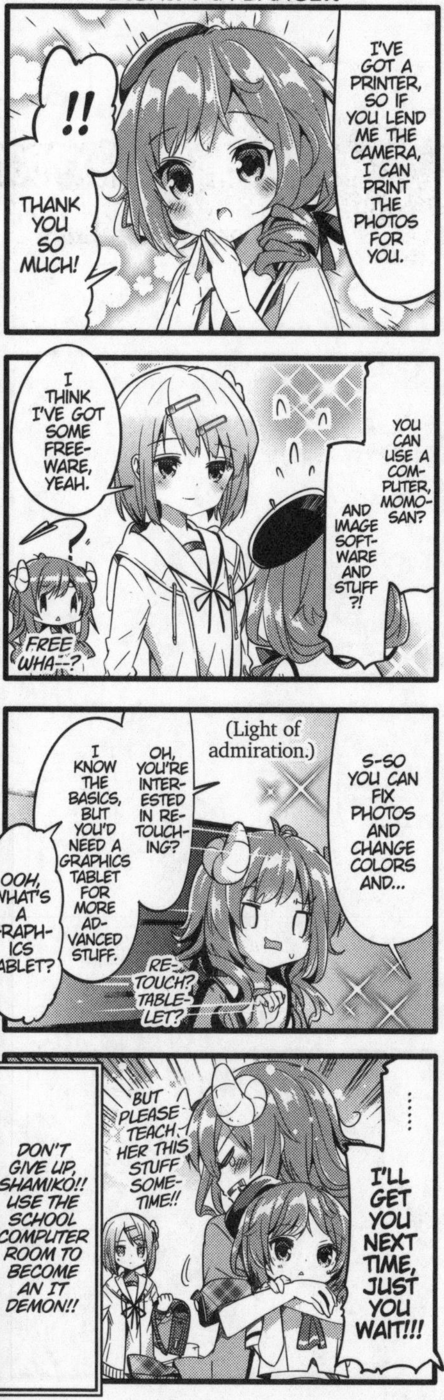
I'VE GOT A PRINTER, SO IF YOU LEND ME THE CAMERA, I CAN PRINT THE PHOTOS FOR YOU.
!!
THANK YOU SO MUCH!
YOU CAN USE A COMPUTER, MOMO-SAN?
AND IMAGE SOFTWARE AND STUFF?!
I THINK I'VE GOT SOME FREEWARE, YEAH.
FREE WHA--?
S-SO YOU CAN FIX PHOTOS AND CHANGE COLORS AND...
(Light of admiration.)
OH, YOU'RE INTERESTED IN RETOUCHING?
I KNOW THE BASICS, BUT YOU'D NEED A GRAPHICS TABLET FOR MORE ADVANCED STUFF.
OOH, /HAT'S A RAPH-ICS ABLET?
RE-TOUCH? TABLE-LET?
......
I'LL GET YOU NEXT TIME, JUST YOU WAIT!!!
BUT PLEASE TEACH HER THIS STUFF SOMETIME!!
DON'T GIVE UP, SHAMIKO!! USE THE SCHOOL COMPUTER ROOM TO BECOME AN IT DEMON!!

SECONDS!!

DEMON GIRL NEXT DOO

(EXTRA 1)

~ A DEMON'S FEELINGS ~

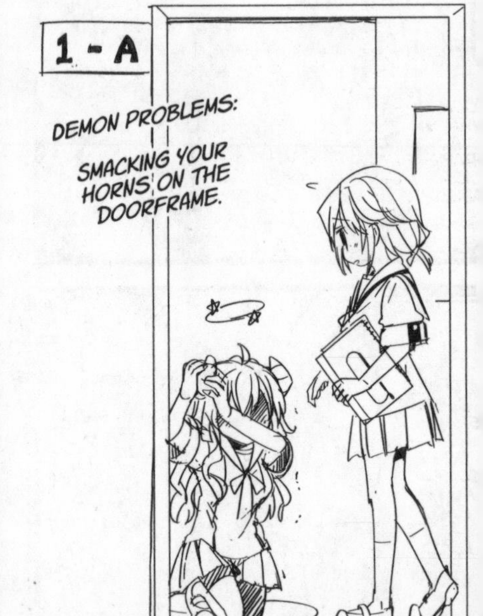
1 - A
DEMON PROBLEMS:
SMACKING YOUR HORNS ON THE DOORFRAME.

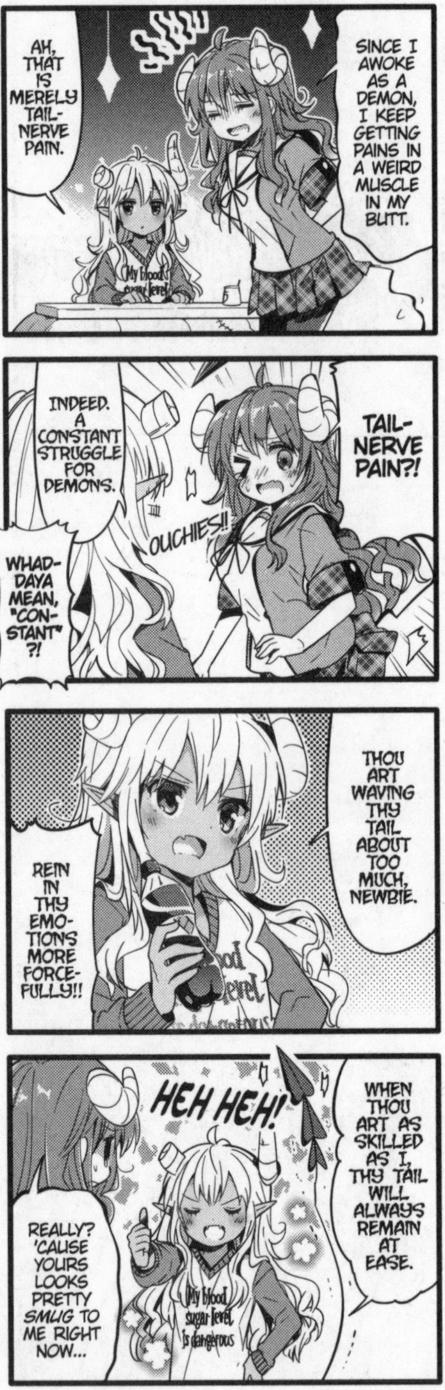
SINCE I AWOKE AS A DEMON, I KEEP GETTING PAINS IN A WEIRD MUSCLE IN MY BUTT.
AH, THAT IS MERELY TAIL-NERVE PAIN.
My blood sugar level
TAIL-NERVE PAIN?!
OUCHIES!!
INDEED. A CONSTANT STRUGGLE FOR DEMONS.
WHADDAYA MEAN, "CONSTANT"?!
THOU ART WAVING THY TAIL ABOUT TOO MUCH, NEWBIE.
REIN IN THY EMOTIONS MORE FORCEFULLY!!
WHEN THOU ART AS SKILLED AS I, THY TAIL WILL ALWAYS REMAIN AT EASE.
HEH HEH!
REALLY? 'CAUSE YOURS LOOKS PRETTY SMUG TO ME RIGHT NOW...
My blood sugar level is dangerous

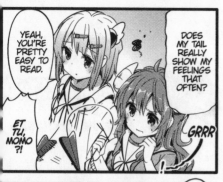

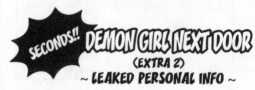

SECONDS!! DEMON GIRL NEXT DOOR (EXTRA 2)

~ LEAKED PERSONAL INFO ~

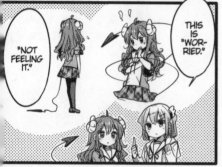

IT TAKES 1.5 SECONDS FOR HER TO FEEL THE COLD.

DOES MY TAIL REALLY SHOW MY FEELINGS THAT OFTEN?
GRRR
YEAH, YOU'RE PRETTY EASY TO READ.
ET TU, MOMO ?!
THIS IS "WOR-RIED."
"NOT FEELING IT."
"NER-VOUS."
AND EXCIT-ED."
AND NOW YOUR TAIL SAYS ...
"HOW CLOSELY HAS SHE BEEN OBSERV-ING ME? THAT'S KINDA SCARY."
I BET.
WHY IS THAT ONE SO SPE-CIFIC?!

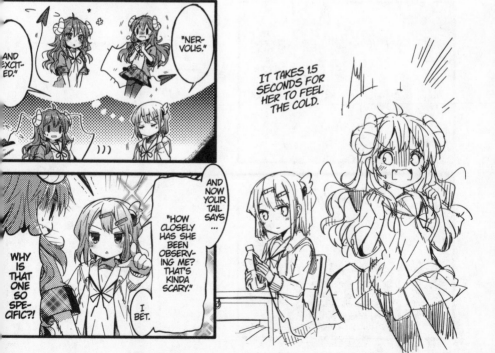

The Demon
Girl Next Door

The Demon Girl Next Door

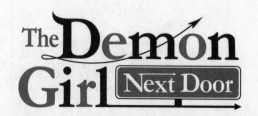

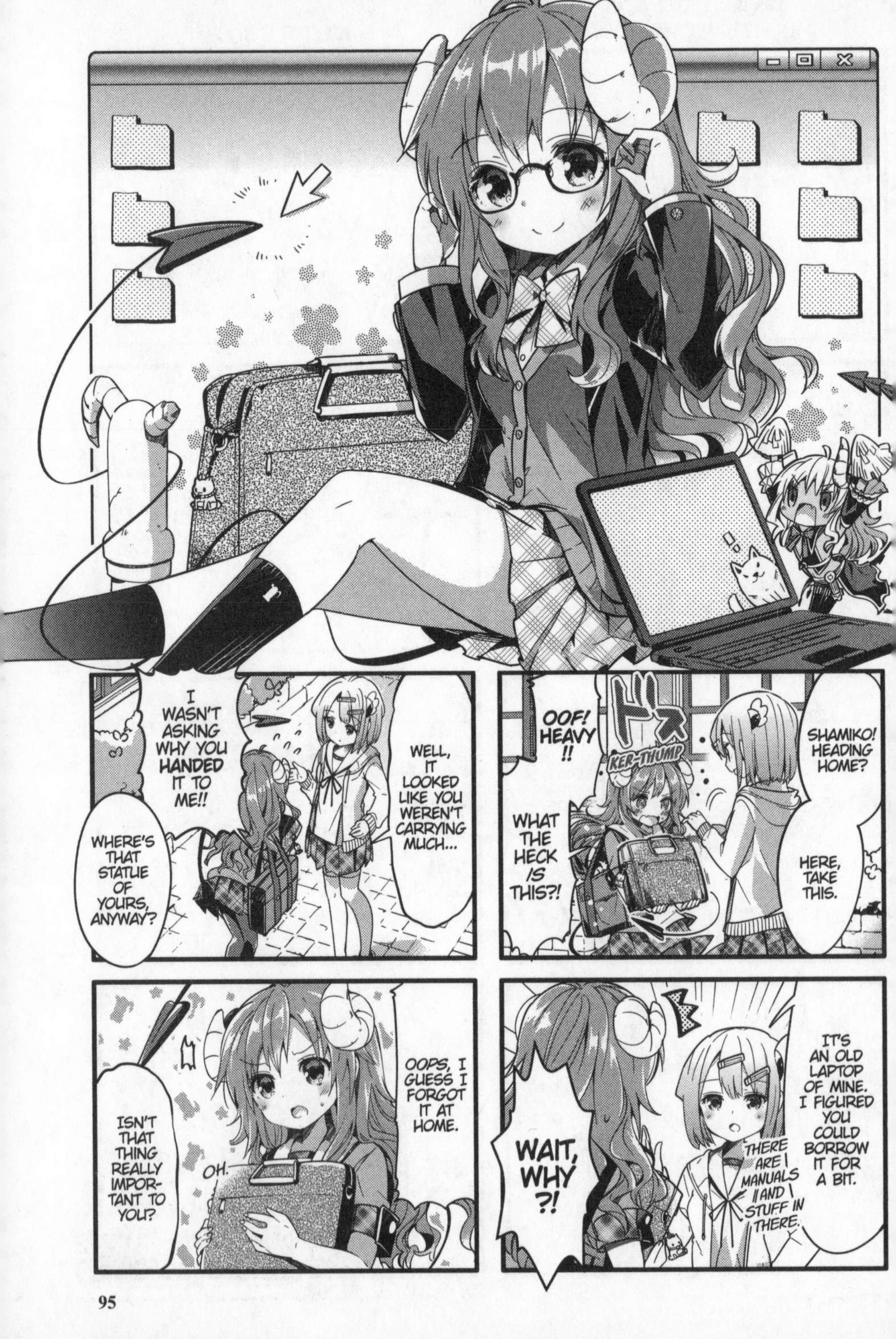
SHAMIKO! HEADING HOME?
HERE, TAKE THIS.
ドス
KER-THUMP
OOF! HEAVY!!
WHAT THE HECK IS THIS?!
WELL, IT LOOKED LIKE YOU WEREN'T CARRYING MUCH...
I WASN'T ASKING WHY YOU HANDED IT TO ME!!
WHERE'S THAT STATUE OF YOURS, ANYWAY?
IT'S AN OLD LAPTOP OF MINE. I FIGURED YOU COULD BORROW IT FOR A BIT.
THERE ARE MANUALS AND STUFF IN THERE.
WAIT, WHY?!
OOPS, I GUESS I FORGOT IT AT HOME.
ISN'T THAT THING REALLY IMPORTANT TO YOU?
OH.

A LITTLE SLOW

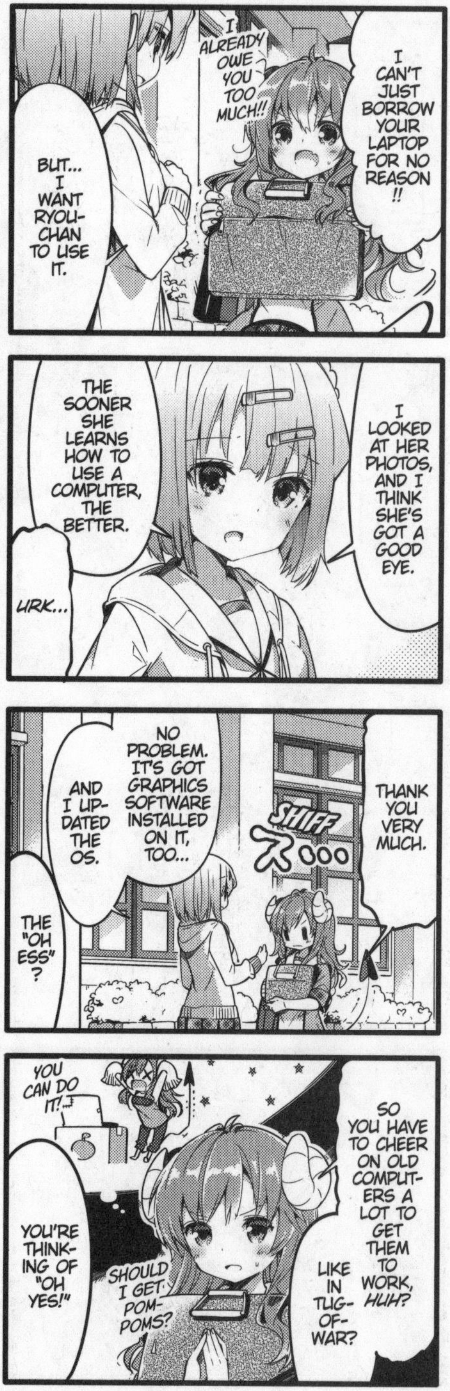
I CAN'T JUST BORROW YOUR LAPTOP FOR NO REASON!!
I ALREADY OWE YOU TOO MUCH!!
BUT... I WANT RYOU-CHAN TO USE IT.
I LOOKED AT HER PHOTOS, AND I THINK SHE'S GOT A GOOD EYE.
THE SOONER SHE LEARNS HOW TO USE A COMPUTER, THE BETTER.
URK...
THANK YOU VERY MUCH.
SHIFF
NO PROBLEM. IT'S GOT GRAPHICS SOFTWARE INSTALLED ON IT, TOO...
AND I UPDATED THE OS.
THE "OH ESS"?
SO YOU HAVE TO CHEER ON OLD COMPUTERS A LOT TO GET THEM TO WORK, HUH?
LIKE IN TUG-OF-WAR?
YOU CAN DO IT!
YOU'RE THINKING OF "OH YES!"
SHOULD I GET POM-POMS?

FOUR YEARS AGO, HDD 1TB, MEMORY 8GB

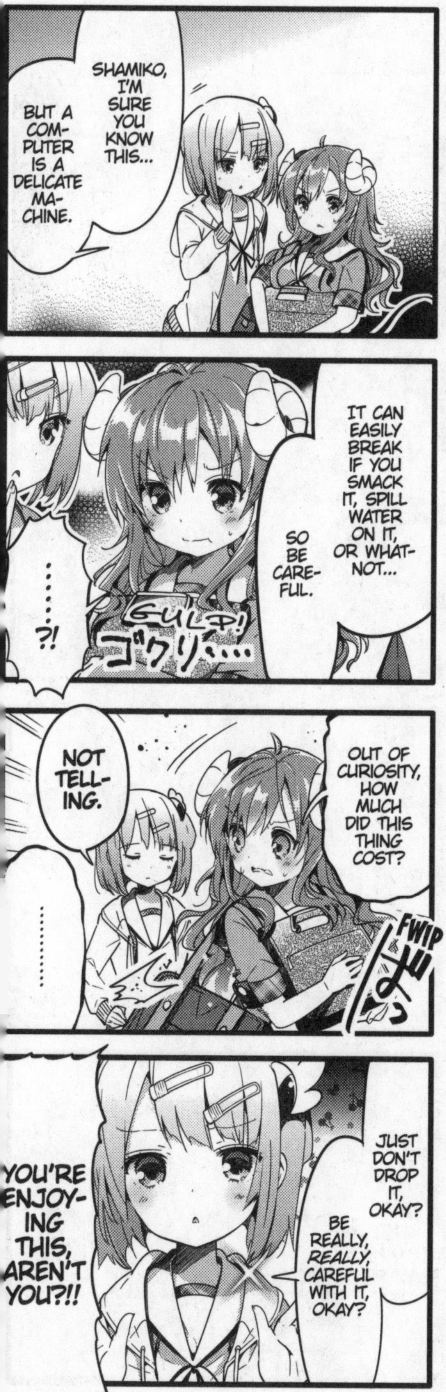
SHAMIKO, I'M SURE YOU KNOW THIS...
BUT A COMPUTER IS A DELICATE MACHINE.
IT CAN EASILY BREAK IF YOU SMACK IT, SPILL WATER ON IT, OR WHATNOT...
SO BE CAREFUL.
GULP!
ゴクリ…
......?!
OUT OF CURIOSITY, HOW MUCH DID THIS THING COST?
NOT TELLING.
FWIP
......
JUST DON'T DROP IT, OKAY?
BE REALLY, *REALLY*, CAREFUL WITH IT, OKAY?
YOU'RE ENJOYING THIS, AREN'T YOU?!!

TRIAL 1: GET PAST THE SPORTS TEAMS

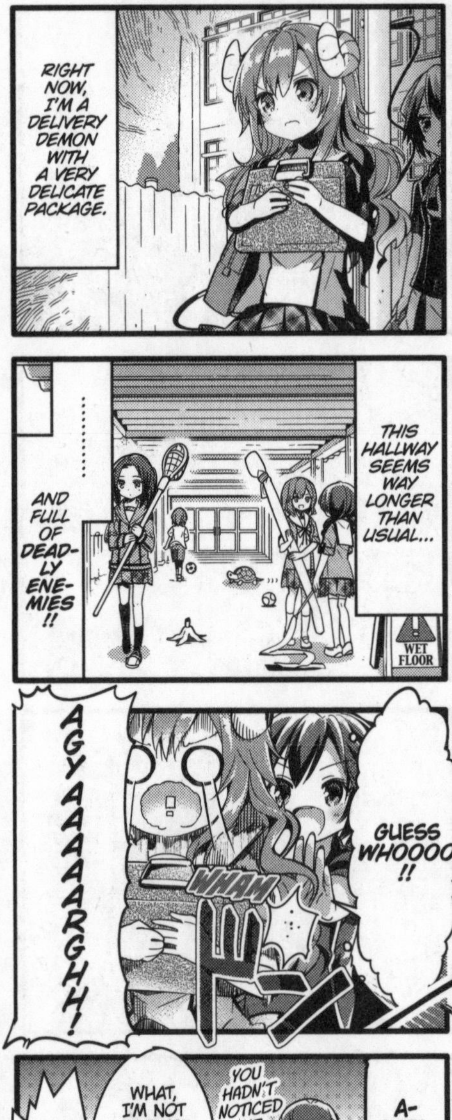
RIGHT NOW, I'M A DELIVERY DEMON WITH A VERY DELICATE PACKAGE.
THIS HALLWAY SEEMS WAY LONGER THAN USUAL...
......
AND FULL OF DEADLY ENEMIES!!
WET FLOOR
GUESS WHOOOO!!
WHAM
AGYAAAAAARGHH!
A-ANRI-CHAN... WHAT THE HECK?!!
YOU HADN'T NOTICED ME.
WHAT, I'M NOT ALLOWED TO PULL A LITTLE PRANK ON MY FRIEND?
NOT AT THE MOMENT, PLEASE!!
TREMBLE
ガク
TREMBLE
ガク

NOT A GOOD SIGN

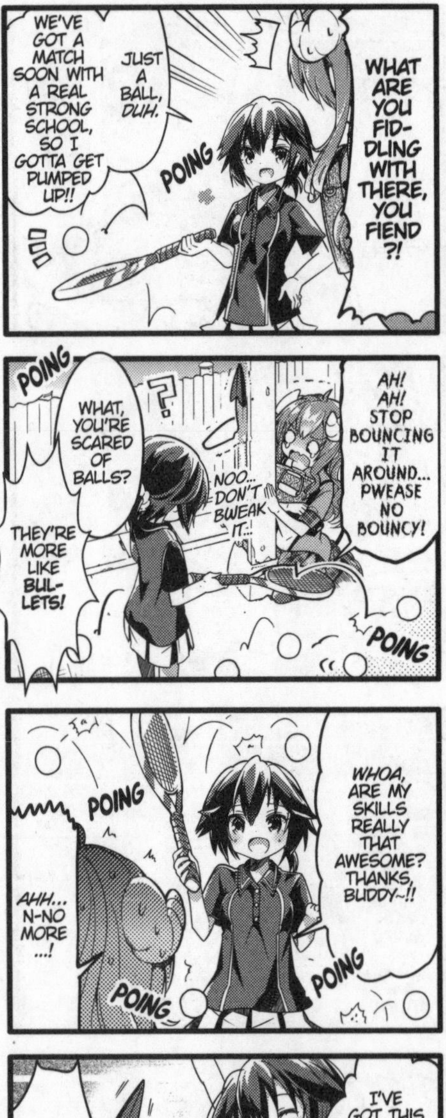
WHAT ARE YOU FIDDLING WITH THERE, YOU FIEND?!
JUST A BALL, DUH.
WE'VE GOT A MATCH SOON WITH A REAL STRONG SCHOOL, SO I GOTTA GET PUMPED UP!!
POING
AH! AH! STOP BOUNCING IT AROUND... PWEASE NO BOUNCY!
NOO... DON'T BWEAK IT...
WHAT, YOU'RE SCARED OF BALLS?
THEY'RE MORE LIKE BULLETS!
POING
POING
WHOA, ARE MY SKILLS REALLY THAT AWESOME? THANKS, BUDDY~!!
POING
AHH... N-NO MORE...!
POING
POING
I'VE GOT THIS SWEET MOVE WHERE I BOUNCE IT INTO THE AIR AND SMASH IT, TOO!!
ARE YOU TRYING TO KILL ME?!

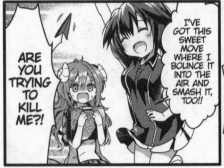

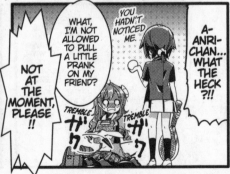

TRIAL 2: OGURA-SAN ON CLEANING DUTY

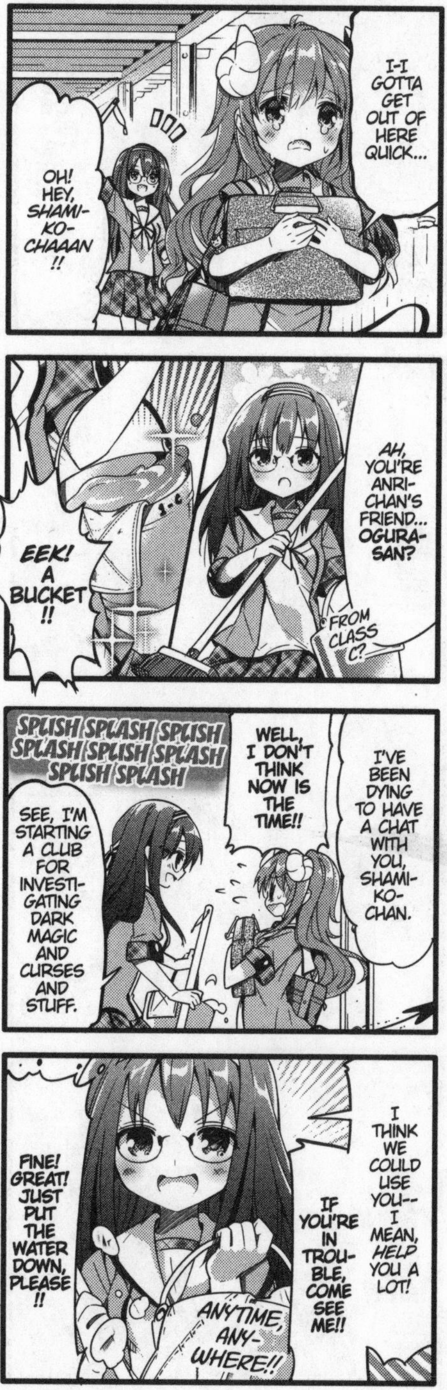
I-I GOTTA GET OUT OF HERE QUICK...
OH! HEY, SHAMI-KO-CHAAAN!!
AH, YOU'RE ANRI-CHAN'S FRIEND... OGURA-SAN?
FROM CLASS C?
EEK! A BUCKET!!
I'VE BEEN DYING TO HAVE A CHAT WITH YOU, SHAMI-KO-CHAN.
WELL, I DON'T THINK NOW IS THE TIME!!
SPLISH SPLASH SPLISH SPLASH SPLISH SPLASH SPLISH SPLASH
SEE, I'M STARTING A CLUB FOR INVESTI-GATING DARK MAGIC AND CURSES AND STUFF.
I THINK WE COULD USE YOU-- I MEAN, HELP YOU A LOT!
IF YOU'RE IN TROU-BLE, COME SEE ME!!
FINE! GREAT! JUST PUT THE WATER DOWN, PLEASE!!
ANYTIME, ANY-WHERE!!

EVER SINCE AROUND CHAPTER TWO

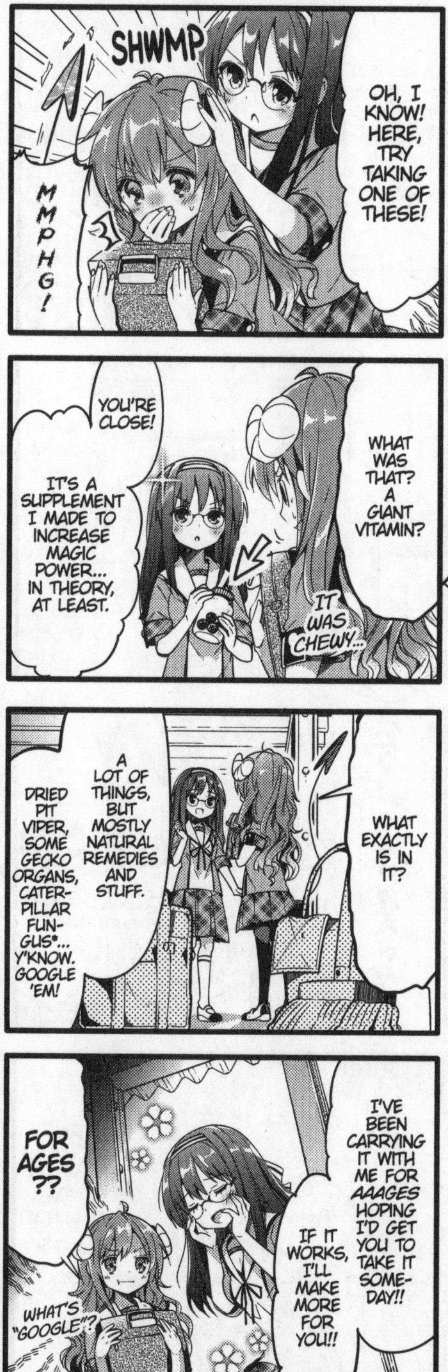
OH, I KNOW! HERE, TRY TAKING ONE OF THESE!
SHWMP
MMPHG!
WHAT WAS THAT? A GIANT VITAMIN?
YOU'RE CLOSE!
IT'S A SUPPLEMENT I MADE TO INCREASE MAGIC POWER... IN THEORY, AT LEAST.
IT WAS CHEWY...
WHAT EXACTLY IS IN IT?
A LOT OF THINGS, BUT MOSTLY NATURAL REMEDIES AND STUFF.
DRIED PIT VIPER, SOME GECKO ORGANS, CATER-PILLAR FUN-GUS*... Y'KNOW. GOOGLE 'EM!
I'VE BEEN CARRYING IT WITH ME FOR AAAGES HOPING I'D GET YOU TO TAKE IT SOME-DAY!!
IF IT WORKS, I'LL MAKE MORE FOR YOU!!
FOR AGES??
WHAT'S "GOOGLE"?

*These are all ingredients used in traditional Chinese medicine.

FINAL BATTLE?

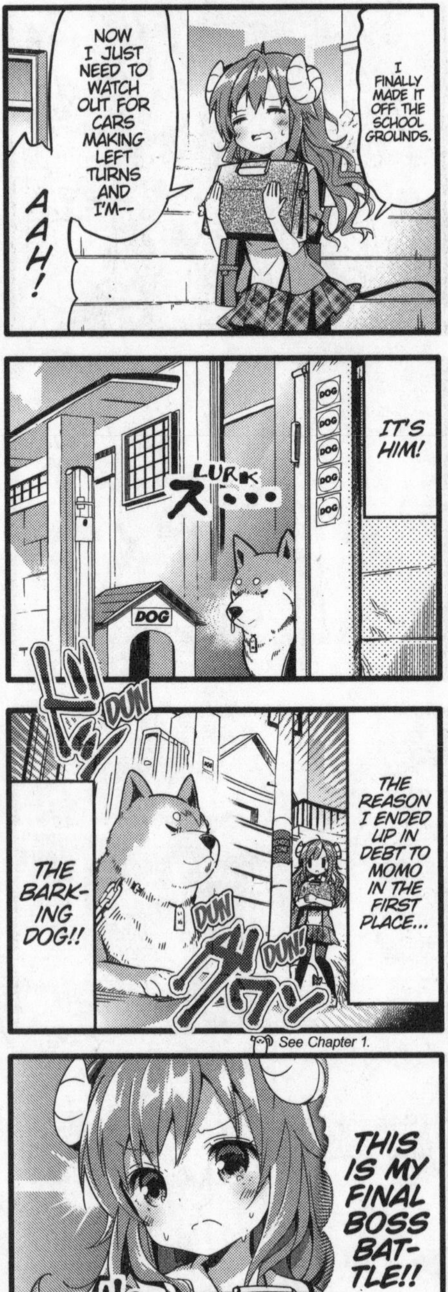
I FINALLY MADE IT OFF THE SCHOOL GROUNDS.
NOW I JUST NEED TO WATCH OUT FOR CARS MAKING LEFT TURNS AND I'M--
AAAH!
IT'S HIM!
LURK
DOG
THE REASON I ENDED UP IN DEBT TO MOMO IN THE FIRST PLACE...
THE BARKING DOG!!
DUN DUN DUN
See Chapter 1.
THIS IS MY FINAL BOSS BATTLE!!

JUST PUT DOWN THE PC AND CALM DOWN

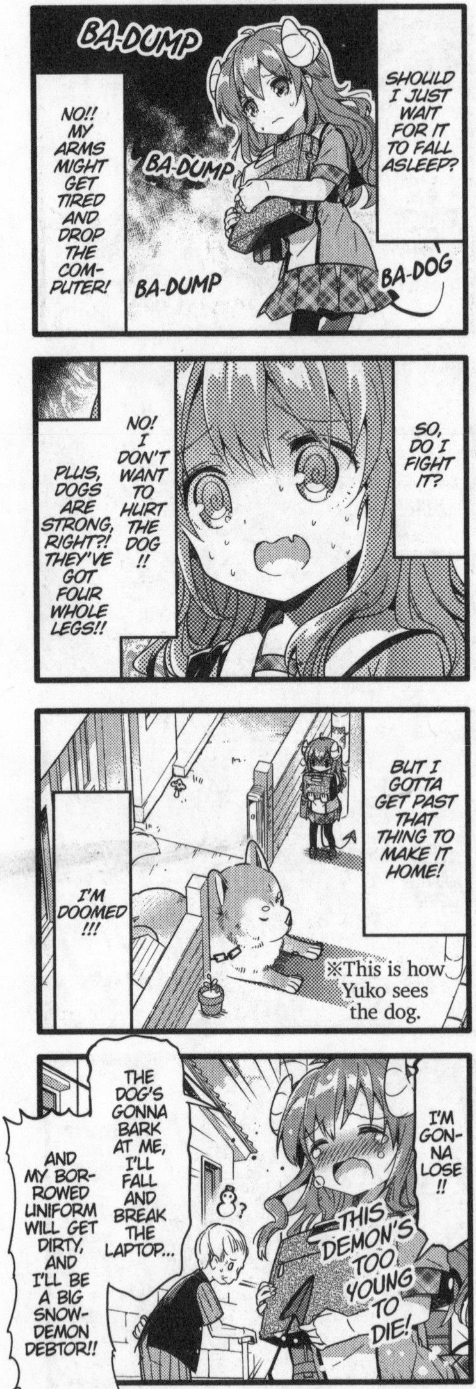
BA-DUMP
SHOULD I JUST WAIT FOR IT TO FALL ASLEEP?
NO!! MY ARMS MIGHT GET TIRED AND DROP THE COMPUTER!
BA-DUMP
BA-DOG
BA-DUMP
SO, DO I FIGHT IT?
NO! I DON'T WANT TO HURT THE DOG!!
PLUS, DOGS ARE STRONG, RIGHT?! THEY'VE GOT FOUR WHOLE LEGS!!
BUT I GOTTA GET PAST THAT THING TO MAKE IT HOME!
I'M DOOMED!!!
※This is how Yuko sees the dog.
I'M GONNA LOSE!!
THE DOG'S GONNA BARK AT ME, I'LL FALL AND BREAK THE LAPTOP...
AND MY BORROWED UNIFORM WILL GET DIRTY, AND I'LL BE A BIG SNOW-DEMON DEBTOR!!
THIS DEMON'S TOO YOUNG TO DIE!

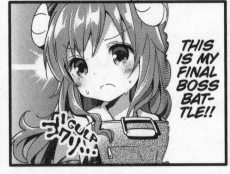

DON'T THINK, JUST FEEL

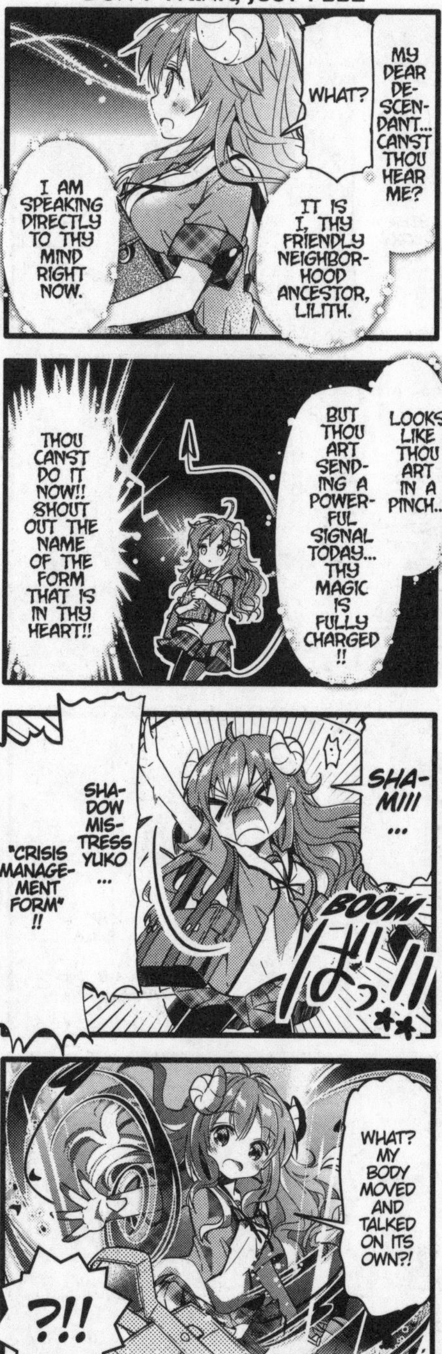
MY DEAR DESCENDANT... CANST THOU HEAR ME?
WHAT?
IT IS I, THY FRIENDLY NEIGHBORHOOD ANCESTOR, LILITH.
I AM SPEAKING DIRECTLY TO THY MIND RIGHT NOW.
LOOKS LIKE THOU ART IN A PINCH...
BUT THOU ART SENDING A POWERFUL SIGNAL TODAY... THY MAGIC IS FULLY CHARGED!!
THOU CANST DO IT NOW!! SHOUT OUT THE NAME OF THE FORM THAT IS IN THY HEART!!
SHA-MIII...
SHADOW MISTRESS YUKO...
BOOM
ぱっ!!
"CRISIS MANAGEMENT FORM"!!
WHAT? MY BODY MOVED AND TALKED ON ITS OWN?!
?!!

EXPOSED WEAKNESS FORM

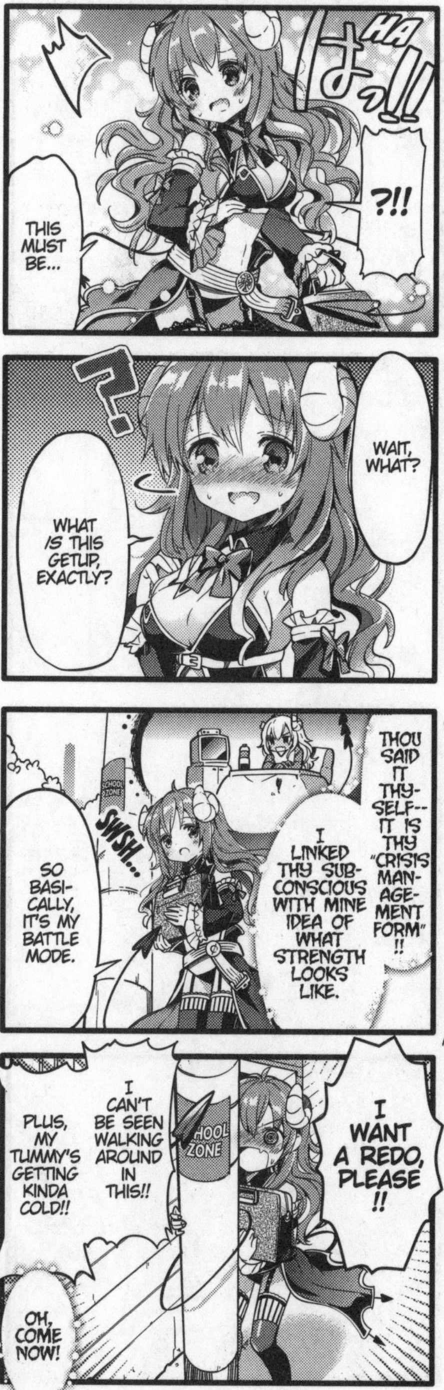
HA
はっ!!
?!!
THIS MUST BE...
?
WAIT, WHAT?
WHAT IS THIS GETUP, EXACTLY?
THOU SAID IT THYSELF-- IT IS THY "CRISIS MANAGEMENT FORM"!!
I LINKED THY SUBCONSCIOUS WITH MINE IDEA OF WHAT STRENGTH LOOKS LIKE.
SWSH...
SCHOOL ZONE
SO BASICALLY, IT'S MY BATTLE MODE.
I WANT A REDO, PLEASE!!
SCHOOL ZONE
I CAN'T BE SEEN WALKING AROUND IN THIS!!
PLUS, MY TUMMY'S GETTING KINDA COLD!!
OH, COME NOW!

A BATTLE FORM THAT SILENCES DOGS

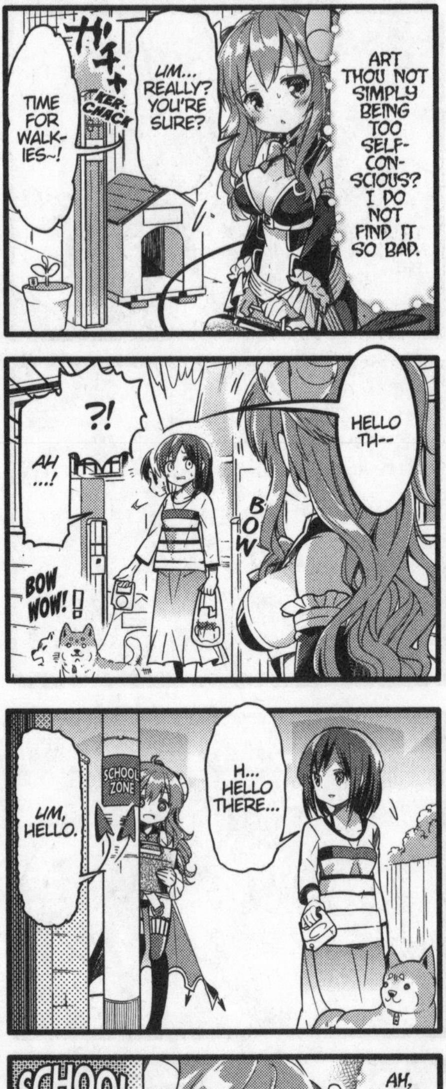

ART THOU NOT SIMPLY BEING TOO SELF-CONSCIOUS? I DO NOT FIND IT SO BAD.
UM... REALLY? YOU'RE SURE?
KER-CHACK
TIME FOR WALKIES~!
HELLO TH--
BOW WOW
?!
AH ...!
BOW WOW! !
H... HELLO THERE...
SCHOOL ZONE
UM, HELLO.
AH, I SEE. THAT IS QUITE AN UNFORTUNATE REACTION. I SHALL AMEND THE COSTUME AT ONCE.
SCHOO
ZO
I... I KNEW IT.
THIS IS A DOUBLE-TAKE KIND OF OUTFIT.

RIGHT, I FORGOT

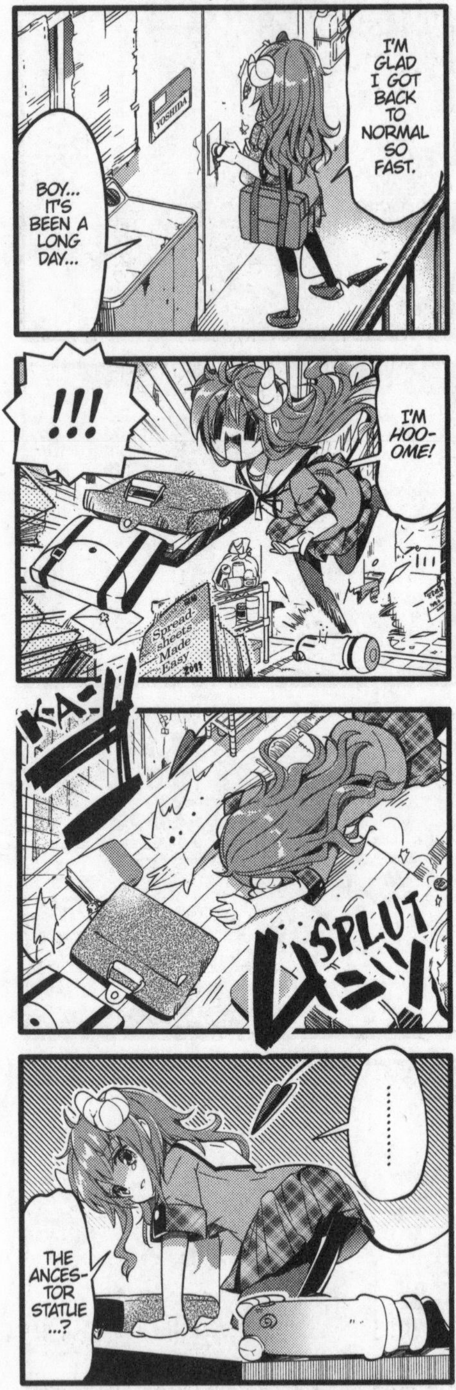

I'M GLAD I GOT BACK TO NORMAL SO FAST.
YOSHIDA
BOY... IT'S BEEN A LONG DAY...
I'M HOO-OME!
!!!
Spread-sheets Made Easy 2011
K-A-
SPLUT
......
THE ANCES-TOR STATUE ...?

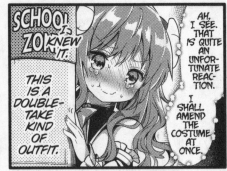

JUDGMENTAL

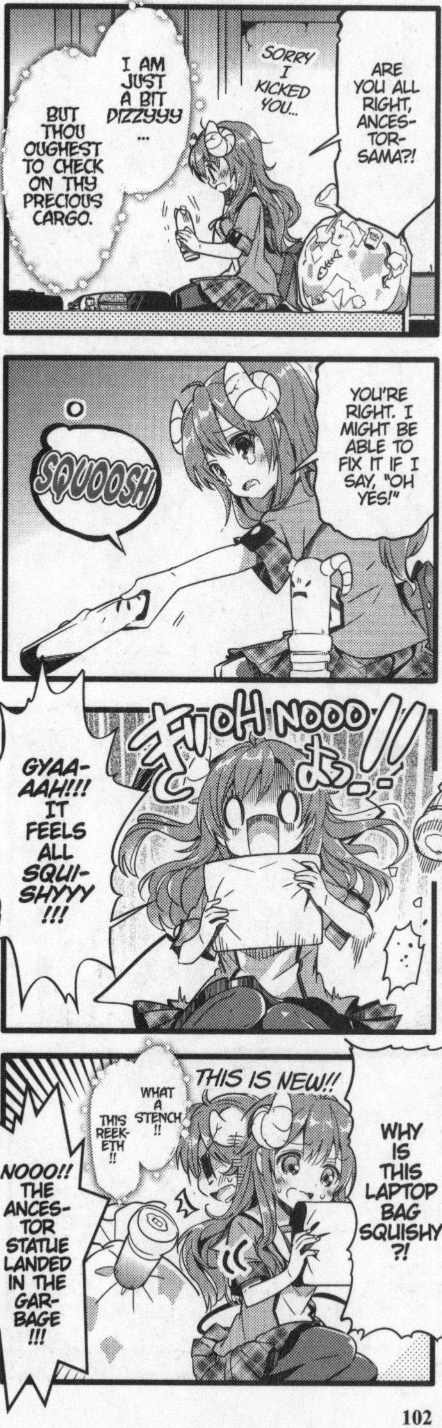

ARE YOU ALL RIGHT, ANCES-TOR-SAMA?!
SORRY I KICKED YOU...
I AM JUST A BIT DIZZYYY ...
BUT THOU OUGHEST TO CHECK ON THY PRECIOUS CARGO.
YOU'RE RIGHT. I MIGHT BE ABLE TO FIX IT IF I SAY, "OH YES!"
SQUOOSH
OH NOOO!!
GYAA-AAH!!! IT FEELS ALL SQUI-SHYYY!!!
WHY IS THIS LAPTOP BAG SQUISHY?!
THIS IS NEW!!
WHAT A STENCH!!
THIS REEK-ETH!!
NOOO!! THE ANCES-TOR STATUE LANDED IN THE GAR-BAGE!!!

TOTAL PINK VICTORY

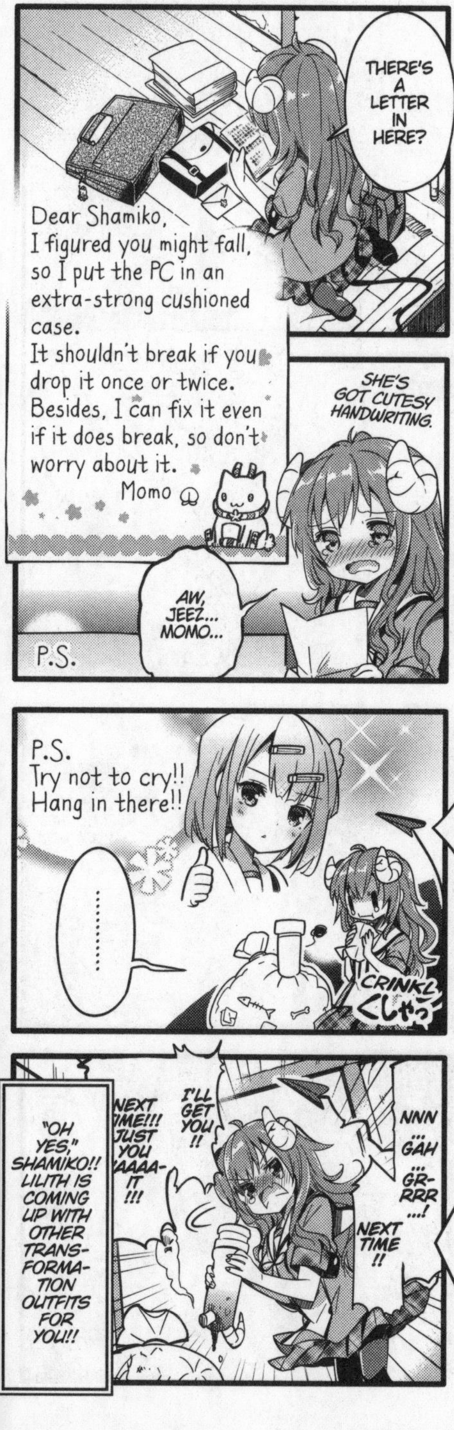

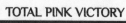

THERE'S A LETTER IN HERE?
Dear Shamiko,
I figured you might fall, so I put the PC in an extra-strong cushioned case.
It shouldn't break if you drop it once or twice.
Besides, I can fix it even if it does break, so don't worry about it.
Momo
SHE'S GOT CUTESY HANDWRITING.
AW, JEEZ... MOMO...
P.S.
P.S. Try not to cry!! Hang in there!!
....
CRINKL
NNN ...GAH ...GR-RRR ...!
NEXT TIME!!
I'LL GET YOU!!
NEXT TIME!!! JUST YOU WAAAA-IT!!!
"OH YES," SHAMIKO!! LILITH IS COMING UP WITH OTHER TRANS-FORMA-TION OUTFITS FOR YOU!!

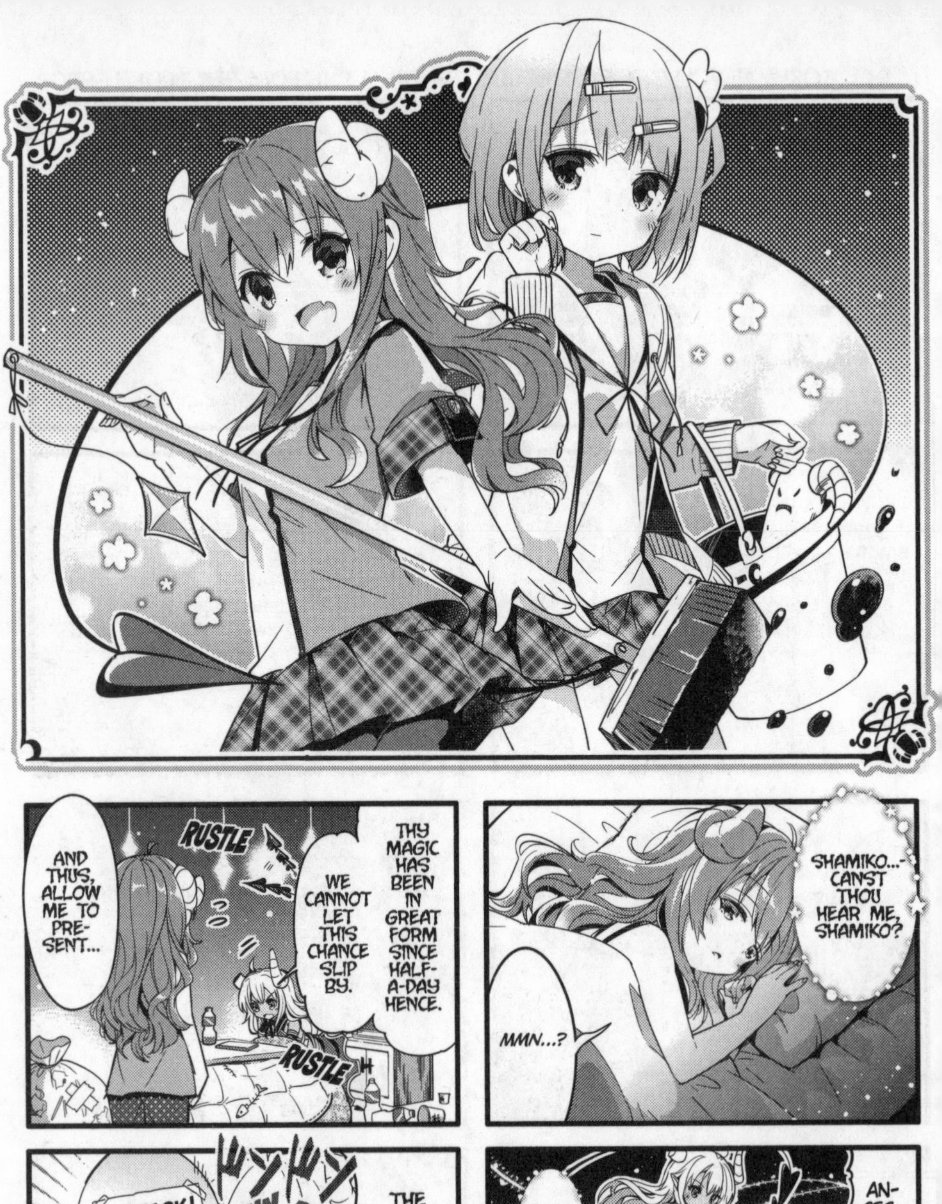
SHAMIKO...-CANST THOU HEAR ME, SHAMIKO?
MMN...?
RUSTLE
THY MAGIC HAS BEEN IN GREAT FORM SINCE HALF-A-DAY HENCE.
WE CANNOT LET THIS CHANCE SLIP BY.
AND THUS, ALLOW ME TO PRE-SENT...
RUSTLE
ANCES-TOR?!
IN-DEED.
'TWAS MUCH EASTER TO CALL ON THEE TODAY.
ドンドン
DUN DUN
THE "INFIL-TRATE MOMO'S SUBCON-SCIOUS AND CONTROL HER" SPECIAL~!!
ATTACK! NEXT-DOOR DREAM
WHAT THE HECK IS THAT GADGET?!
PAFF PAFF
パフパフ

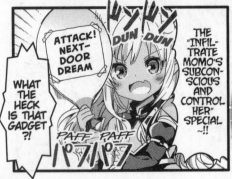

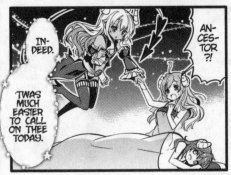

ENDING THE PINK REIGN OF TERROR

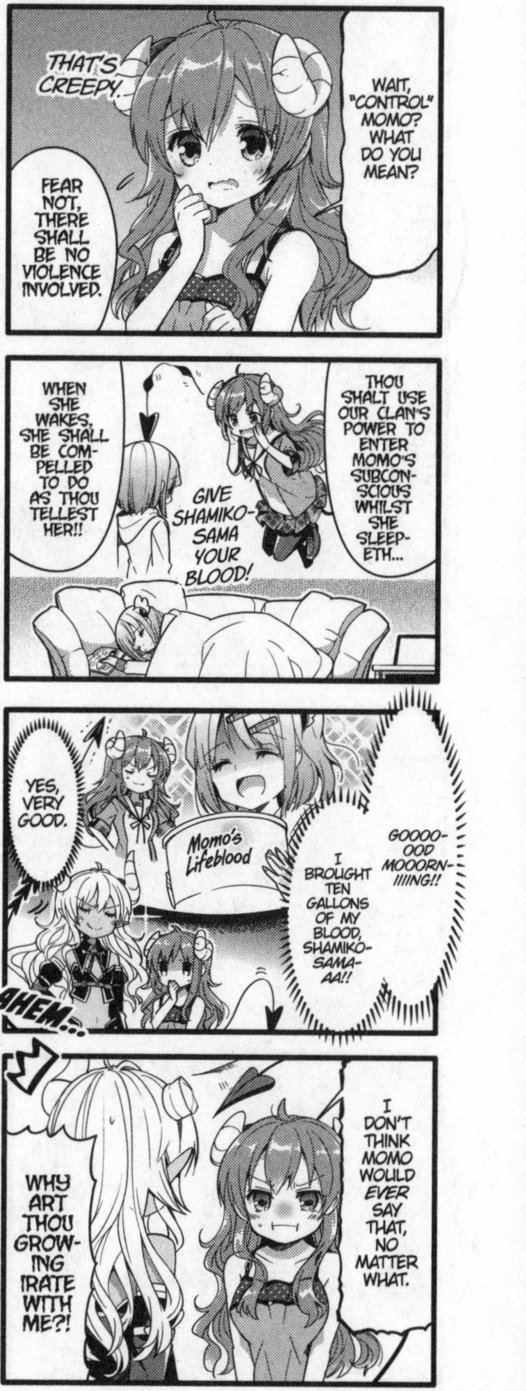
WAIT, "CONTROL" MOMO? WHAT DO YOU MEAN?
THAT'S CREEPY.
FEAR NOT, THERE SHALL BE NO VIOLENCE INVOLVED.
THOU SHALT USE OUR CLAN'S POWER TO ENTER MOMO'S SUBCONSCIOUS WHILST SHE SLEEPETH...
WHEN SHE WAKES, SHE SHALL BE COMPELLED TO DO AS THOU TELLEST HER!!
GIVE SHAMIKO-SAMA YOUR BLOOD!
GOOOO-OOD MOOORN-IIIING!!
I BROUGHT TEN GALLONS OF MY BLOOD, SHAMIKO-SAMA-AA!!
YES, VERY GOOD.
Momo's Lifeblood
AHEM...
I DON'T THINK MOMO WOULD EVER SAY THAT, NO MATTER WHAT.
WHY ART THOU GROWING IRATE WITH ME?!

DON'T WORRY IF YOU GET REPORTED

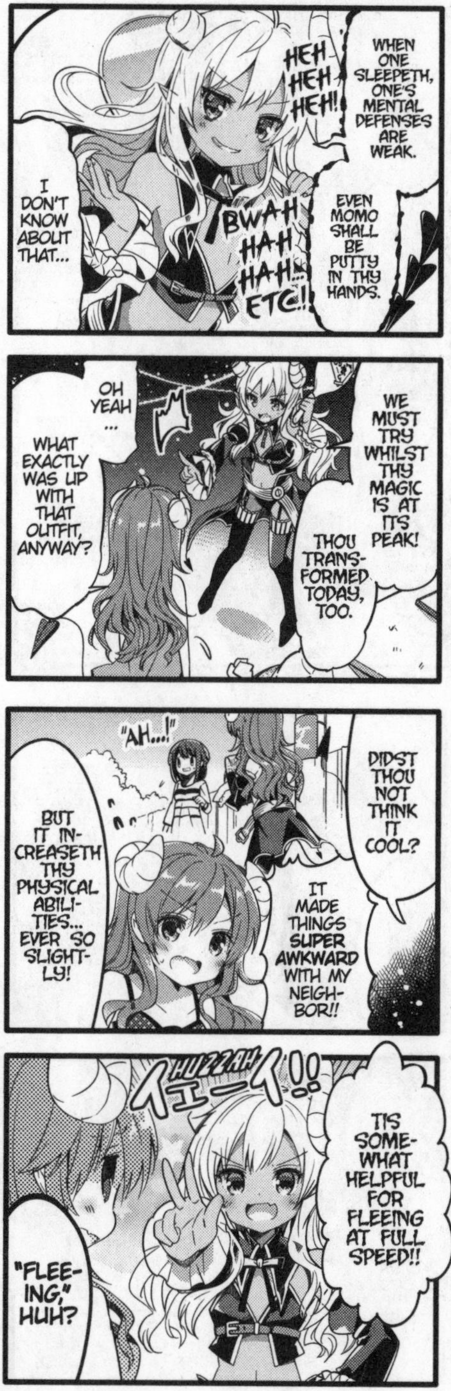
WHEN ONE SLEEPETH, ONE'S MENTAL DEFENSES ARE WEAK.
HEH HEH HEH!
EVEN MOMO SHALL BE PUTTY IN THY HANDS.
BWAH HAH HAH!! ETC.!!
I DON'T KNOW ABOUT THAT...
WE MUST TRY WHILST THY MAGIC IS AT ITS PEAK!
THOU TRANSFORMED TODAY, TOO.
OH YEAH...
WHAT EXACTLY WAS UP WITH THAT OUTFIT, ANYWAY?
DIDST THOU NOT THINK IT COOL?
IT MADE THINGS SUPER AWKWARD WITH MY NEIGHBOR!!
"AH...!"
BUT IT INCREASETH THY PHYSICAL ABILITIES... EVER SO SLIGHTLY!
HUZZAH
イェーイ!!
'TIS SOMEWHAT HELPFUL FOR FLEEING AT FULL SPEED!!
"FLEEING," HUH?

TREASURED MEMORIES

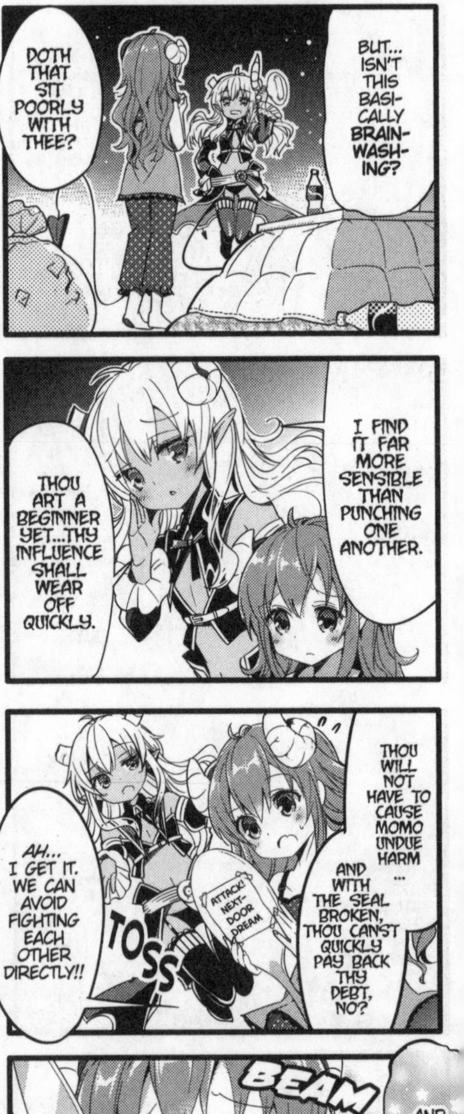
BUT... ISN'T THIS BASICALLY BRAINWASHING?
DOTH THAT SIT POORLY WITH THEE?
I FIND IT FAR MORE SENSIBLE THAN PUNCHING ONE ANOTHER.
THOU ART A BEGINNER YET...THY INFLUENCE SHALL WEAR OFF QUICKLY.
THOU WILL NOT HAVE TO CAUSE MOMO UNDUE HARM ...
AND WITH THE SEAL BROKEN, THOU CAN'ST QUICKLY PAY BACK THY DEBT, NO?
ATTACK! NEXT-DOOR DREAM
TOSS
AH... I GET IT. WE CAN AVOID FIGHTING EACH OTHER DIRECTLY!!
BEAM
AND IF WE DON'T HAVE TO PUNCH EACH OTHER...
I WON'T GET DRAGGED INTO RUNNING AND ENDING UP SORE ALL OVER AND STUFF!
I AM SORRY THOU HAST SUFFERED SO.

FREEZE FRAME

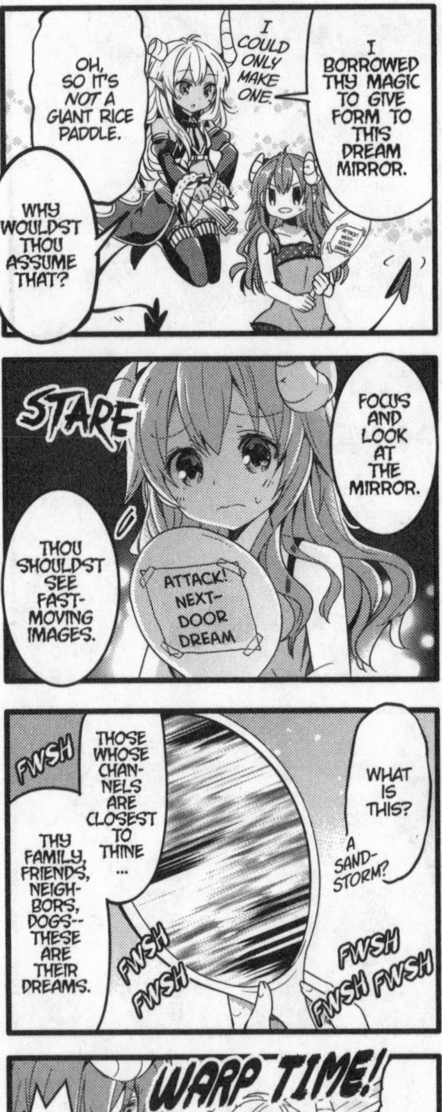
I BORROWED THY MAGIC TO GIVE FORM TO THIS DREAM MIRROR.
I COULD ONLY MAKE ONE.
OH, SO IT'S NOT A GIANT RICE PADDLE.
WHY WOULDST THOU ASSUME THAT?
FOCUS AND LOOK AT THE MIRROR.
STARE
THOU SHOULDST SEE FAST-MOVING IMAGES.
ATTACK! NEXT-DOOR DREAM
WHAT IS THIS?
A SANDSTORM?
THOSE WHOSE CHANNELS ARE CLOSEST TO THINE ...
FWSH
THY FAMILY, FRIENDS, NEIGHBORS, DOGS--THESE ARE THEIR DREAMS.
FWSH FWSH
FWSH FWSH FWSH
WARP TIME!
WHEN THOU SEEST MOMO'S DREAM ...
SMASH THE MIRROR ON THAT EXACT FRAME!
WHAT IS THIS, A FIGHTING GAME?!

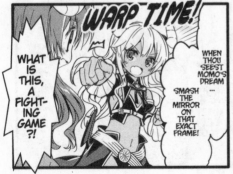

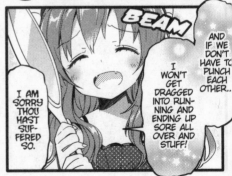

ENLIGHTENMENT IN THE MIRROR

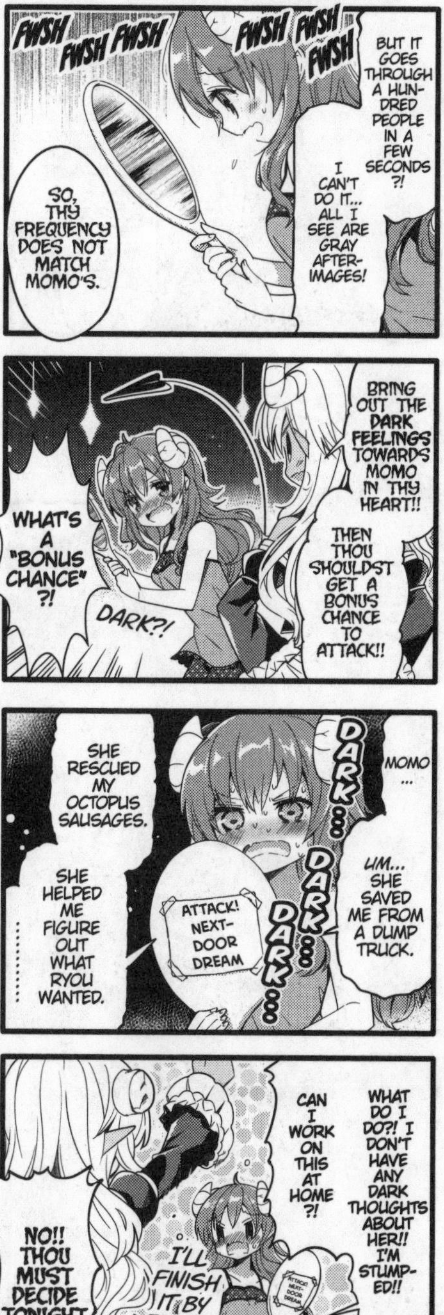
FWSH FWSH FWSH
FWSH FWSH FWSH
BUT IT GOES THROUGH A HUNDRED PEOPLE IN A FEW SECONDS ?!
I CAN'T DO IT... ALL I SEE ARE GRAY AFTER-IMAGES!
SO, THY FREQUENCY DOES NOT MATCH MOMO'S.
BRING OUT THE DARK FEELINGS TOWARDS MOMO IN THY HEART!!
THEN THOU SHOULDST GET A BONUS CHANCE TO ATTACK!!
DARK?!
WHAT'S A "BONUS CHANCE" ?!
MOMO ...
UM... SHE SAVED ME FROM A DUMP TRUCK.
DARK... DARK... DARK... DARK...
SHE RESCUED MY OCTOPUS SAUSAGES.
SHE HELPED ME FIGURE OUT WHAT RYOU WANTED.
......
ATTACK! NEXT-DOOR DREAM
WHAT DO I DO?! I DON'T HAVE ANY DARK THOUGHTS ABOUT HER!! I'M STUMPED!!
CAN I WORK ON THIS AT HOME ?!
I'LL FINISH IT BY FRIDAY!
NO!! THOU MUST DECIDE TONIGHT !!

BRINGING BACK THAT FORM

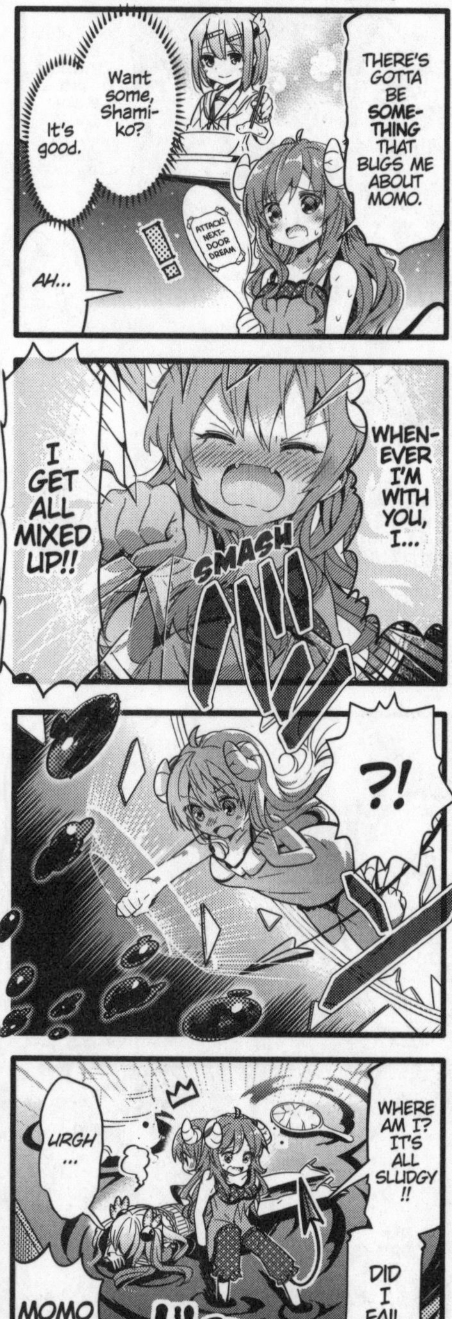
THERE'S GOTTA BE SOMETHING THAT BUGS ME ABOUT MOMO.
Want some, Shamiko?
It's good.
!
ATTACK! NEXT-DOOR DREAM
AH...
WHENEVER I'M WITH YOU, I...
I GET ALL MIXED UP!!
SMASH
?!
WHERE AM I? IT'S ALL SLUDGY !!
DID I FAIL ?!
URGH ...
MOMO ?!!
SPLAT

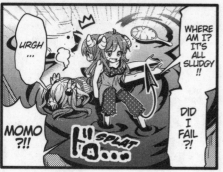

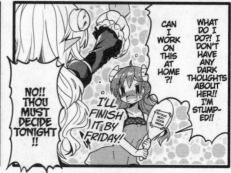

DIDN'T QUITE GRAB HER

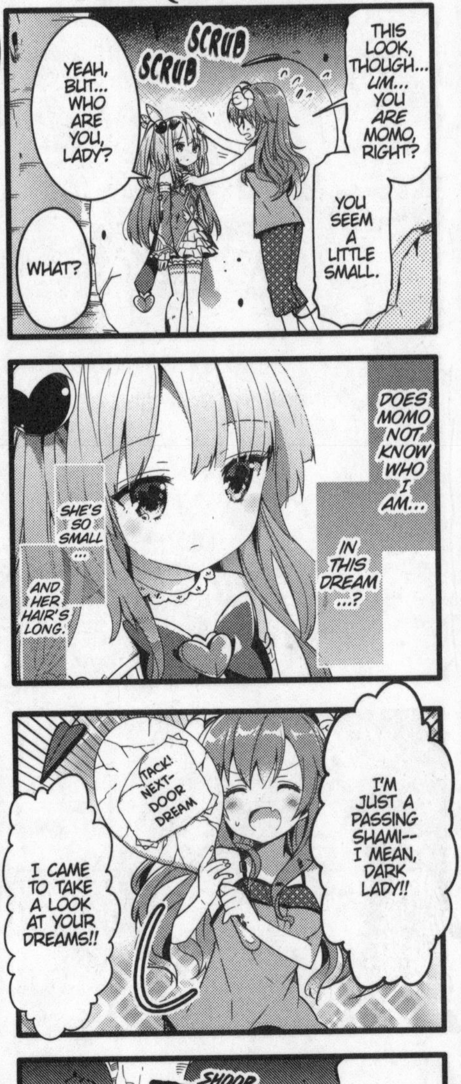
THIS LOOK, THOUGH... UM... YOU ARE MOMO, RIGHT?
SCRUB
SCRUB
YOU SEEM A LITTLE SMALL.
YEAH, BUT... WHO ARE YOU, LADY?
WHAT?
DOES MOMO NOT KNOW WHO I AM...
IN THIS DREAM...?
SHE'S SO SMALL...
AND HER HAIR'S LONG.
I'M JUST A PASSING SHAMI-- I MEAN, DARK LADY!!
TACK! NEXT-DOOR DREAM
I CAME TO TAKE A LOOK AT YOUR DREAMS!!
SO, UM...THIS SURE IS A WEIRD ONE, HUH? IT'S KINDA MUDDY... OR LIVER-Y?
SHOOP
......
SHE'S TUNING ME OUT!!

IMPORTED EYE JUICE

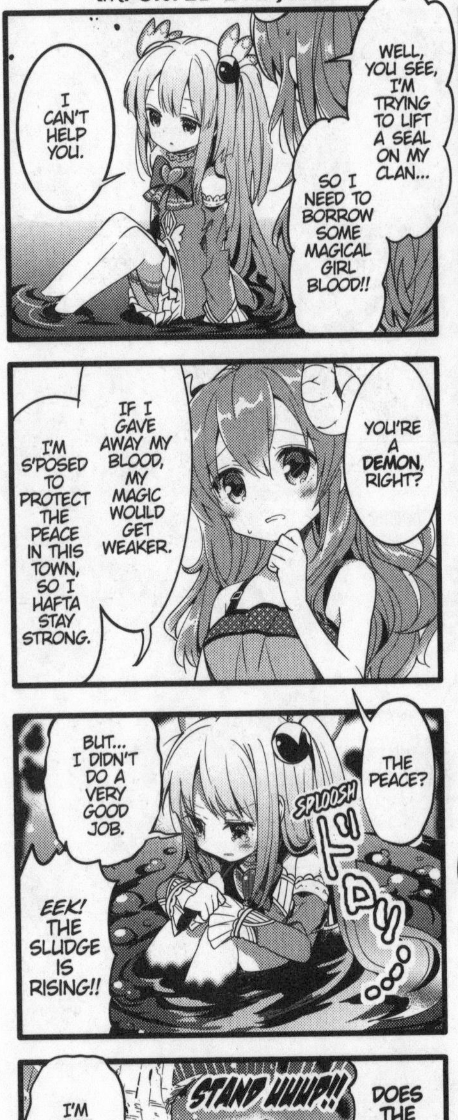
WELL, YOU SEE, I'M TRYING TO LIFT A SEAL ON MY CLAN...
SO I NEED TO BORROW SOME MAGICAL GIRL BLOOD!!
I CAN'T HELP YOU.
YOU'RE A DEMON, RIGHT?
IF I GAVE AWAY MY BLOOD, MY MAGIC WOULD GET WEAKER.
I'M S'POSED TO PROTECT THE PEACE IN THIS TOWN, SO I HAFTA STAY STRONG.
THE PEACE?
SPLOOSH
BUT... I DIDN'T DO A VERY GOOD JOB.
EEK! THE SLUDGE IS RISING!!
DOES THE MUD IN-CREASE WHEN YOU CRY, LITTLE MOMO?!
STAND UUUP!!
I'M NOT CRYING. IT'S EYE JUICE.
DON'T WORRY ABOUT THAT BIT RIGHT NOW!!

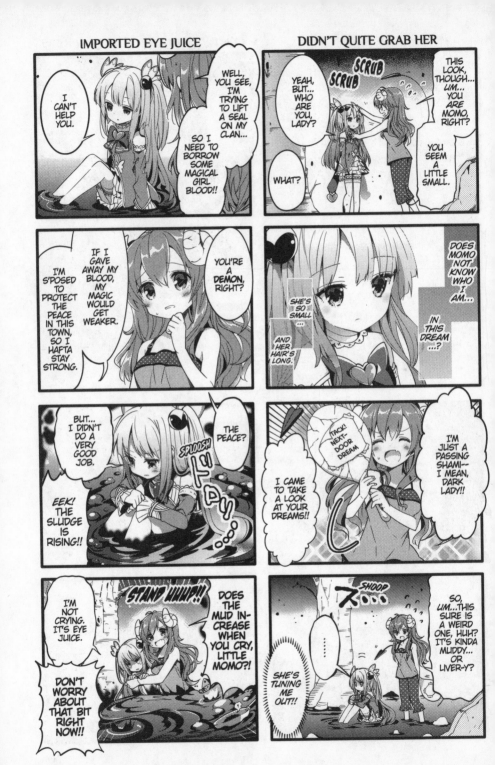

CONTROLLING THE SUBCONSCIOUS

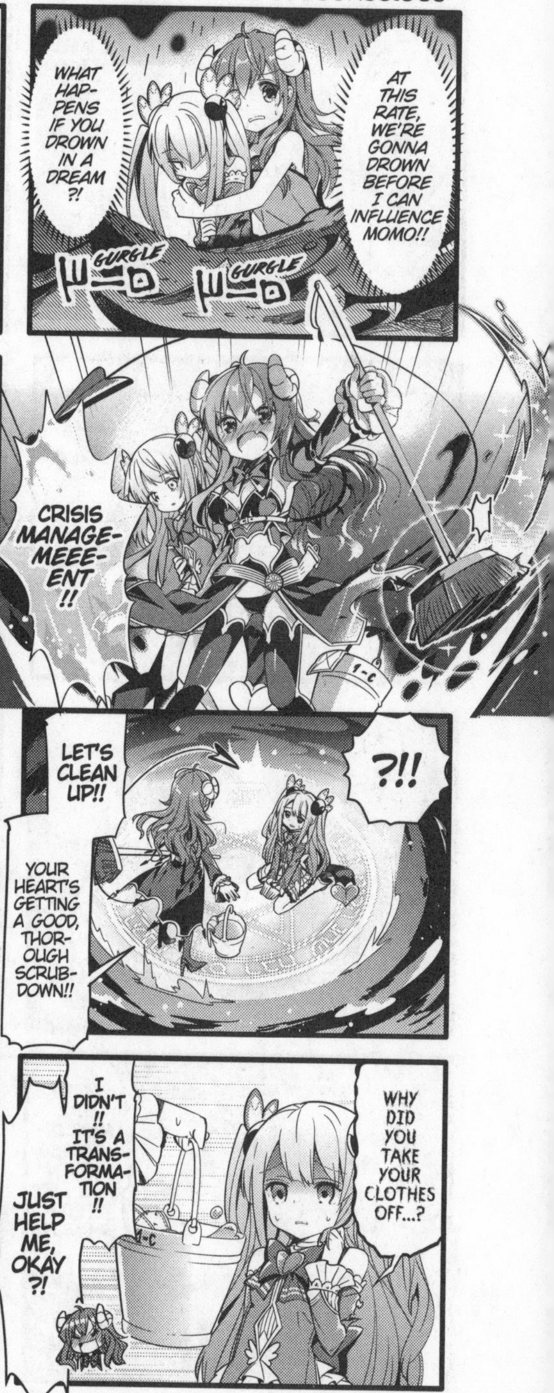
AT THIS RATE, WE'RE GONNA DROWN BEFORE I CAN INFLUENCE MOMO!!
WHAT HAPPENS IF YOU DROWN IN A DREAM?!
GURGLE
GURGLE
CRISIS MANAGEMEEEENT!!
?!!
LET'S CLEAN UP!!
YOUR HEART'S GETTING A GOOD, THOROUGH SCRUBDOWN!!
WHY DID YOU TAKE YOUR CLOTHES OFF...?
I DIDN'T!! IT'S A TRANSFORMATION!!
JUST HELP ME, OKAY?!

TIME'S UP

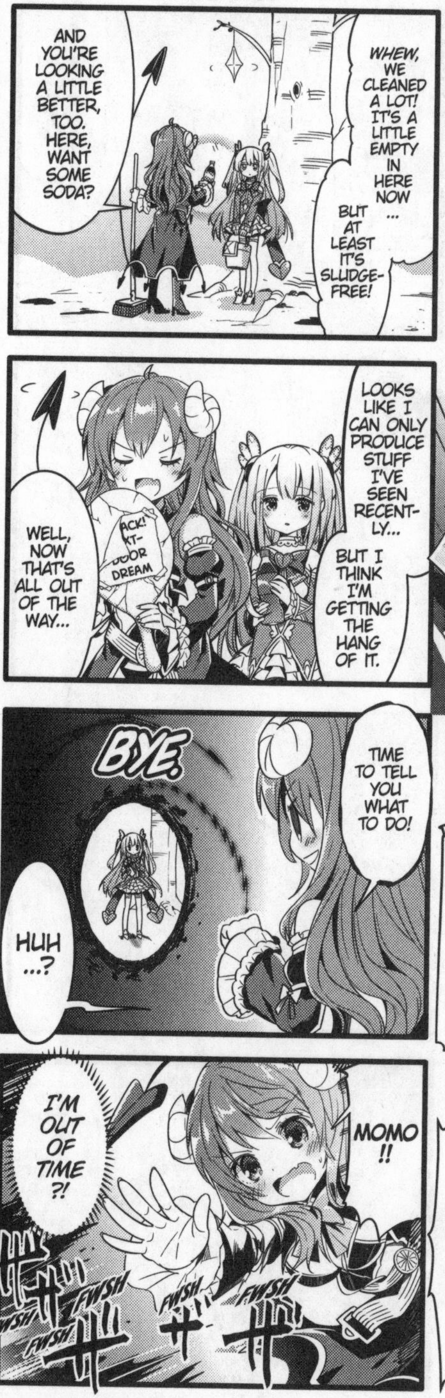
WHEW, WE CLEANED A LOT! IT'S A LITTLE EMPTY IN HERE NOW...
BUT AT LEAST IT'S SLUDGE-FREE!
AND YOU'RE LOOKING A LITTLE BETTER, TOO. HERE, WANT SOME SODA?
LOOKS LIKE I CAN ONLY PRODUCE STUFF I'VE SEEN RECENTLY...
BUT I THINK I'M GETTING THE HANG OF IT.
WELL, NOW THAT'S ALL OUT OF THE WAY...
TIME TO TELL YOU WHAT TO DO!
BYE.
HUH...?
MOMO!!
I'M OUT OF TIME?!
FWSH
FWSH
FWSH
FWSH

FISH FILLET, MOMO-STYLE

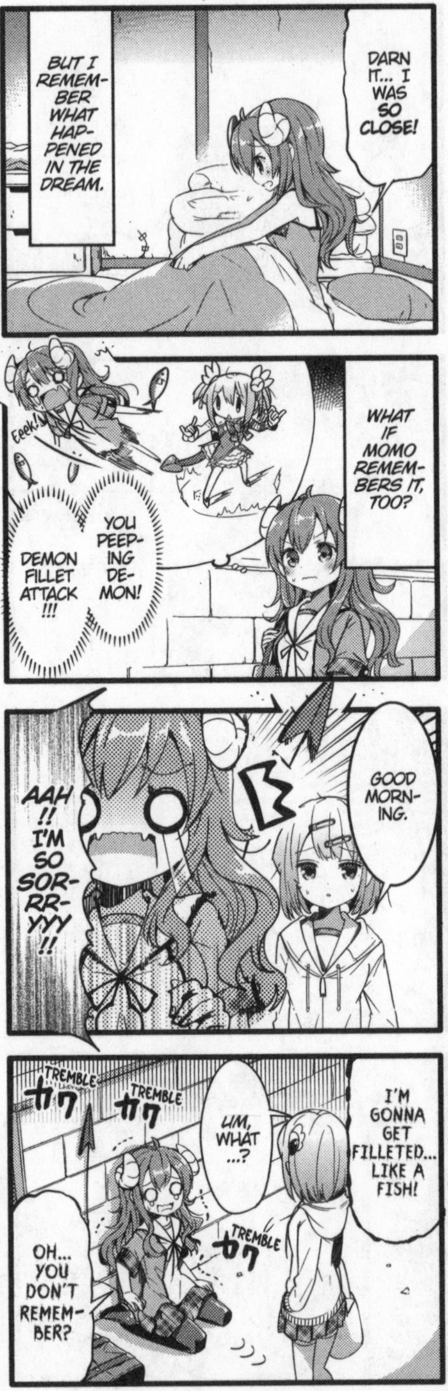
DARN IT... I WAS SO CLOSE!
BUT I REMEMBER WHAT HAPPENED IN THE DREAM.
WHAT IF MOMO REMEMBERS IT, TOO?
Eeek!
YOU PEEPING DEMON!
DEMON FILLET ATTACK!!!
GOOD MORNING.
AAH!! I'M SO SORRRYYY!!
I'M GONNA GET FILLETED... LIKE A FISH!
UM, WHAT ...?
TREMBLE
TREMBLE
TREMBLE
OH... YOU DON'T REMEMBER?

SHAMIKO-SAN'S AFTER-EFFECT

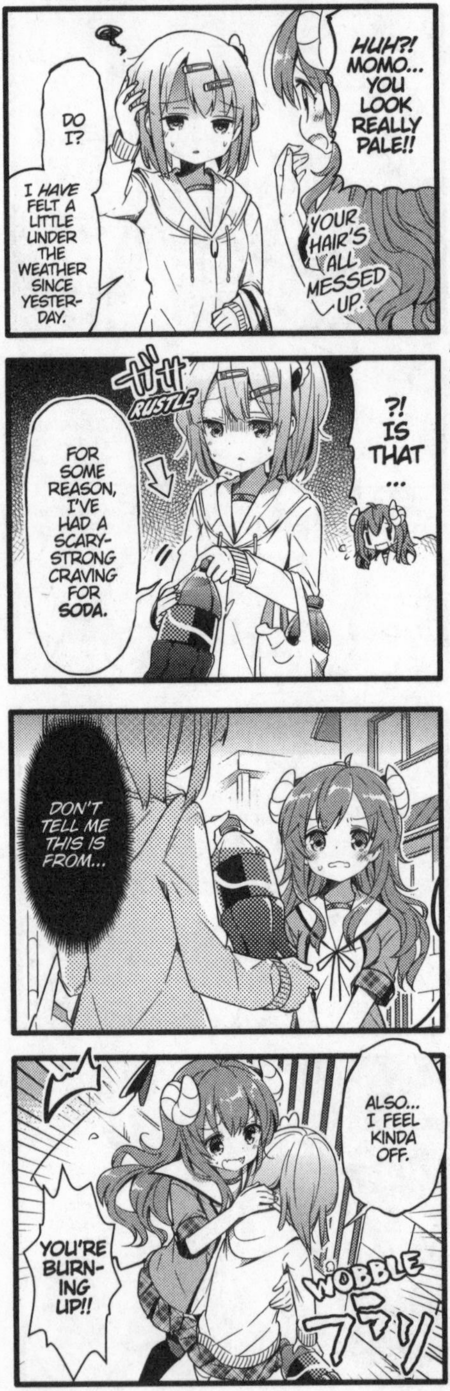
HUH?! MOMO... YOU LOOK REALLY PALE!!
YOUR HAIR'S ALL MESSED UP.
DO I?
I HAVE FELT A LITTLE UNDER THE WEATHER SINCE YESTERDAY.
?! IS THAT ...
RUSTLE
FOR SOME REASON, I'VE HAD A SCARY-STRONG CRAVING FOR SODA.
DON'T TELL ME THIS IS FROM...
ALSO... I FEEL KINDA OFF.
YOU'RE BURNING UP!!
WOBBLE

CAN'T SAY IT OUT LOUD

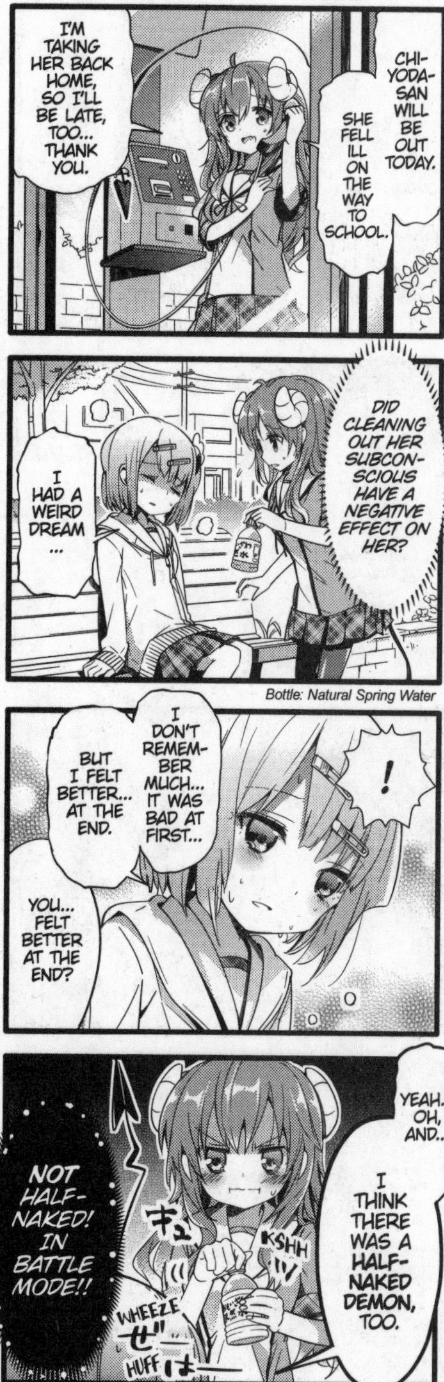
CHI-YODA-SAN WILL BE OUT TODAY.
SHE FELL ILL ON THE WAY TO SCHOOL.
I'M TAKING HER BACK HOME, SO I'LL BE LATE, TOO... THANK YOU.
DID CLEANING OUT HER SUBCON-SCIOUS HAVE A NEGATIVE EFFECT ON HER?
I HAD A WEIRD DREAM...
!
I DON'T REMEM-BER MUCH... IT WAS BAD AT FIRST...
BUT I FELT BETTER... AT THE END.
YOU... FELT BETTER AT THE END?
YEAH... OH, AND...
I THINK THERE WAS A HALF-NAKED DEMON, TOO.
KSHH
NOT HALF-NAKED! IN BATTLE MODE!!
WHEEZE
HUFF

Bottle: Natural Spring Water

MONEY FOR THE PAY PHONE AND WATER

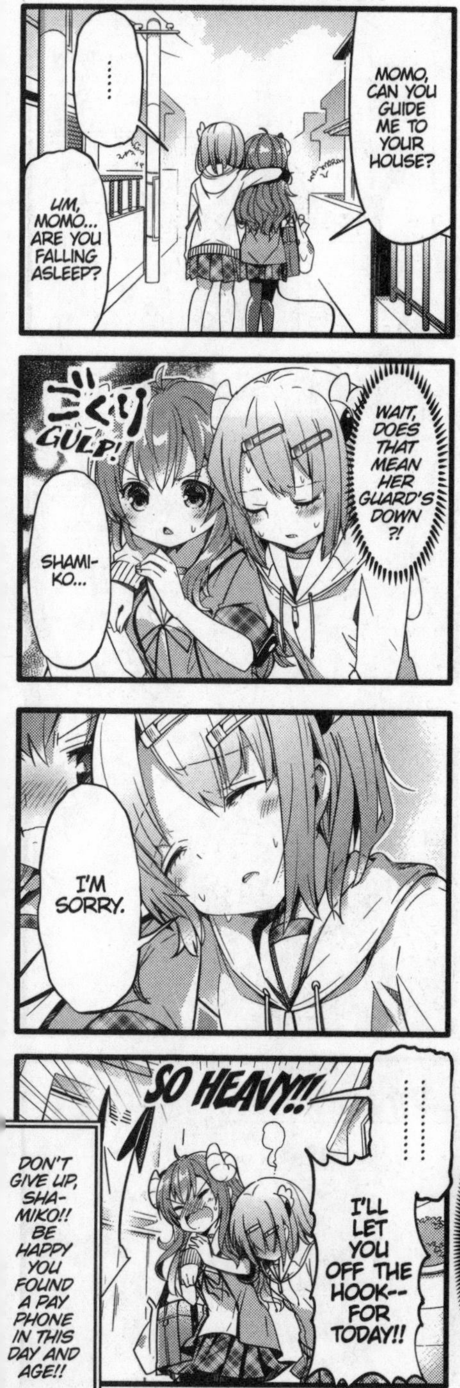
MOMO, CAN YOU GUIDE ME TO YOUR HOUSE?
......
UM, MOMO... ARE YOU FALLING ASLEEP?
WAIT, DOES THAT MEAN HER GUARD'S DOWN?!
GULP!
SHAMI-KO...
I'M SORRY.
......
SO HEAVY!!
I'LL LET YOU OFF THE HOOK--FOR TODAY!!
DON'T GIVE UP, SHA-MIKO!! BE HAPPY YOU FOUND A PAY PHONE IN THIS DAY AND AGE!!

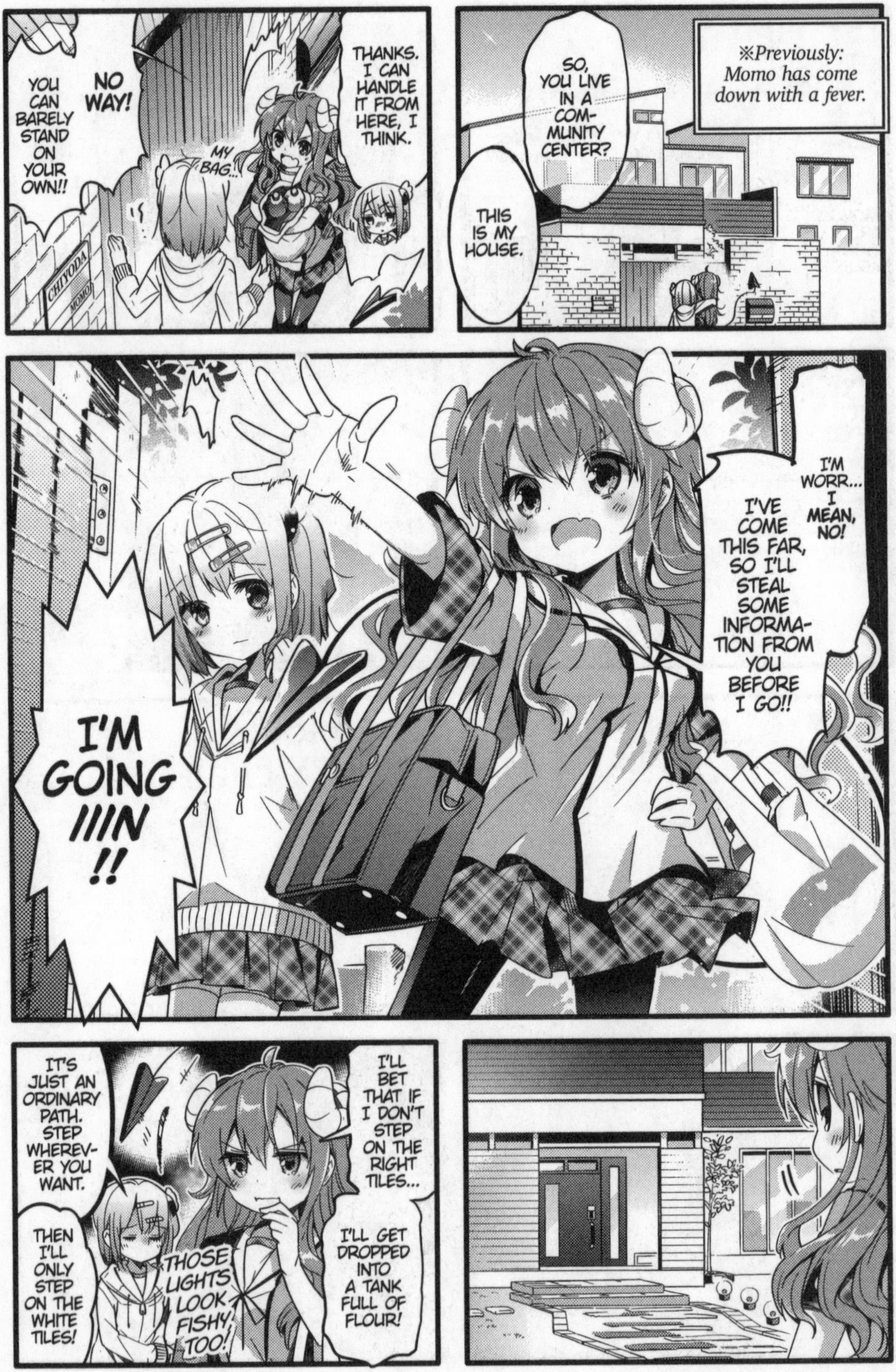
※Previously: Momo has come down with a fever.
SO, YOU LIVE IN A COMMUNITY CENTER?
THIS IS MY HOUSE.
THANKS. I CAN HANDLE IT FROM HERE, I THINK.
MY BAG...
NO WAY!
YOU CAN BARELY STAND ON YOUR OWN!!
CHIYODA
MOMO
I'M WORR... I MEAN, NO!
I'VE COME THIS FAR, SO I'LL STEAL SOME INFORMATION FROM YOU BEFORE I GO!!
I'M GOING IIIN!!
I'LL BET THAT IF I DON'T STEP ON THE RIGHT TILES...
I'LL GET DROPPED INTO A TANK FULL OF FLOUR!
IT'S JUST AN ORDINARY PATH. STEP WHEREVER YOU WANT.
THEN I'LL ONLY STEP ON THE WHITE TILES!
THOSE LIGHTS LOOK FISHY, TOO!

WHAT DOES THE "CHAN" DO?

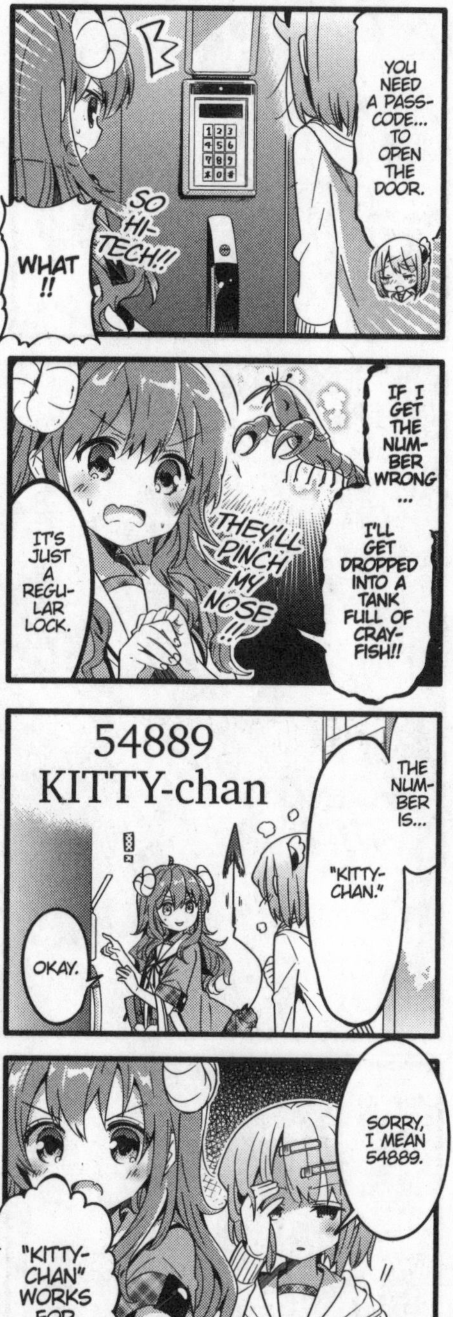
YOU NEED A PASSCODE... TO OPEN THE DOOR.
SO HI-TECH!!
WHAT !!
IF I GET THE NUMBER WRONG ...
I'LL GET DROPPED INTO A TANK FULL OF CRAYFISH!!
THEY'LL PINCH MY NOSE!!
IT'S JUST A REGULAR LOCK.
THE NUMBER IS...
"KITTY-CHAN."
54889
KITTY-chan
OKAY.
SORRY, I MEAN 54889.
"KITTY-CHAN" WORKS FOR ME!

IT CAN TRANSFORM YOU INTO LOTS OF THINGS

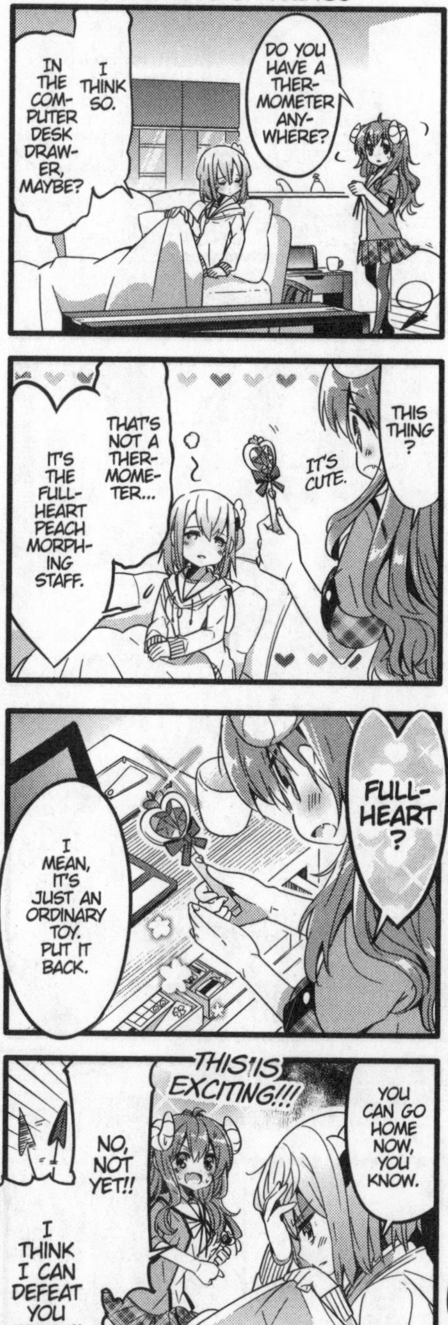
DO YOU HAVE A THERMOMETER ANYWHERE?
I THINK SO.
IN THE COMPUTER DESK DRAWER, MAYBE?
THIS THING?
IT'S CUTE.
THAT'S NOT A THERMOMETER...
IT'S THE FULL-HEART PEACH MORPHING STAFF.
FULL-HEART?
I MEAN, IT'S JUST AN ORDINARY TOY. PUT IT BACK.
THIS IS EXCITING!!!
YOU CAN GO HOME NOW, YOU KNOW.
NO, NOT YET!!
I THINK I CAN DEFEAT YOU TODAY!!

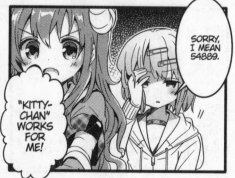

PERFECT FOR PLAYING

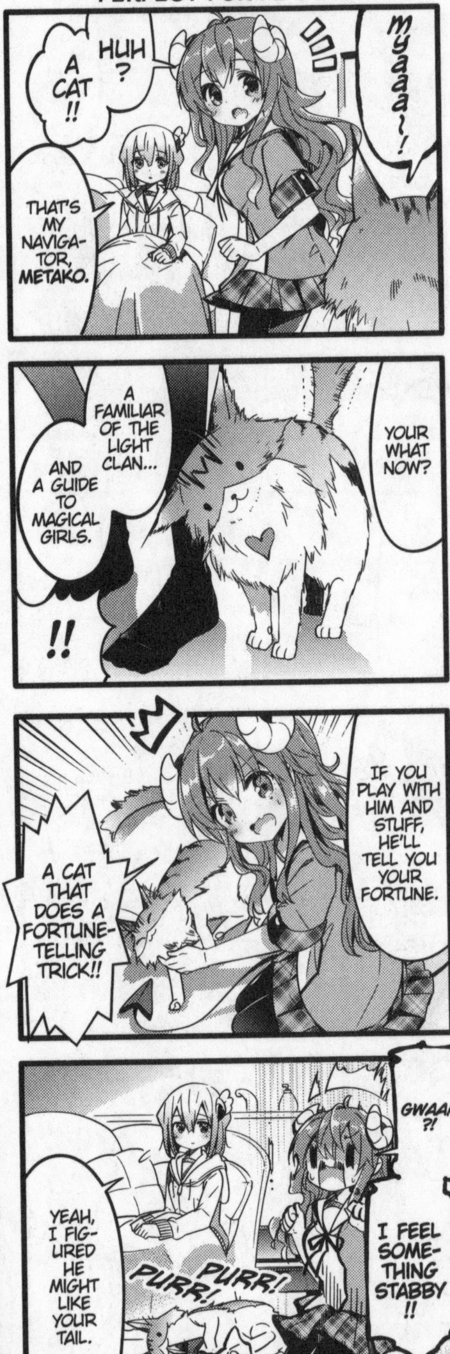
myaaa~!
HUH?
A CAT!!
THAT'S MY NAVIGATOR, METAKO.
YOUR WHAT NOW?
A FAMILIAR OF THE LIGHT CLAN...
AND A GUIDE TO MAGICAL GIRLS.
!!
IF YOU PLAY WITH HIM AND STUFF, HE'LL TELL YOU YOUR FORTUNE.
A CAT THAT DOES A FORTUNE-TELLING TRICK!!
GWAAH?!
I FEEL SOMETHING STABBY!!
PURR! PURR!
YEAH, I FIGURED HE MIGHT LIKE YOUR TAIL.

NEEDS A TUNE-UP

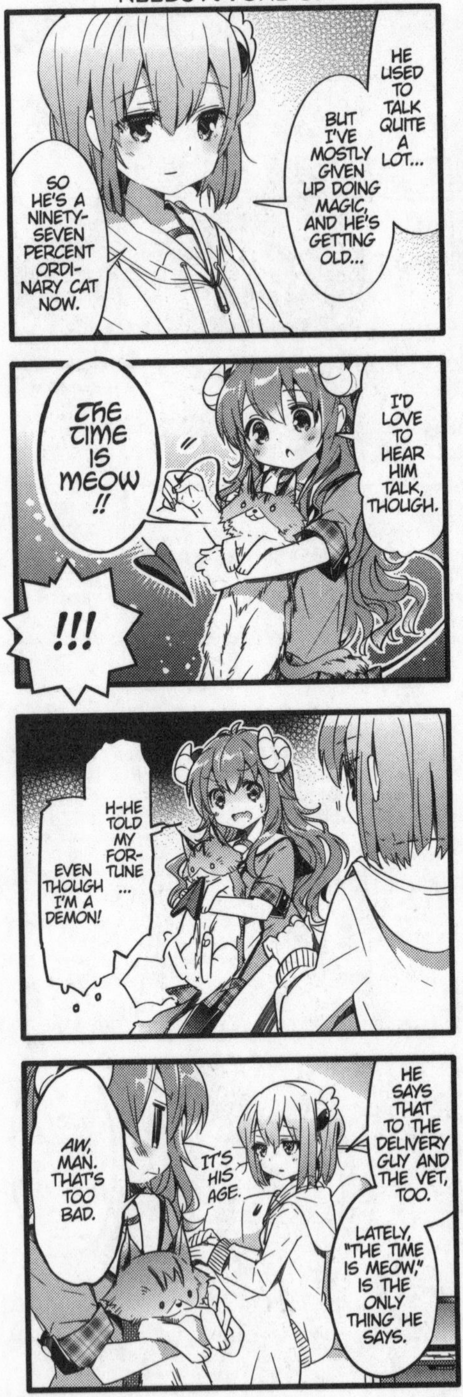
HE USED TO TALK QUITE A LOT...
BUT I'VE MOSTLY GIVEN UP DOING MAGIC, AND HE'S GETTING OLD...
SO HE'S A NINETY-SEVEN PERCENT ORDINARY CAT NOW.
I'D LOVE TO HEAR HIM TALK, THOUGH.
THE TIME IS MEOW!!
!!!
H-HE TOLD MY FORTUNE...
EVEN THOUGH I'M A DEMON!
HE SAYS THAT TO THE DELIVERY GUY AND THE VET, TOO.
IT'S HIS AGE.
LATELY, "THE TIME IS MEOW," IS THE ONLY THING HE SAYS.
AW, MAN. THAT'S TOO BAD.

THE QUALITY CAN DEGRADE

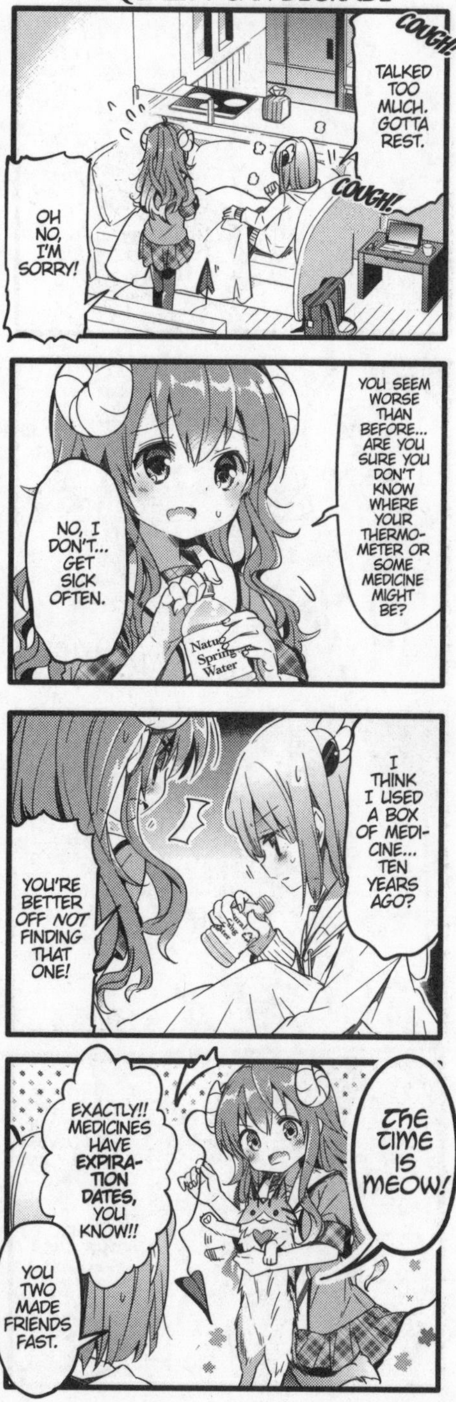
COUGH!
TALKED TOO MUCH. GOTTA REST.
COUGH!
OH NO, I'M SORRY!
YOU SEEM WORSE THAN BEFORE... ARE YOU SURE YOU DON'T KNOW WHERE YOUR THERMOMETER OR SOME MEDICINE MIGHT BE?
NO, I DON'T... GET SICK OFTEN.
I THINK I USED A BOX OF MEDICINE... TEN YEARS AGO?
YOU'RE BETTER OFF NOT FINDING THAT ONE!
THE TIME IS MEOW!
EXACTLY!! MEDICINES HAVE EXPIRATION DATES, YOU KNOW!!
YOU TWO MADE FRIENDS FAST.

THE NEW REFRIGERATOR TRAP

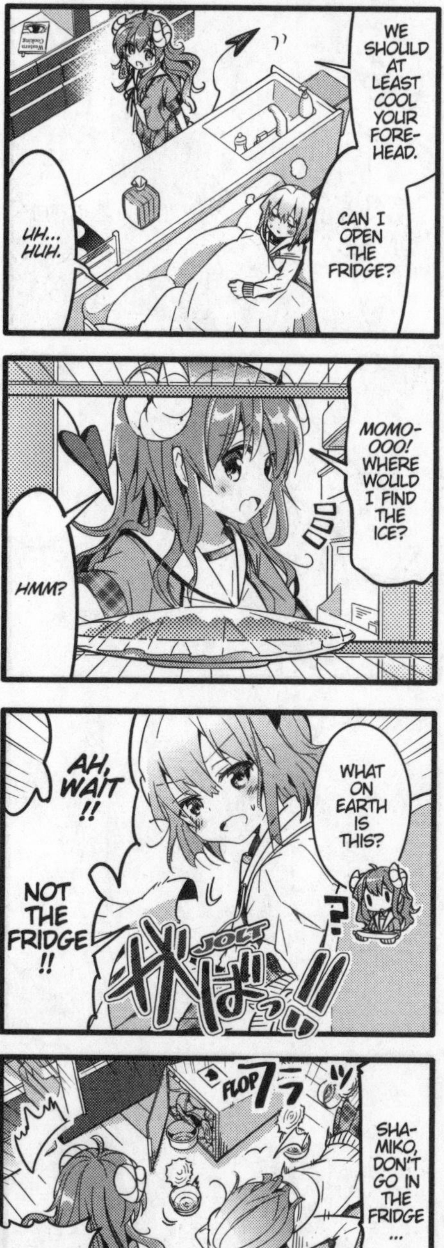
WE SHOULD AT LEAST COOL YOUR FOREHEAD.
CAN I OPEN THE FRIDGE?
UH... HUH.
MOMO-OOO! WHERE WOULD I FIND THE ICE?
HMM?
WHAT ON EARTH IS THIS?
AH, WAIT!!
NOT THE FRIDGE!!
JOLT
FLOP
SHAMIKO, DON'T GO IN THE FRIDGE...
MOMO?!
URGH...

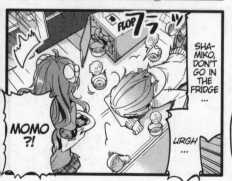

GOOD GRAVY

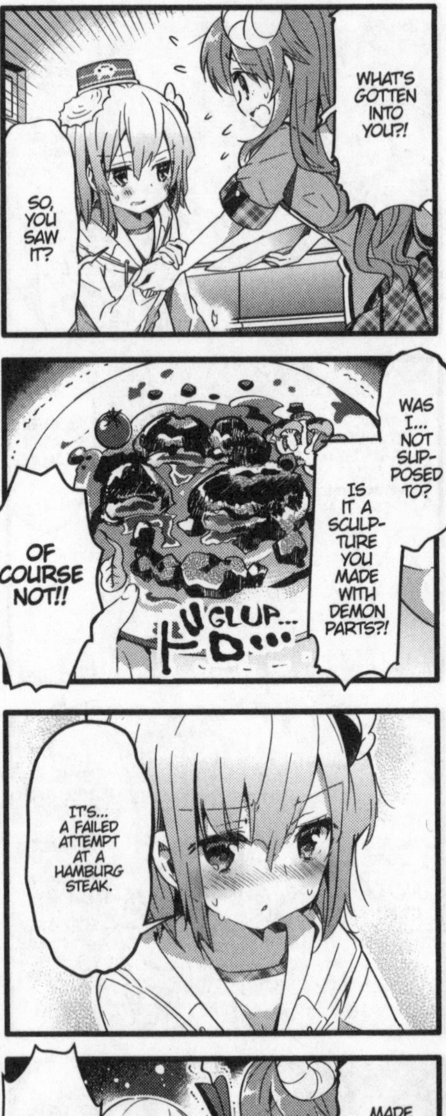
WHAT'S GOTTEN INTO YOU?!
SO, YOU SAW IT?
WAS I... NOT SUPPOSED TO?
IS IT A SCULPTURE YOU MADE WITH DEMON PARTS?!
OF COURSE NOT!!
GLUP...
IT'S... A FAILED ATTEMPT AT A HAMBURG STEAK.
MADE WITH HIGH-QUALITY GRUDGE-FILLED DEMON MEAT, RIGHT?
IT'S SO DARK AND EVIL!
IT'S JUST ORDINARY GROUND BEEF!!

THE CAUSE

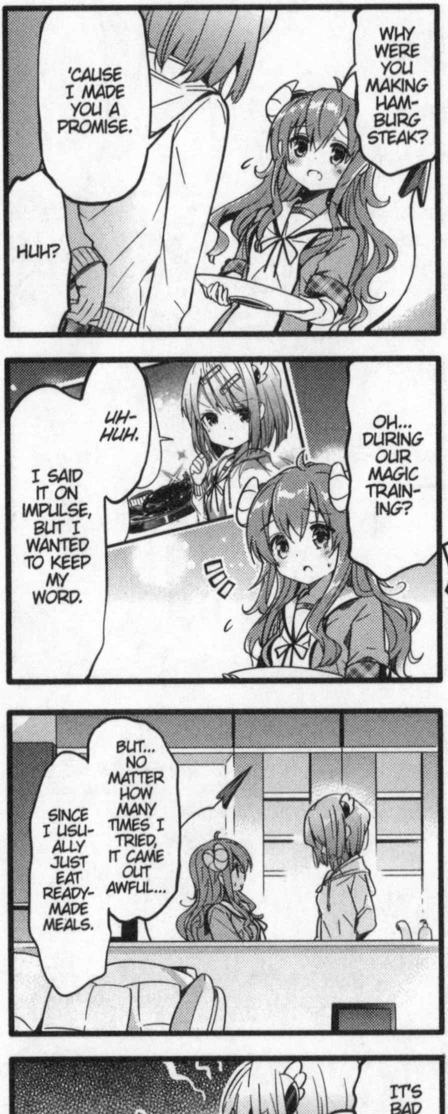
WHY WERE YOU MAKING HAMBURG STEAK?
'CAUSE I MADE YOU A PROMISE.
HUH?
OH... DURING OUR MAGIC TRAINING?
UH-HUH.
I SAID IT ON IMPULSE, BUT I WANTED TO KEEP MY WORD.
BUT... NO MATTER HOW MANY TIMES I TRIED, IT CAME OUT AWFUL...
SINCE I USUALLY JUST EAT READY-MADE MEALS.
IT'S BAD TO WASTE FOOD, SO I'VE BEEN EATING IT...
BUT I CAN ONLY MANAGE A BITE OR TWO AT A TIME.
MAYBE *THAT'S* WHY YOU GOT SICK?

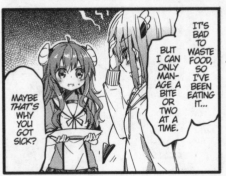

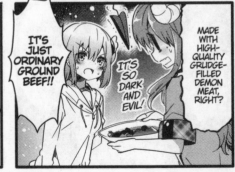

CURVEBALL

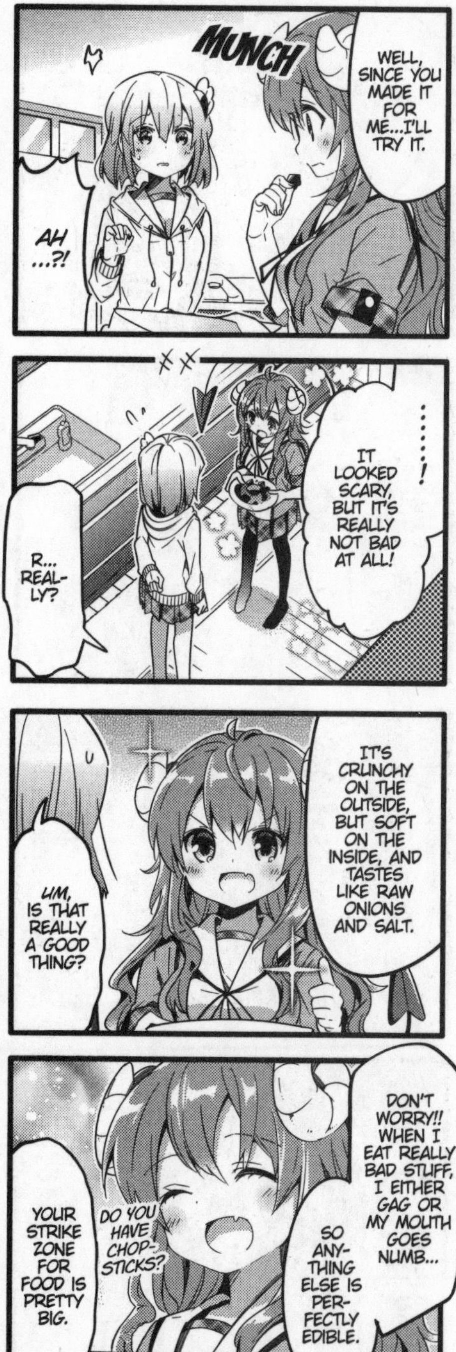
MUNCH
WELL, SINCE YOU MADE IT FOR ME...I'LL TRY IT.
AH ...?!
......!
IT LOOKED SCARY, BUT IT'S REALLY NOT BAD AT ALL!
R... REALLY?
IT'S CRUNCHY ON THE OUTSIDE, BUT SOFT ON THE INSIDE, AND TASTES LIKE RAW ONIONS AND SALT.
UM, IS THAT REALLY A GOOD THING?
DON'T WORRY!! WHEN I EAT REALLY BAD STUFF, I EITHER GAG OR MY MOUTH GOES NUMB...
SO ANYTHING ELSE IS PERFECTLY EDIBLE.
DO YOU HAVE CHOPSTICKS?
YOUR STRIKE ZONE FOR FOOD IS PRETTY BIG.

※Due to her family's circumstances, she's developed a high tolerance for sketchy food. Please be careful when eating on very hot days.

A PEACH IS EASILY BRUISED

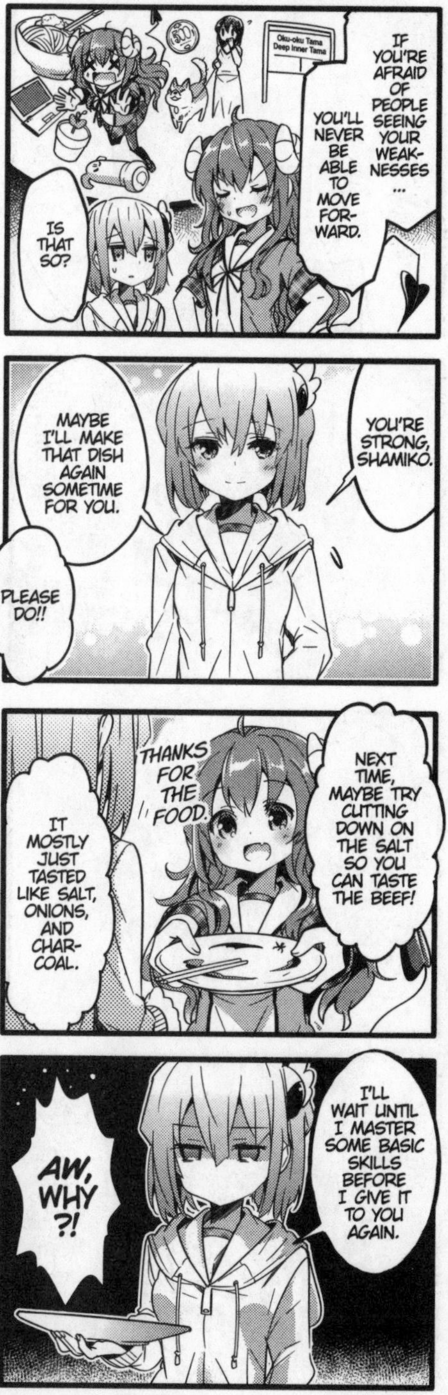
IF YOU'RE AFRAID OF PEOPLE SEEING YOUR WEAKNESSES...
YOU'LL NEVER BE ABLE TO MOVE FORWARD.
Oku-oku Tama
Deep Inner Tama
500
IS THAT SO?
YOU'RE STRONG, SHAMIKO.
MAYBE I'LL MAKE THAT DISH AGAIN SOMETIME FOR YOU.
PLEASE DO!!
NEXT TIME, MAYBE TRY CUTTING DOWN ON THE SALT SO YOU CAN TASTE THE BEEF!
THANKS FOR THE FOOD.
IT MOSTLY JUST TASTED LIKE SALT, ONIONS, AND CHARCOAL.
I'LL WAIT UNTIL I MASTER SOME BASIC SKILLS BEFORE I GIVE IT TO YOU AGAIN.
AW, WHY?!

MORE LIKE TOFU STEAK

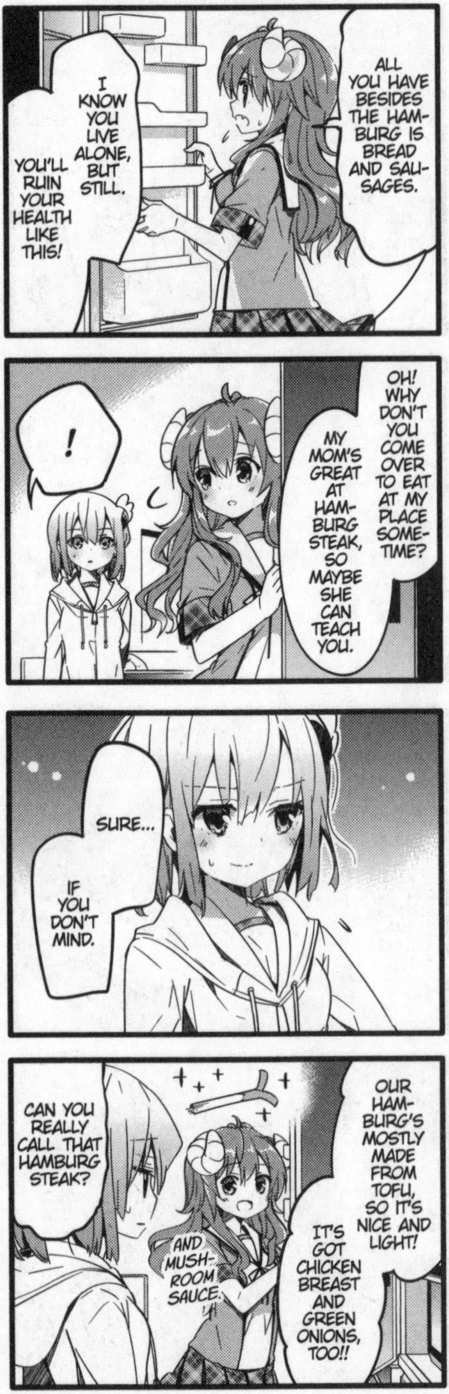
ALL YOU HAVE BESIDES THE HAMBURG IS BREAD AND SAUSAGES.
I KNOW YOU LIVE ALONE, BUT STILL.
YOU'LL RUIN YOUR HEALTH LIKE THIS!
OH! WHY DON'T YOU COME OVER TO EAT AT MY PLACE SOMETIME?
MY MOM'S GREAT AT HAMBURG STEAK, SO MAYBE SHE CAN TEACH YOU.
!
SURE...
IF YOU DON'T MIND.
OUR HAMBURG'S MOSTLY MADE FROM TOFU, SO IT'S NICE AND LIGHT!
IT'S GOT CHICKEN BREAST AND GREEN ONIONS, TOO!!
AND MUSHROOM SAUCE.
CAN YOU REALLY CALL THAT HAMBURG STEAK?

AN EARLY "GET YOU NEXT TIME!"

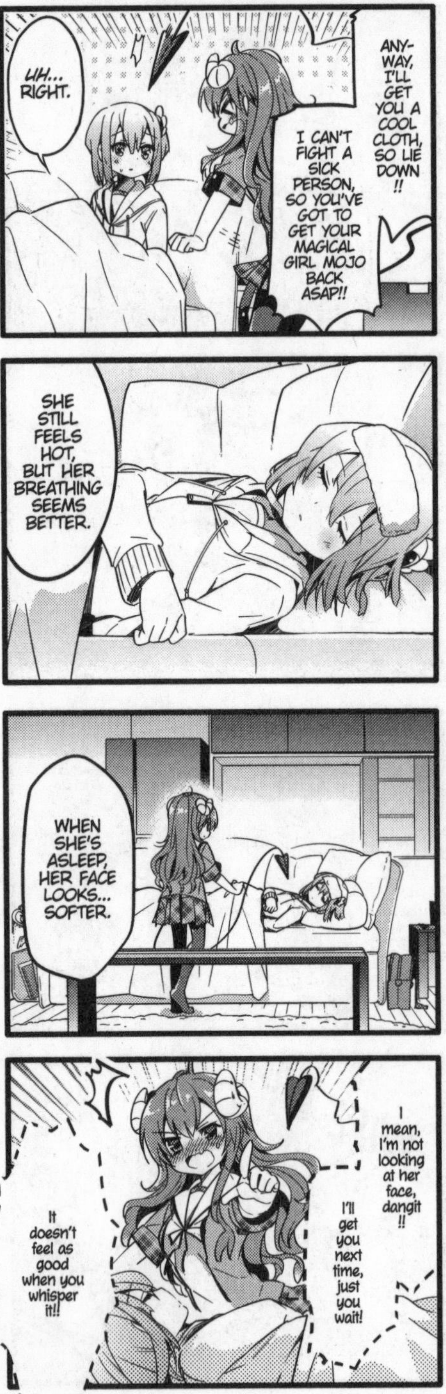
ANYWAY, I'LL GET YOU A COOL CLOTH, SO LIE DOWN!!
I CAN'T FIGHT A SICK PERSON, SO YOU'VE GOT TO GET YOUR MAGICAL GIRL MOJO BACK ASAP!!
UH... RIGHT.
SHE STILL FEELS HOT, BUT HER BREATHING SEEMS BETTER.
WHEN SHE'S ASLEEP, HER FACE LOOKS... SOFTER.
I mean, I'm not looking at her face, dangit!!
I'll get you next time, just you wait!
It doesn't feel as good when you whisper it!!

A DEMON WHO NOTICES THINGS

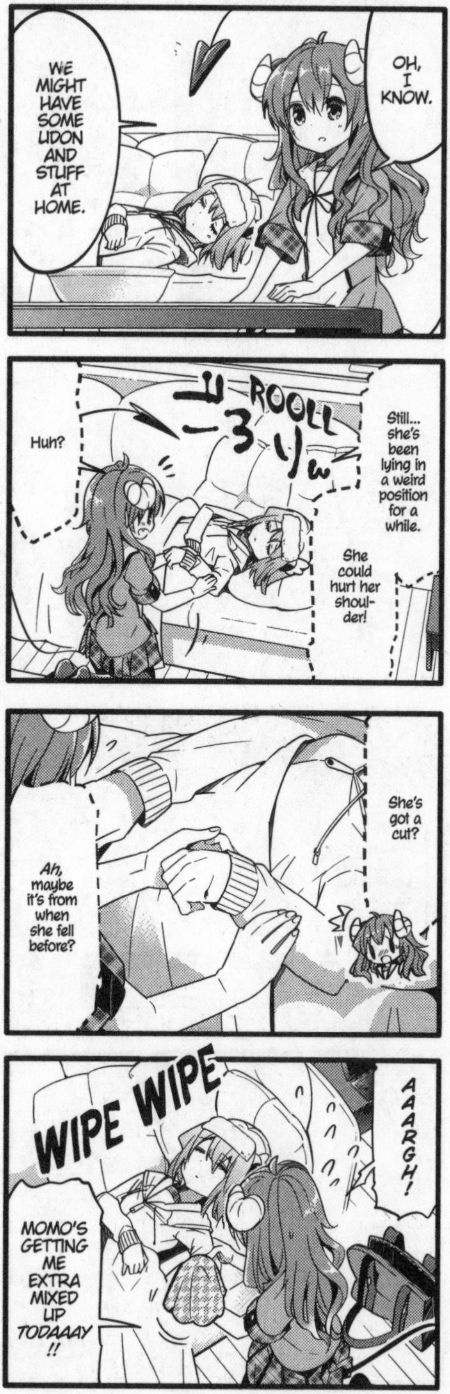

OH, I KNOW.
WE MIGHT HAVE SOME UDON AND STUFF AT HOME.
Still... she's been lying in a weird position for a while.
She could hurt her shoulder!
ROOLL
Huh?
She's got a cut?
Ah, maybe it's from when she fell before?
AAARGH!
WIPE WIPE
MOMO'S GETTING ME EXTRA MIXED UP TODAAAY!!

THE TIME IS MEOW

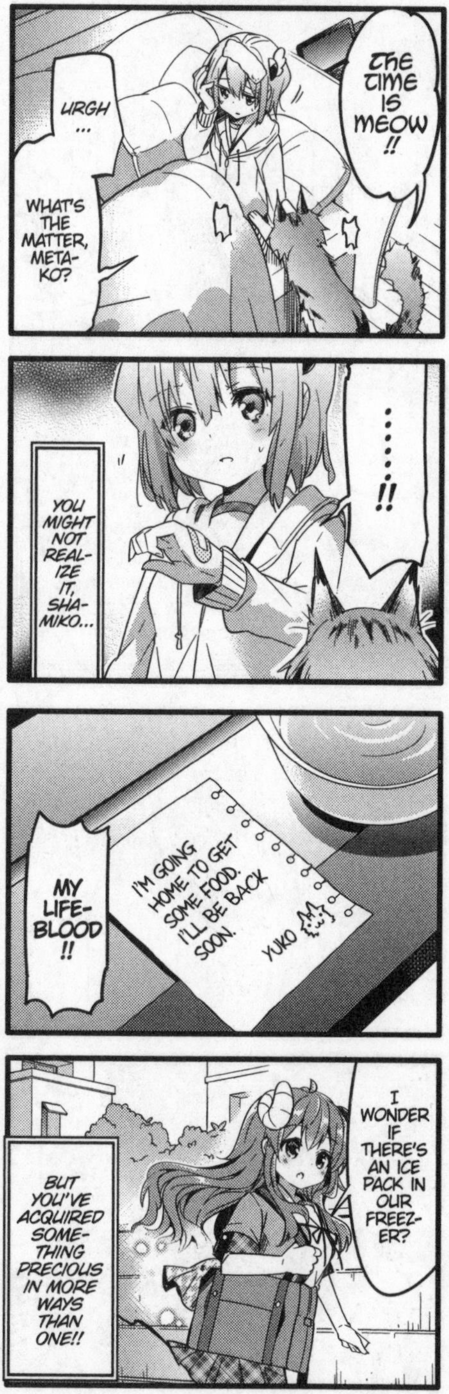

THE TIME IS MEOW!!
URGH...
WHAT'S THE MATTER, METAKO?
......!!
YOU MIGHT NOT REALIZE IT, SHAMIKO...
I'M GOING HOME TO GET SOME FOOD. I'LL BE BACK SOON.
YUKO
MY LIFE-BLOOD!!
I WONDER IF THERE'S AN ICE PACK IN OUR FREEZER?
BUT YOU'VE ACQUIRED SOMETHING PRECIOUS IN MORE WAYS THAN ONE!!

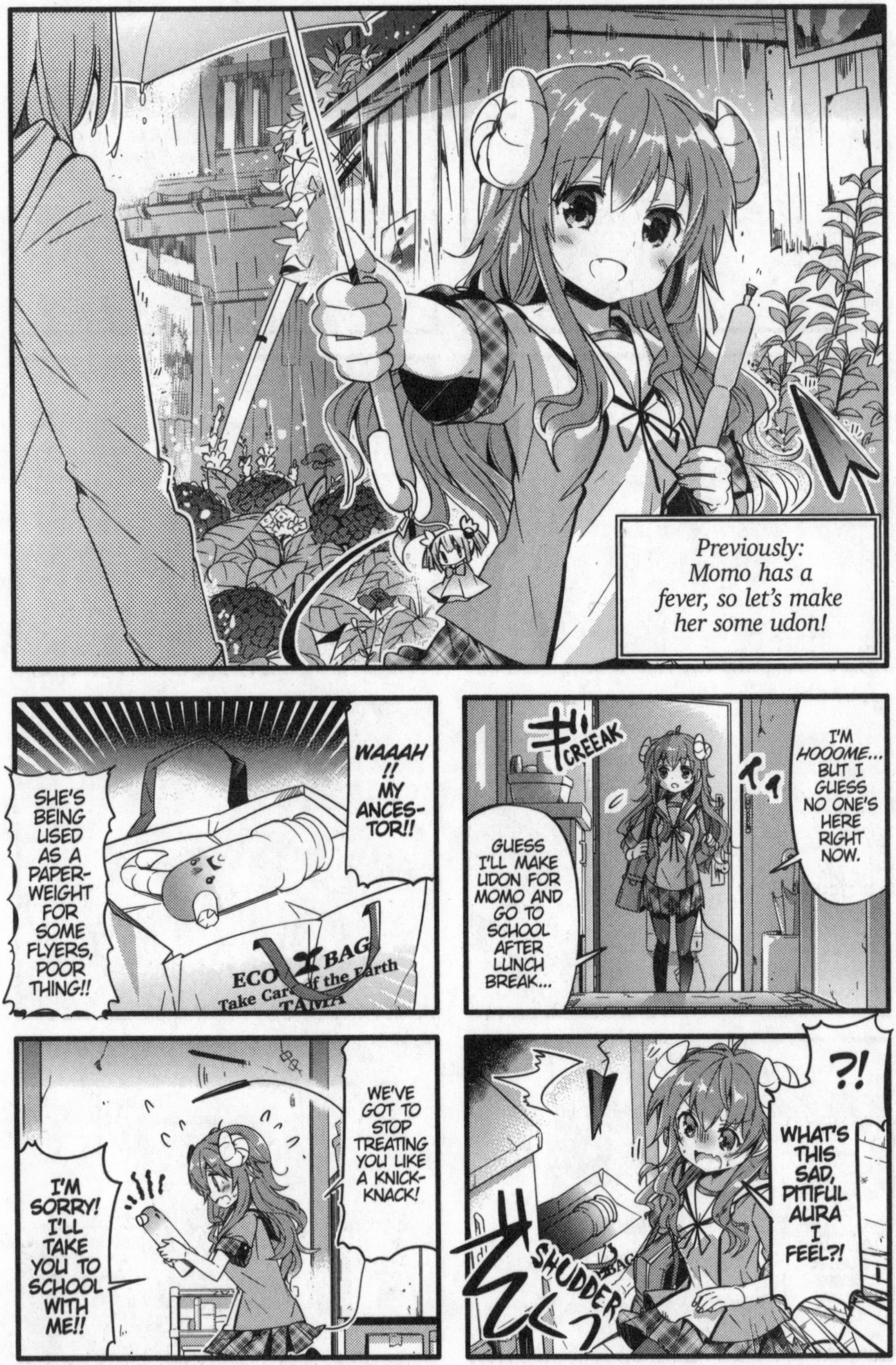
Previously: Momo has a fever, so let's make her some udon!
CREEAK
I'M HOOOME... BUT I GUESS NO ONE'S HERE RIGHT NOW.
GUESS I'LL MAKE UDON FOR MOMO AND GO TO SCHOOL AFTER LUNCH BREAK...
WAAAH!! MY ANCESTOR!!
SHE'S BEING USED AS A PAPERWEIGHT FOR SOME FLYERS, POOR THING!!
?!
WHAT'S THIS SAD, PITIFUL AURA I FEEL?!
SHUDDER
WE'VE GOT TO STOP TREATING YOU LIKE A KNICK-KNACK!
I'M SORRY! I'LL TAKE YOU TO SCHOOL WITH ME!!

THE TIME IS MEOW?

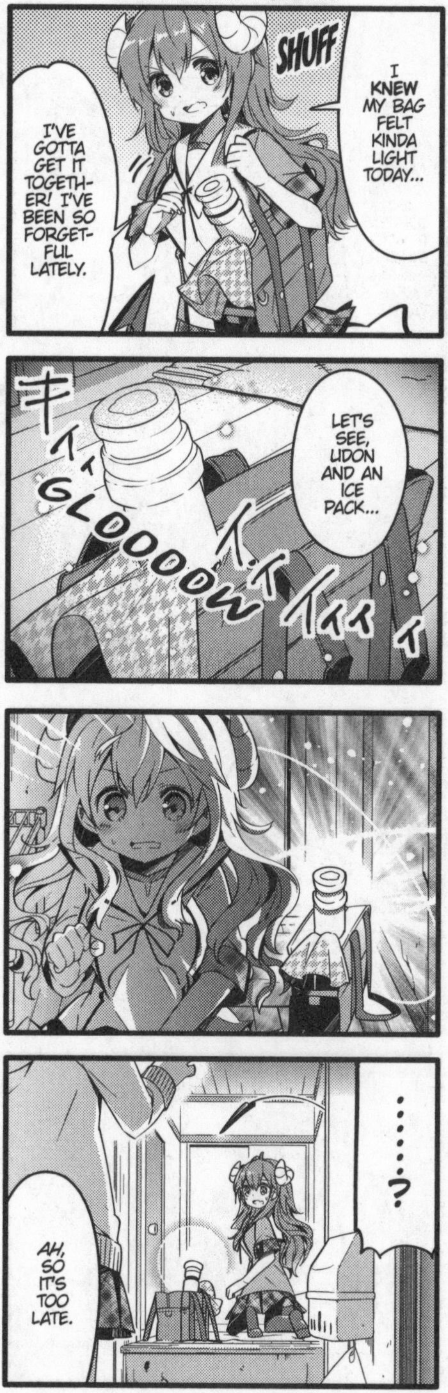
SHUFF
I KNEW MY BAG FELT KINDA LIGHT TODAY...
I'VE GOTTA GET IT TOGETHER! I'VE BEEN SO FORGETFUL LATELY.
LET'S SEE, UDON AND AN ICE PACK...
キィィィィィィ
GLOOOOOW
......?
AH, SO IT'S TOO LATE.

MYSTERY DECORATION

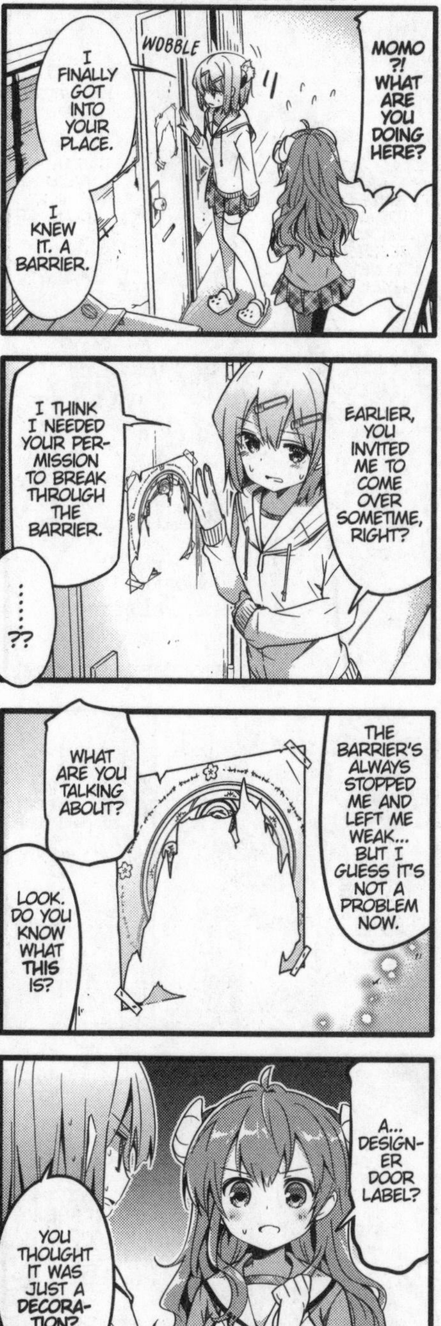
MOMO?! WHAT ARE YOU DOING HERE?
WOBBLE
I FINALLY GOT INTO YOUR PLACE.
I KNEW IT. A BARRIER.
EARLIER, YOU INVITED ME TO COME OVER SOMETIME, RIGHT?
I THINK I NEEDED YOUR PERMISSION TO BREAK THROUGH THE BARRIER.
......??
THE BARRIER'S ALWAYS STOPPED ME AND LEFT ME WEAK... BUT I GUESS IT'S NOT A PROBLEM NOW.
WHAT ARE YOU TALKING ABOUT?
LOOK. DO YOU KNOW WHAT THIS IS?
A... DESIGNER DOOR LABEL?
YOU THOUGHT IT WAS JUST A DECORATION?

PRIORITIES

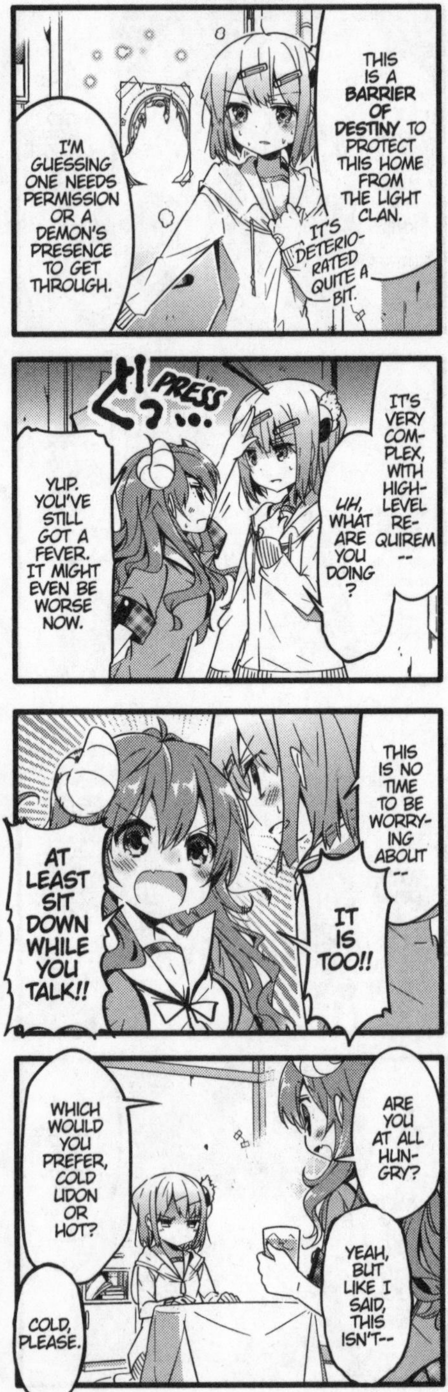
THIS IS A BARRIER OF DESTINY TO PROTECT THIS HOME FROM THE LIGHT CLAN.
I'M GUESSING ONE NEEDS PERMISSION OR A DEMON'S PRESENCE TO GET THROUGH.
IT'S DETERIO-RATED QUITE A BIT.
IT'S VERY COM-PLEX, WITH HIGH-LEVEL RE-QUIREM--
PRESS
UH, WHAT ARE YOU DOING?
YUP. YOU'VE STILL GOT A FEVER. IT MIGHT EVEN BE WORSE NOW.
THIS IS NO TIME TO BE WORRY-ING ABOUT--
AT LEAST SIT DOWN WHILE YOU TALK!!
IT IS TOO!!
ARE YOU AT ALL HUN-GRY?
WHICH WOULD YOU PREFER, COLD UDON OR HOT?
YEAH, BUT LIKE I SAID, THIS ISN'T--
COLD, PLEASE.

COOKING LESSONS

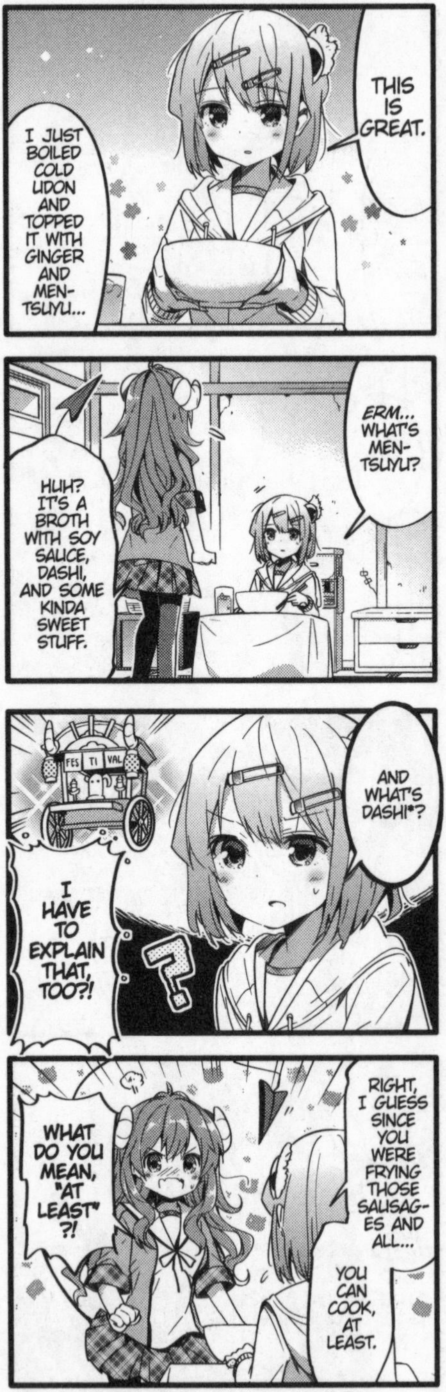
THIS IS GREAT.
I JUST BOILED COLD UDON AND TOPPED IT WITH GINGER AND MEN-TSUYU...
ERM... WHAT'S MEN-TSUYU?
HUH? IT'S A BROTH WITH SOY SAUCE, DASHI, AND SOME KINDA SWEET STUFF.
AND WHAT'S DASHI*?
FES TI VAL
I HAVE TO EXPLAIN THAT, TOO?!
RIGHT, I GUESS SINCE YOU WERE FRYING THOSE SAUSAG-ES AND ALL...
WHAT DO YOU MEAN, "AT LEAST"?!
YOU CAN COOK, AT LEAST.

Dashi is soup stock made from dried kelp and bonito flakes. The word can also mean a float in a festival procession.

CLUELESS DEMON

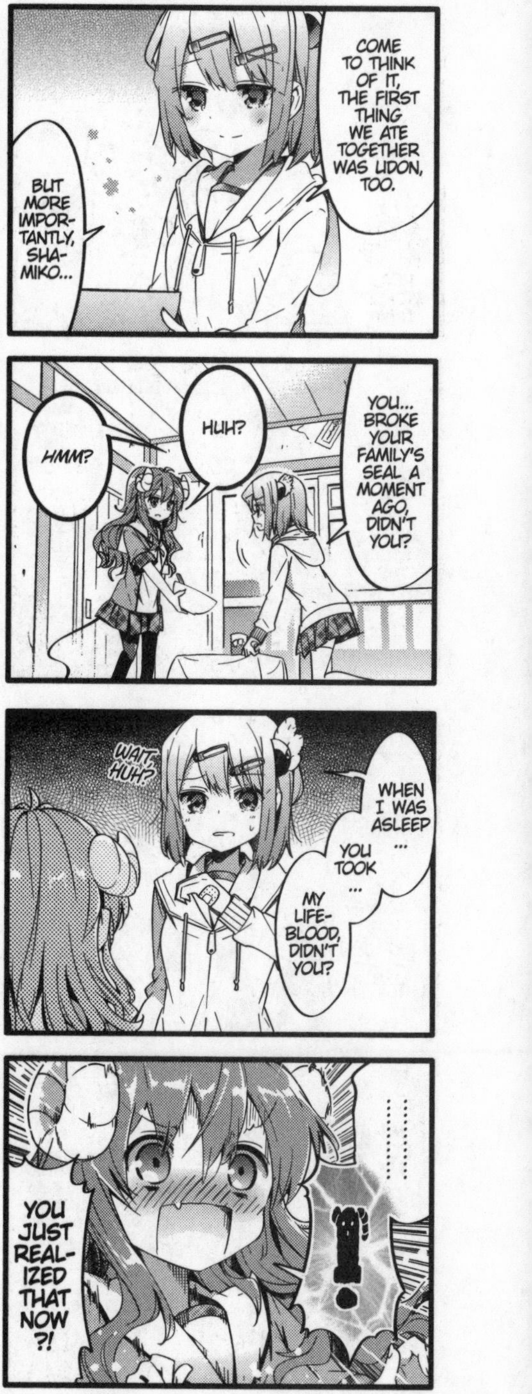
COME TO THINK OF IT, THE FIRST THING WE ATE TOGETHER WAS UDON, TOO.
BUT MORE IMPORTANTLY, SHAMIKO...
YOU... BROKE YOUR FAMILY'S SEAL A MOMENT AGO, DIDN'T YOU?
HUH?
HMM?
WHEN I WAS ASLEEP...
YOU TOOK...
MY LIFE-BLOOD, DIDN'T YOU?
WAIT, HUH?
......
!
YOU JUST REALIZED THAT NOW?!

GOSSIP GIRL

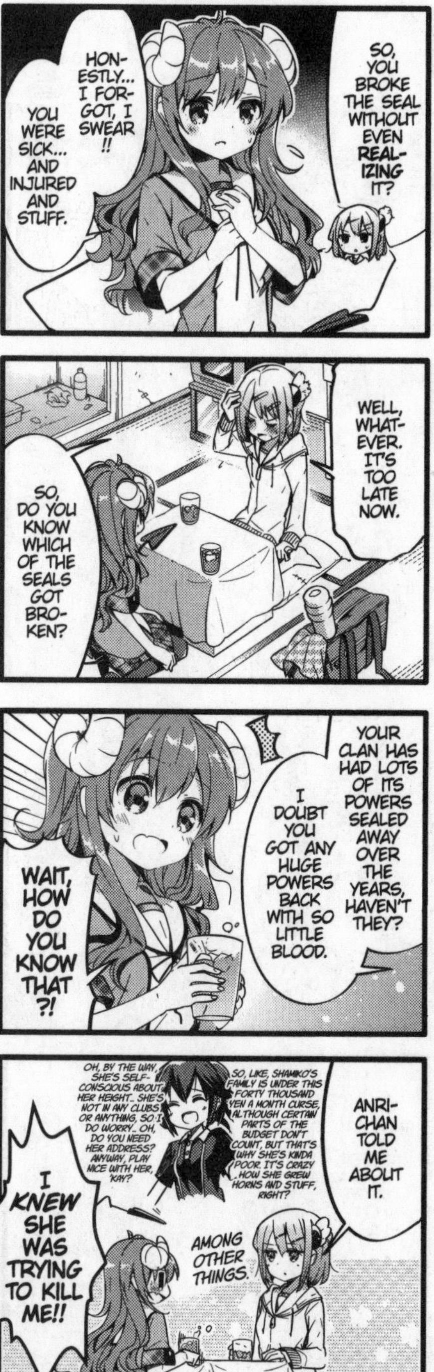
SO, YOU BROKE THE SEAL WITHOUT EVEN REALIZING IT?
HONESTLY... I FORGOT, I SWEAR!!
YOU WERE SICK... AND INJURED AND STUFF.
WELL, WHATEVER. IT'S TOO LATE NOW.
SO, DO YOU KNOW WHICH OF THE SEALS GOT BROKEN?
YOUR CLAN HAS HAD LOTS OF ITS POWERS SEALED AWAY OVER THE YEARS, HAVEN'T THEY?
I DOUBT YOU GOT ANY HUGE POWERS BACK WITH SO LITTLE BLOOD.
WAIT, HOW DO YOU KNOW THAT?!
ANRI-CHAN TOLD ME ABOUT IT.
SO, LIKE, SHAMIKO'S FAMILY IS UNDER THIS FORTY THOUSAND YEN A MONTH CURSE, ALTHOUGH CERTAIN PARTS OF THE BUDGET DON'T COUNT, BUT THAT'S WHY SHE'S KINDA POOR. IT'S CRAZY HOW SHE GREW HORNS AND STUFF, RIGHT?
OH, BY THE WAY, SHE'S SELF-CONSCIOUS ABOUT HER HEIGHT... SHE'S NOT IN ANY CLUBS OR ANYTHING, SO I DO WORRY... OH, DO YOU NEED HER ADDRESS? ANYWAY, PLAY NICE WITH HER, 'KAY?
AMONG OTHER THINGS.
I KNEW SHE WAS TRYING TO KILL ME!!

ANCESTRAL WISDOM

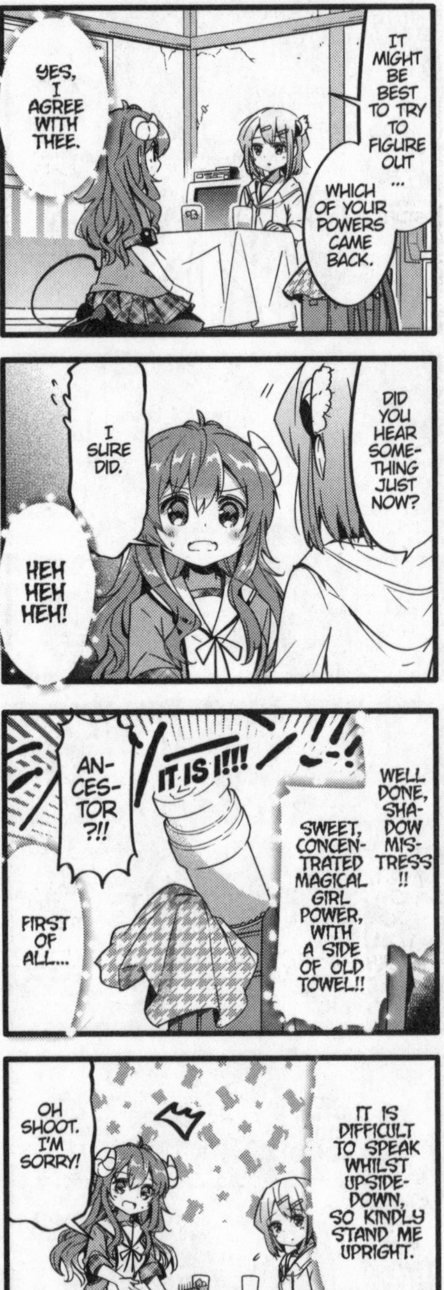
IT MIGHT BE BEST TO TRY TO FIGURE OUT ...
WHICH OF YOUR POWERS CAME BACK.
YES, I AGREE WITH THEE.
DID YOU HEAR SOMETHING JUST NOW?
I SURE DID.
HEH HEH HEH!
WELL DONE, SHADOW MISTRESS!!
IT IS I!!!
ANCESTOR?!!
SWEET, CONCENTRATED MAGICAL GIRL POWER, WITH A SIDE OF OLD TOWEL!!
FIRST OF ALL...
IT IS DIFFICULT TO SPEAK WHILST UPSIDE-DOWN, SO KINDLY STAND ME UPRIGHT.
OH SHOOT. I'M SORRY!

WOW...I SUFFERED FOR *THAT*?

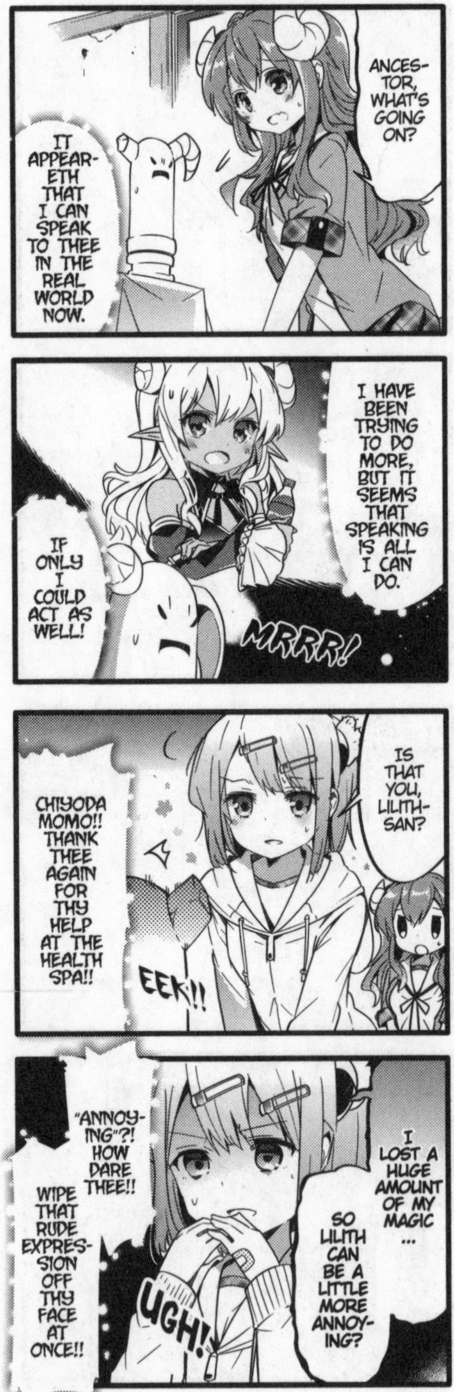
ANCESTOR, WHAT'S GOING ON?
IT APPEARETH THAT I CAN SPEAK TO THEE IN THE REAL WORLD NOW.
I HAVE BEEN TRYING TO DO MORE, BUT IT SEEMS THAT SPEAKING IS ALL I CAN DO.
IF ONLY I COULD ACT AS WELL!
MRRRR!
IS THAT YOU, LILITH-SAN?
CHIYODA MOMO!! THANK THEE AGAIN FOR THY HELP AT THE HEALTH SPA!!
EEK!!
I LOST A HUGE AMOUNT OF MY MAGIC ...
SO LILITH CAN BE A LITTLE MORE ANNOYING?
"ANNOYING"?! HOW DARE THEE!!
WIPE THAT RUDE EXPRESSION OFF THY FACE AT ONCE!!
UGH!

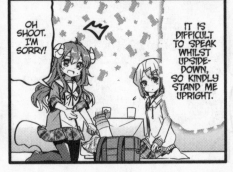

BONUS

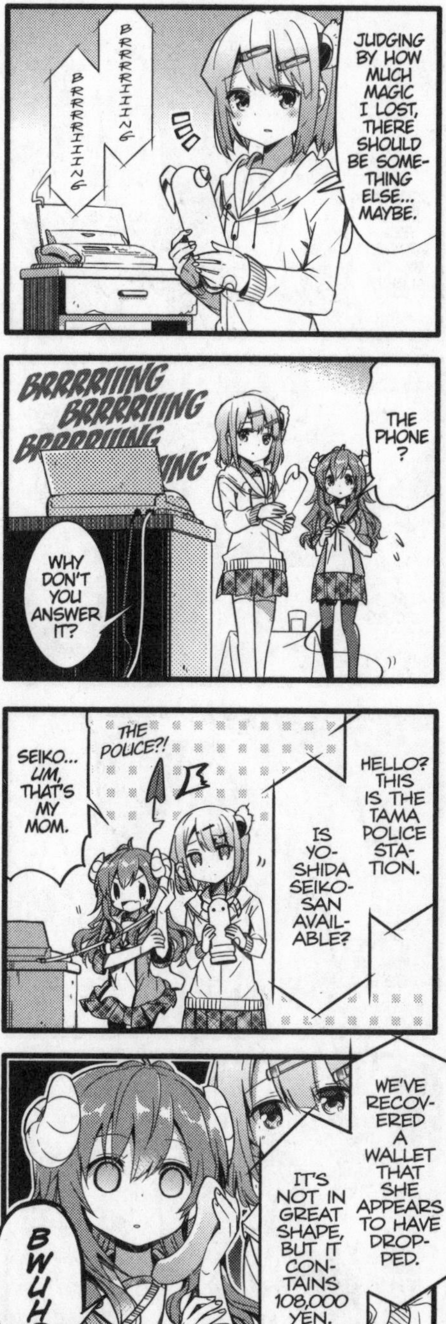
BRRRRIIING
BRRRRIIING
JUDGING BY HOW MUCH MAGIC I LOST, THERE SHOULD BE SOMETHING ELSE... MAYBE.
BRRRRIIING BRRRRIIING
THE PHONE?
WHY DON'T YOU ANSWER IT?
HELLO? THIS IS THE TAMA POLICE STATION.
IS YOSHIDA SEIKO-SAN AVAILABLE?
THE POLICE?!
SEIKO... UM, THAT'S MY MOM.
WE'VE RECOVERED A WALLET THAT SHE APPEARS TO HAVE DROPPED.
IT'S NOT IN GREAT SHAPE, BUT IT CONTAINS 108,000 YEN.
BWUH?

OUT OF THIS WORLD

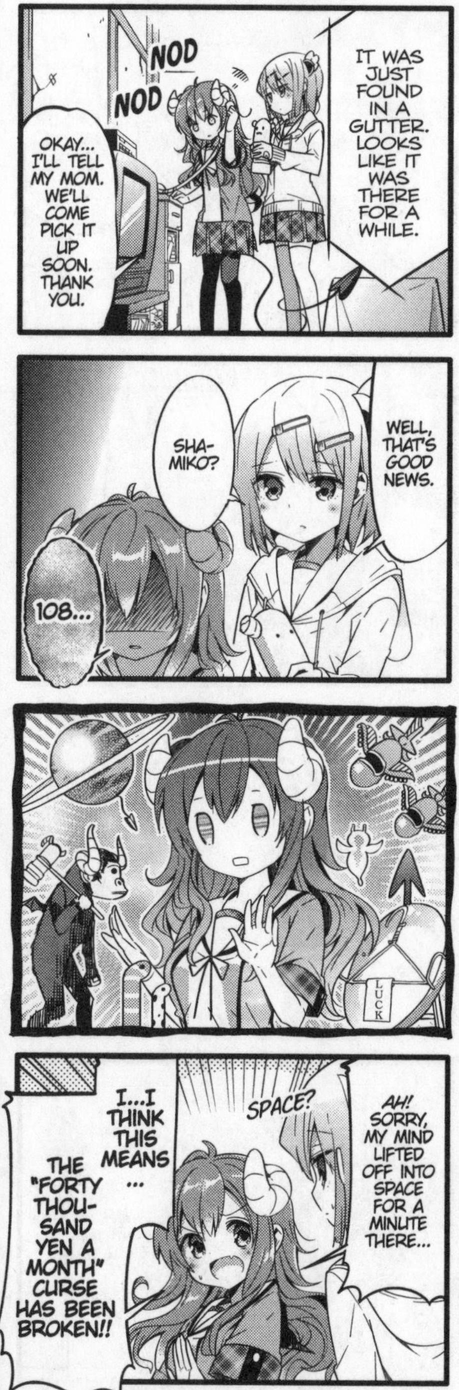
IT WAS JUST FOUND IN A GUTTER. LOOKS LIKE IT WAS THERE FOR A WHILE.
NOD
NOD
OKAY... I'LL TELL MY MOM. WE'LL COME PICK IT UP SOON. THANK YOU.
WELL, THAT'S GOOD NEWS.
SHAMIKO?
108...
LUCK
AH! SORRY, MY MIND LIFTED OFF INTO SPACE FOR A MINUTE THERE...
SPACE?
I...I THINK THIS MEANS...
THE "FORTY THOUSAND YEN A MONTH" CURSE HAS BEEN BROKEN!!

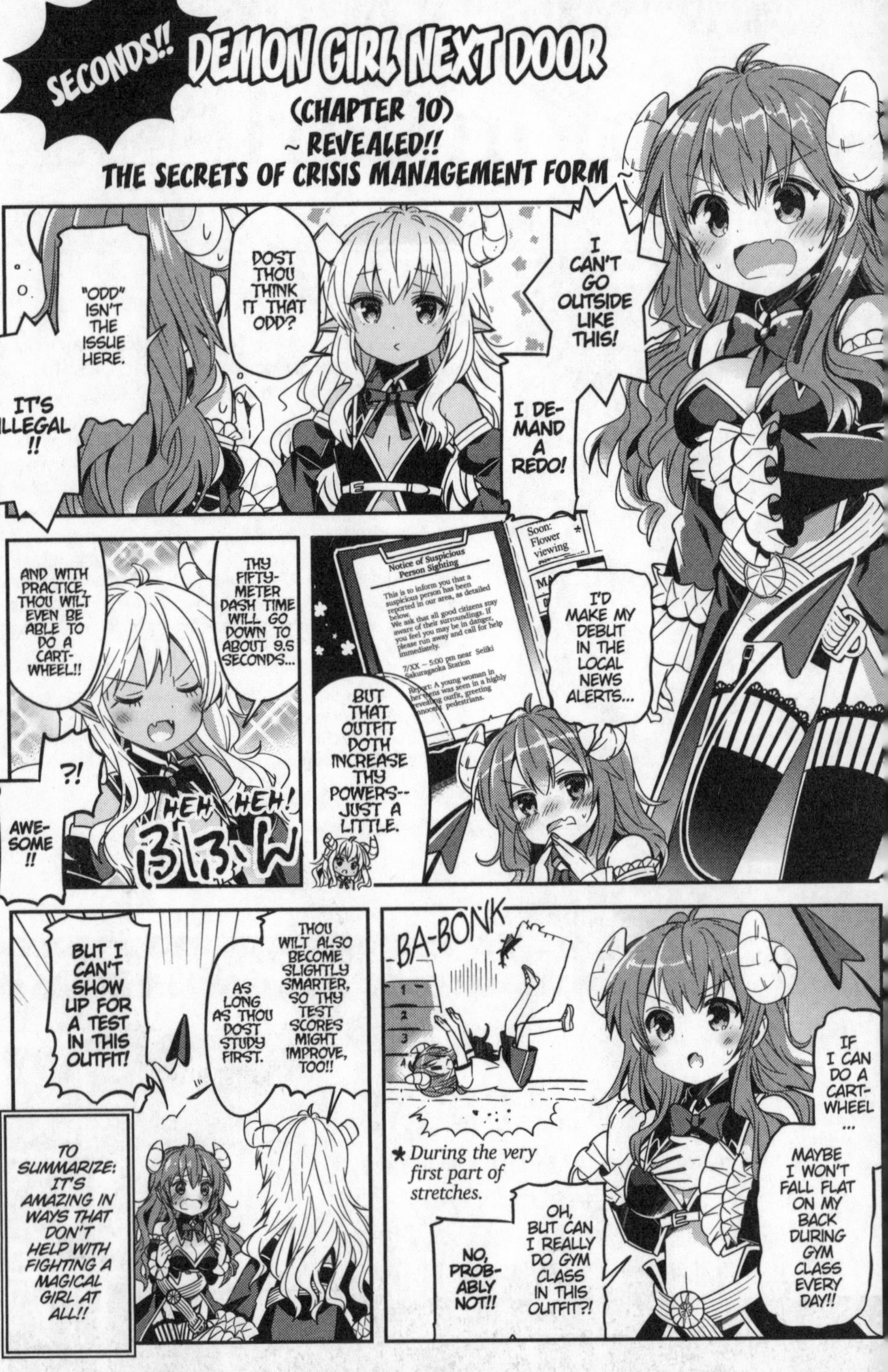
SECONDS!!
DEMON GIRL NEXT DOOR
(CHAPTER 10)
~ REVEALED!!
THE SECRETS OF CRISIS MANAGEMENT FORM ~
I CAN'T GO OUTSIDE LIKE THIS!
I DEMAND A REDO!
DOST THOU THINK IT THAT ODD?
"ODD" ISN'T THE ISSUE HERE.
IT'S ILLEGAL!!
Soon: Flower viewing *
Notice of Suspicious Person Sighting
This is to inform you that a suspicious person has been reported in our area, as detailed below.
We ask that all good citizens stay aware of their surroundings. If you feel you may be in danger, please run away and call for help immediately.
7/XX ~ 5:00 pm near Seiiki Sakuragaoka Station
Report: A young woman in her teens was seen in a highly revealing outfit, greeting innocent pedestrians.
I'D MAKE MY DEBUT IN THE LOCAL NEWS ALERTS...
BUT THAT OUTFIT DOTH INCREASE THY POWERS--JUST A LITTLE.
THY FIFTY-METER DASH TIME WILL GO DOWN TO ABOUT 9.5 SECONDS...
AND WITH PRACTICE, THOU WILT EVEN BE ABLE TO DO A CARTWHEEL!!
HEH HEH!
?!
AWESOME!!
IF I CAN DO A CARTWHEEL...
MAYBE I WON'T FALL FLAT ON MY BACK DURING GYM CLASS EVERY DAY!!
BA-BONK
* During the very first part of stretches.
OH, BUT CAN I REALLY DO GYM CLASS IN THIS OUTFIT?!
NO, PROBABLY NOT!!
THOU WILT ALSO BECOME SLIGHTLY SMARTER, SO THY TEST SCORES MIGHT IMPROVE, TOO!!
AS LONG AS THOU DOST STUDY FIRST.
BUT I CAN'T SHOW UP FOR A TEST IN THIS OUTFIT!
TO SUMMARIZE: IT'S AMAZING IN WAYS THAT DON'T HELP WITH FIGHTING A MAGICAL GIRL AT ALL!!

SEVEN SEAS ENTERTAINMENT PRESENTS

The Demon Girl Next Door

story and art by **IZUMO ITO** VOLUME 1

TRANSLATION
Jenny McKeon

ADAPTATION
Kim Kindya

LETTERING AND RETOUCH
Laura Heo

COVER DESIGN
KC Fabellon

PROOFREADER
Dawn Davis
Danielle King

EDITOR
Shanti Whitesides

PREPRESS TECHNICIAN
Rhiannon Rasmussen-Silverstein

PRODUCTION MANAGER
Lissa Pattillo

MANAGING EDITOR
Julie Davis

ASSOCIATE PUBLISHER
Adam Arnold

PUBLISHER
Jason DeAngelis

Machikado Mazoku Volume 1
© IZUMO ITO 2015
Originally published in Japan in 2015 by HOUBUNSHA CO., LTD., Tokyo.
English translation rights arranged with HOUBUNSHA CO., LTD., Tokyo,
through TOHAN CORPORATION, Tokyo.

Seven Seas press and purchase enquiries can be sent to Marketing Manager
Lianne Sentar at press@gomanga.com. Information regarding the distribution
and purchase of digital editions is available from Digital Manager CK Russell
at digital@gomanga.com.

Seven Seas and the Seven Seas logo are trademarks of
Seven Seas Entertainment. All rights reserved.

ISBN: 978-1-64827-118-2

Printed in Canada

First Printing: January 2021

10 9 8 7 6 5 4 3 2 1

FOLLOW US ONLINE: www.sevenseasentertainment.com

READING DIRECTIONS

This book reads from *right to left*, Japanese style.
If this is your first time reading manga, you start
reading from the top right panel on each page and
take it from there. If you get lost, just follow the
numbered diagram here. It may seem backwards at
first, but you'll get the hang of it! Have fun!!

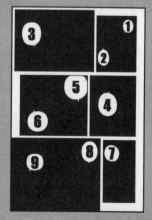

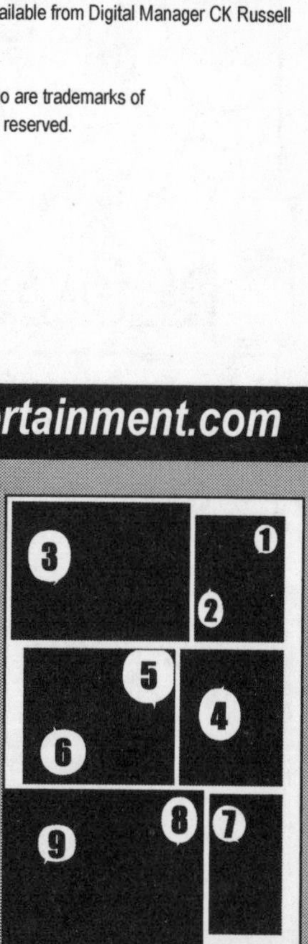

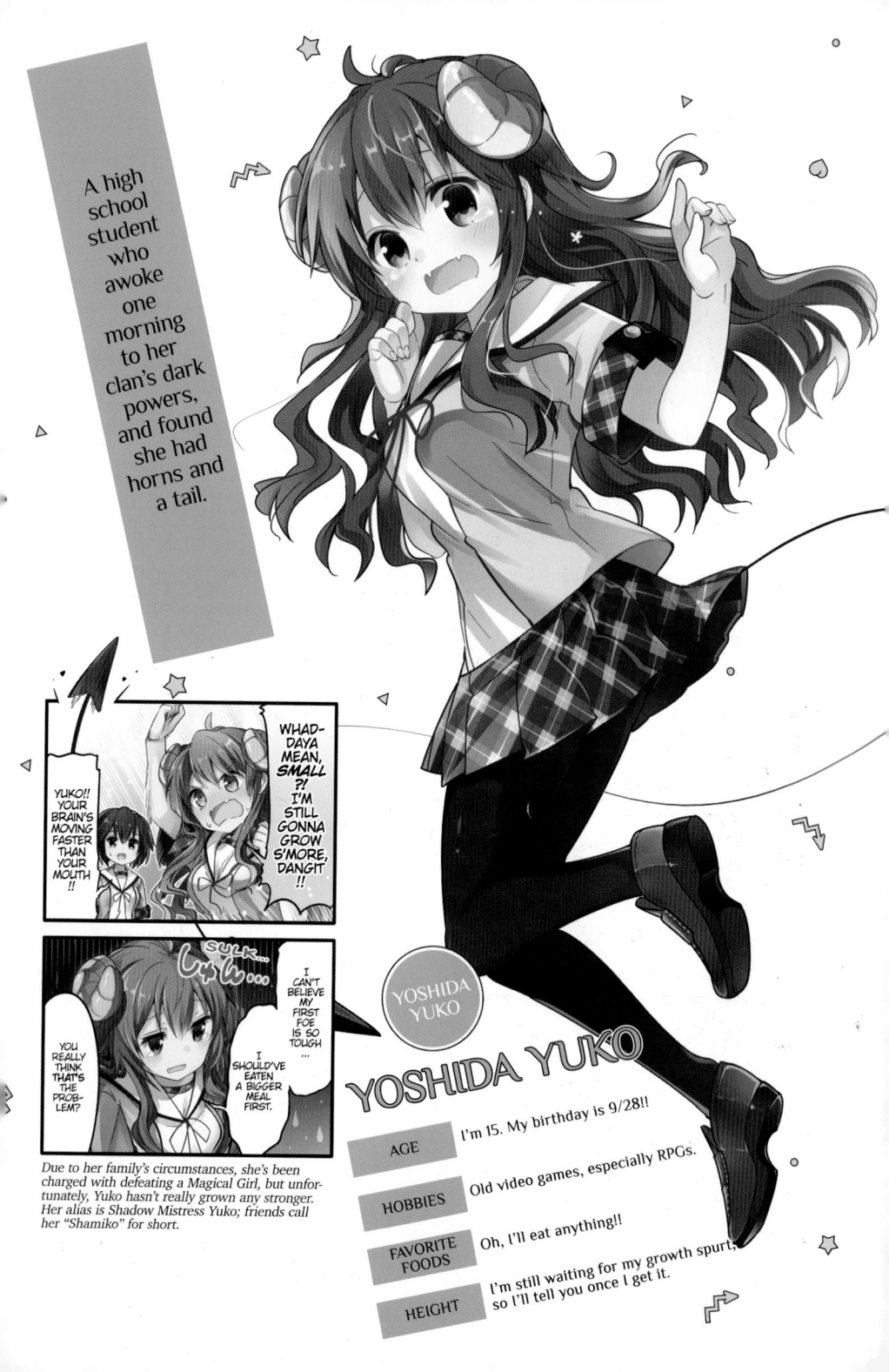

A high school student who awoke one morning to her clan's dark powers, and found she had horns and a tail.

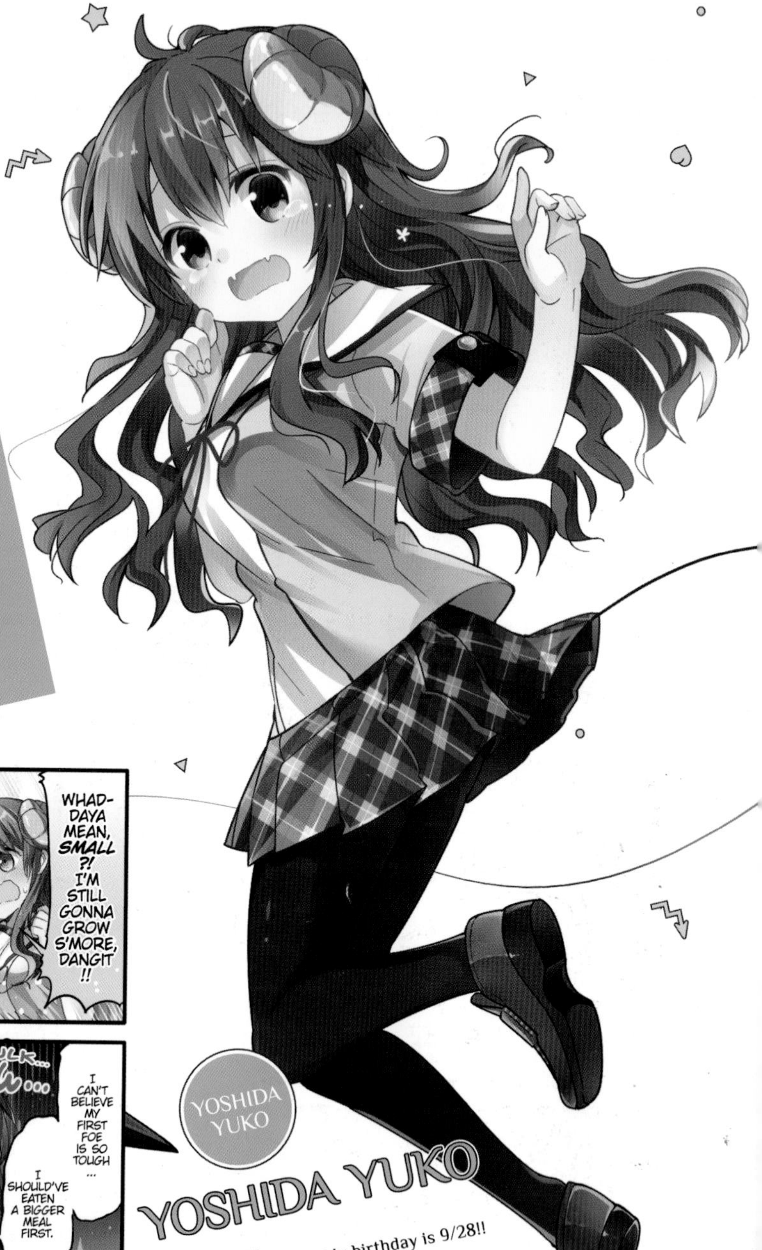
YOSHIDA YUKO

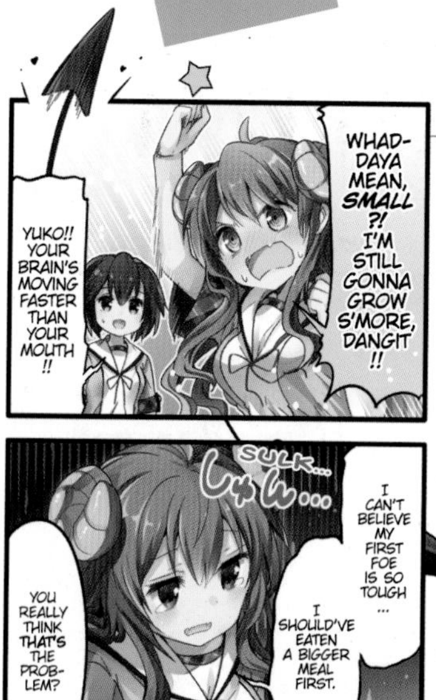
WHADDAYA MEAN, **SMALL** ?! I'M STILL GONNA GROW S'MORE, DANGIT !!
YUKO!! YOUR BRAIN'S MOVING FASTER THAN YOUR MOUTH !!
SULK... しゅん...
I CAN'T BELIEVE MY FIRST FOE IS SO TOUGH ...
I SHOULD'VE EATEN A BIGGER MEAL FIRST.
YOU REALLY THINK **THAT'S** THE PROBLEM?

Due to her family's circumstances, she's been charged with defeating a Magical Girl, but unfortunately, Yuko hasn't really grown any stronger. Her alias is Shadow Mistress Yuko; friends call her "Shamiko" for short.

YOSHIDA YUKO

AGE	I'm 15. My birthday is 9/28!!
HOBBIES	Old video games, especially RPGs.
FAVORITE FOODS	Oh, I'll eat anything!!
HEIGHT	I'm still waiting for my growth spurt, so I'll tell you once I get it.

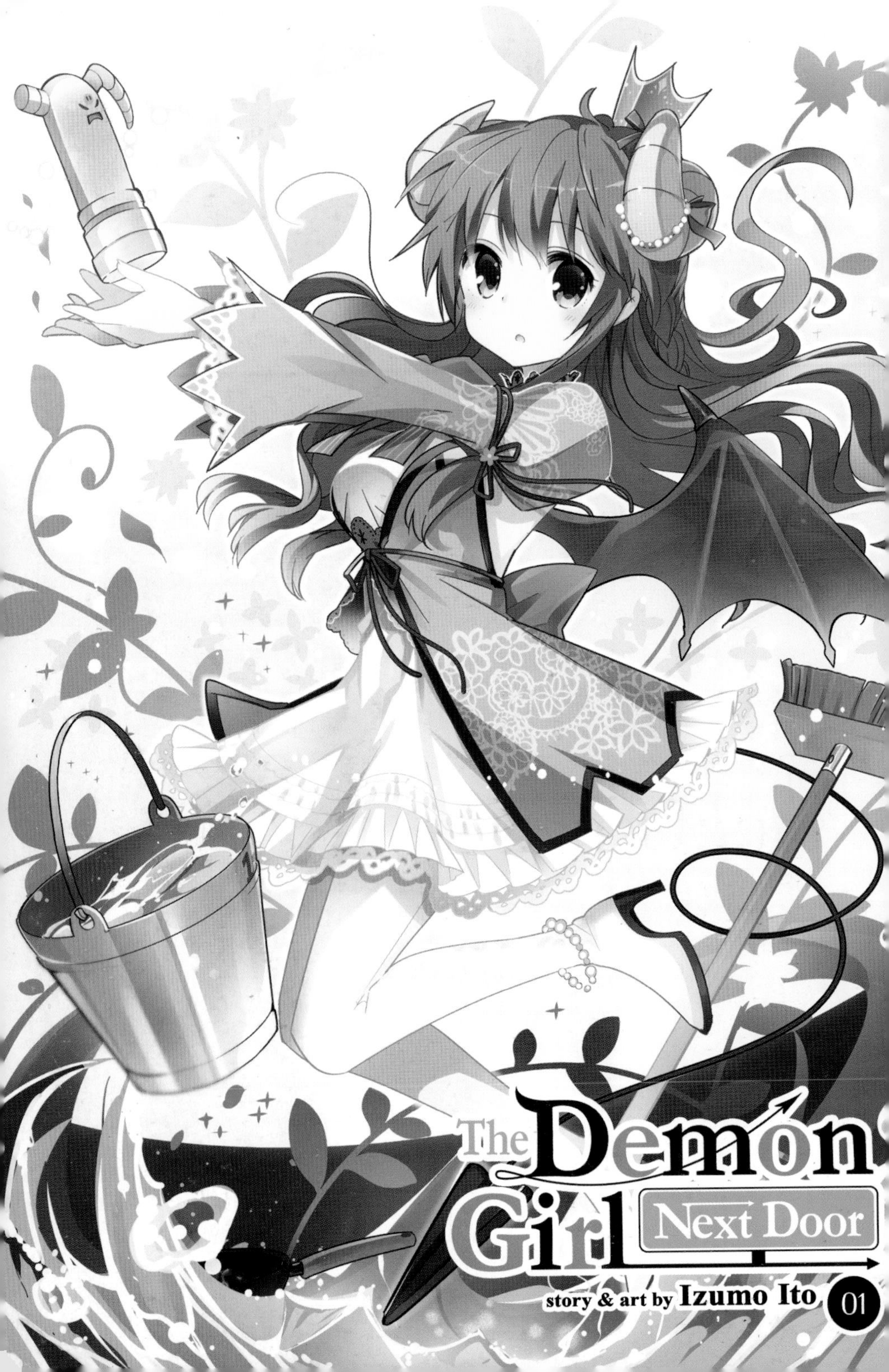
The Demon Girl Next Door
story & art by Izumo Ito
01

SHAMIKO'S MUSCLE-TRAINING SQUAD

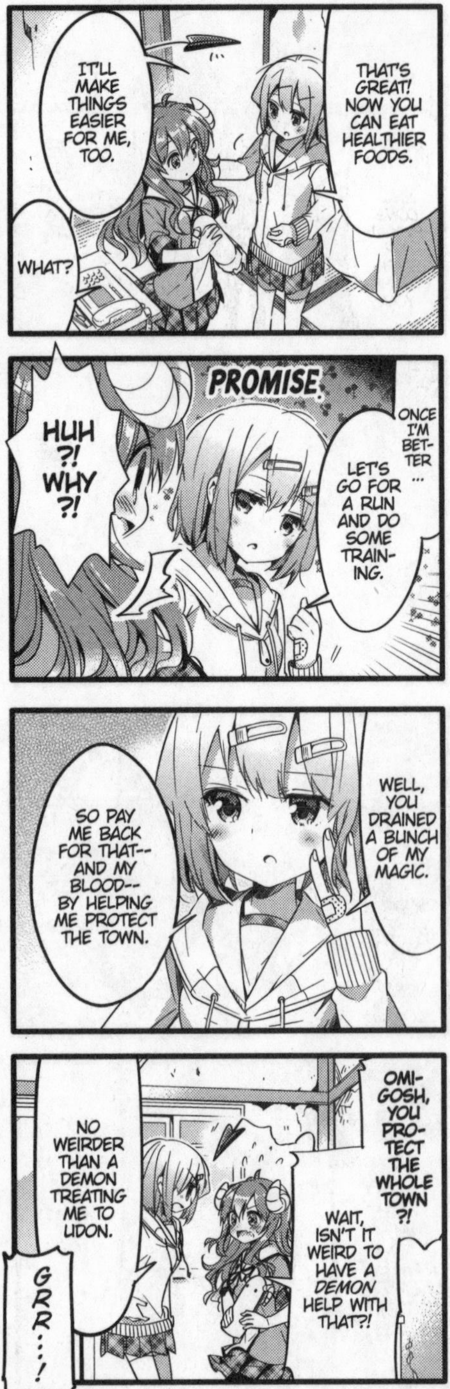
THAT'S GREAT! NOW YOU CAN EAT HEALTHIER FOODS.
IT'LL MAKE THINGS EASIER FOR ME, TOO.
WHAT?
PROMISE
ONCE I'M BETTER...
LET'S GO FOR A RUN AND DO SOME TRAINING.
HUH?! WHY?!
WELL, YOU DRAINED A BUNCH OF MY MAGIC.
SO PAY ME BACK FOR THAT--AND MY BLOOD--BY HELPING ME PROTECT THE TOWN.
OMIGOSH, YOU PROTECT THE WHOLE TOWN?!
WAIT, ISN'T IT WEIRD TO HAVE A *DEMON* HELP WITH THAT?!
NO WEIRDER THAN A DEMON TREATING ME TO UDON.
GRR...!

PLAYING DIRTY

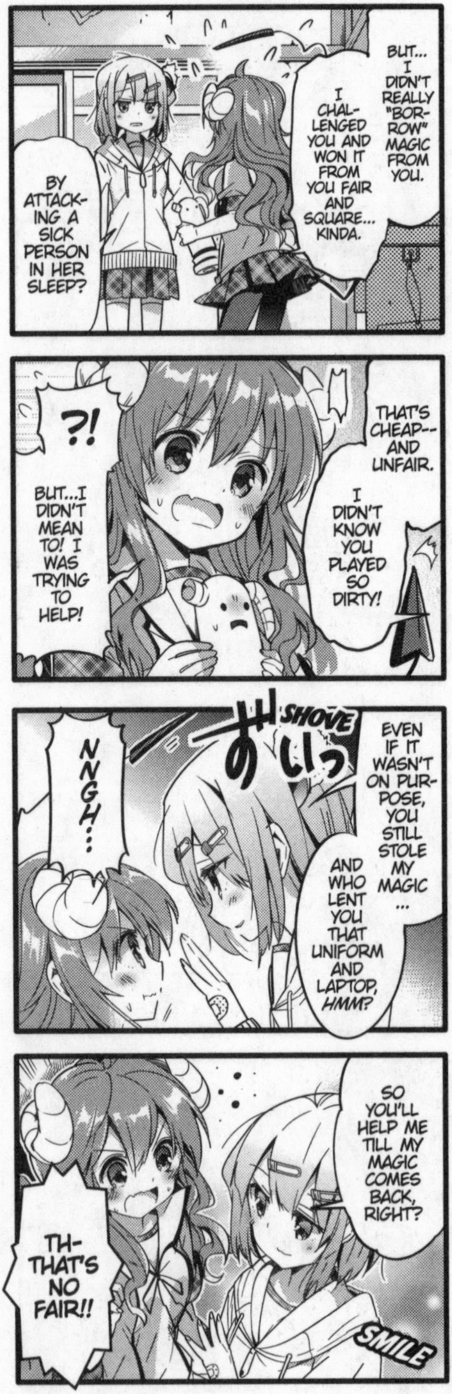
BUT... I DIDN'T REALLY "BORROW" MAGIC FROM YOU.
I CHALLENGED YOU AND WON IT FROM YOU FAIR AND SQUARE... KINDA.
BY ATTACKING A SICK PERSON IN HER SLEEP?
THAT'S CHEAP--AND UNFAIR.
I DIDN'T KNOW YOU PLAYED SO DIRTY!
?!
BUT...I DIDN'T MEAN TO! I WAS TRYING TO HELP!
SHOVE
EVEN IF IT WASN'T ON PURPOSE, YOU STILL STOLE MY MAGIC...
AND WHO LENT YOU THAT UNIFORM AND LAPTOP, *HMM?*
NNGH...!
SO YOU'LL HELP ME TILL MY MAGIC COMES BACK, RIGHT?
SMILE
TH-THAT'S NO FAIR!!

HEAVE-HO!

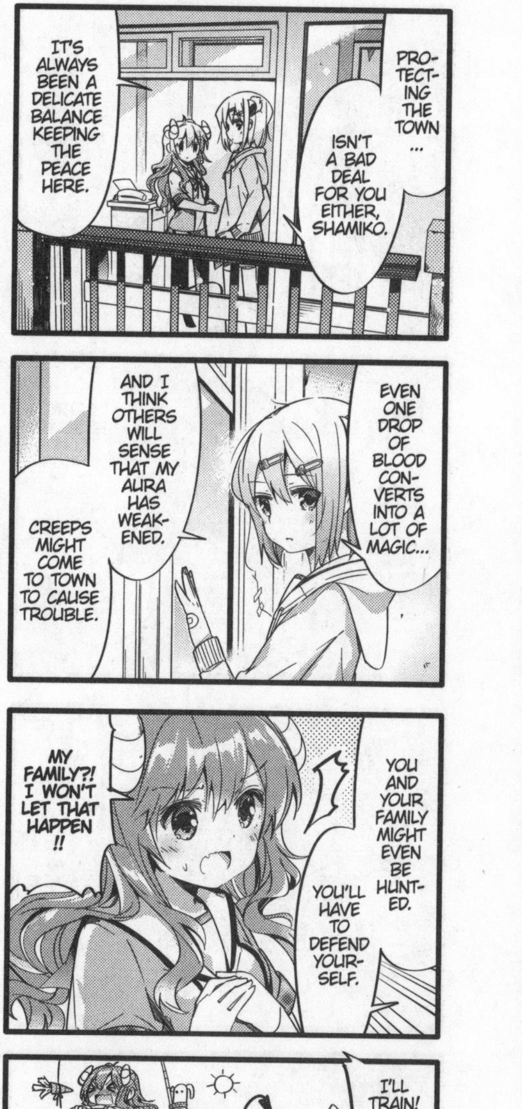
PROTECTING THE TOWN...
ISN'T A BAD DEAL FOR YOU EITHER, SHAMIKO.
IT'S ALWAYS BEEN A DELICATE BALANCE KEEPING THE PEACE HERE.
EVEN ONE DROP OF BLOOD CONVERTS INTO A LOT OF MAGIC...
AND I THINK OTHERS WILL SENSE THAT MY AURA HAS WEAKENED.
CREEPS MIGHT COME TO TOWN TO CAUSE TROUBLE.
YOU AND YOUR FAMILY MIGHT EVEN BE HUNTED.
YOU'LL HAVE TO DEFEND YOURSELF.
MY FAMILY?! I WON'T LET THAT HAPPEN!!
6 TONS
I'LL TRAIN! I'LL CARRY A STEEL BAT!!
AND I'LL PULL ONE OF THOSE BIG ROLLING THINGIES!!
WHATEVER IT TAKES!!
YOUR IDEA OF TRAINING IS SO OUT-OF-DATE.

A LOT OF LONG STORIES

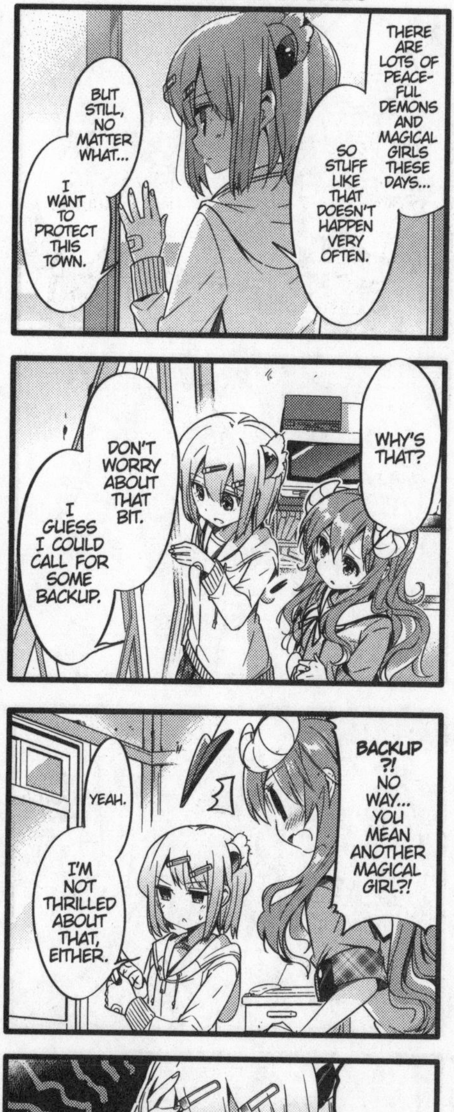
THERE ARE LOTS OF PEACEFUL DEMONS AND MAGICAL GIRLS THESE DAYS...
SO STUFF LIKE THAT DOESN'T HAPPEN VERY OFTEN.
BUT STILL, NO MATTER WHAT...
I WANT TO PROTECT THIS TOWN.
WHY'S THAT?
DON'T WORRY ABOUT THAT BIT.
I GUESS I COULD CALL FOR SOME BACKUP.
BACKUP?! NO WAY... YOU MEAN ANOTHER MAGICAL GIRL?!
YEAH.
I'M NOT THRILLED ABOUT THAT, EITHER.
GOTTA FIND SOMEONE SANE WHO WON'T EAT SHAMIKO ALIVE.
NOT THIS ONE... DEFINITELY NOT THIS ONE...
WHAT, ARE MOST OF THEM INSANE?!

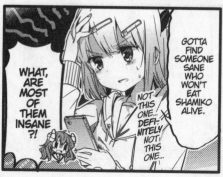

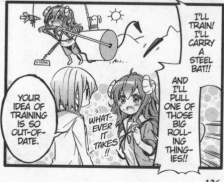

SOUL DAMAGE

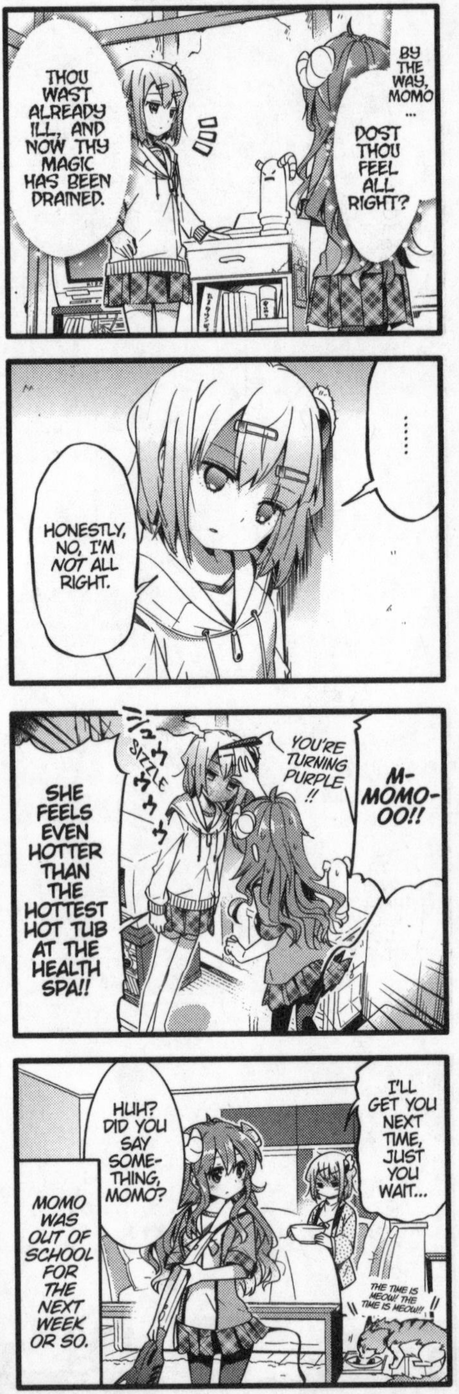
BY THE WAY, MOMO ...
DOST THOU FEEL ALL RIGHT?
THOU WAST ALREADY ILL, AND NOW THY MAGIC HAS BEEN DRAINED.
......
HONESTLY, NO, I'M *NOT* ALL RIGHT.
M-MOMO-OO!!
YOU'RE TURNING PURPLE!!
SIZZLE
SHE FEELS EVEN HOTTER THAN THE HOTTEST HOT TUB AT THE HEALTH SPA!!
I'LL GET YOU NEXT TIME, JUST YOU WAIT...
THE TIME IS MEOW! THE TIME IS MEOW!!
HUH? DID YOU SAY SOMETHING, MOMO?
MOMO WAS OUT OF SCHOOL FOR THE NEXT WEEK OR SO.

IN A CORNER OF THIS TOWN

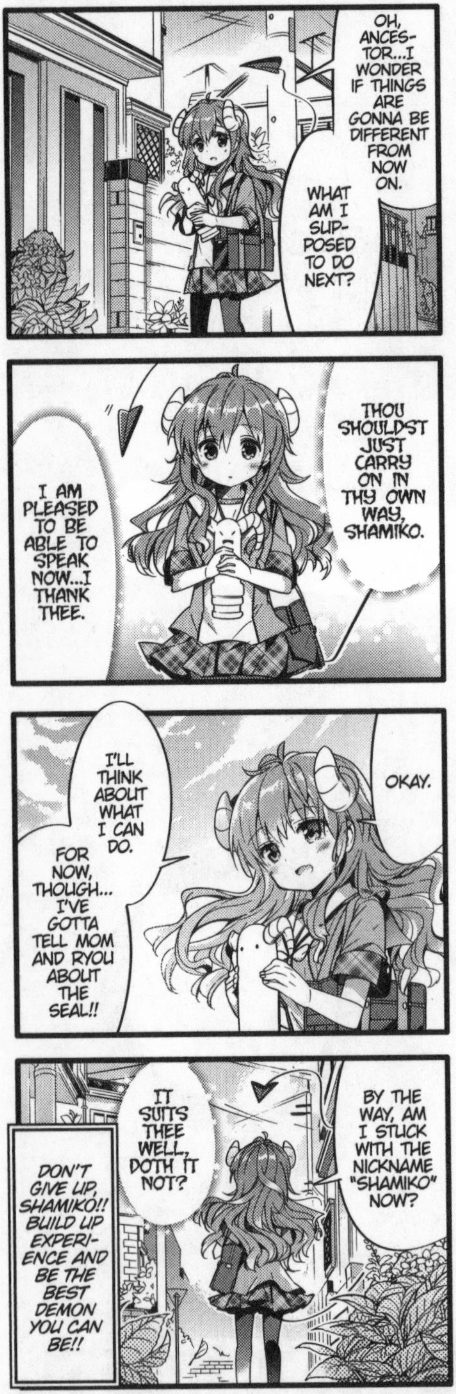
OH, ANCESTOR...I WONDER IF THINGS ARE GONNA BE DIFFERENT FROM NOW ON.
WHAT AM I SUPPOSED TO DO NEXT?
THOU SHOULDST JUST CARRY ON IN THY OWN WAY, SHAMIKO.
I AM PLEASED TO BE ABLE TO SPEAK NOW...I THANK THEE.
OKAY.
I'LL THINK ABOUT WHAT I CAN DO.
FOR NOW, THOUGH... I'VE GOTTA TELL MOM AND RYOU ABOUT THE SEAL!!
BY THE WAY, AM I STUCK WITH THE NICKNAME "SHAMIKO" NOW?
IT SUITS THEE WELL, DOTH IT NOT?
DON'T GIVE UP, SHAMIKO!! BUILD UP EXPERIENCE AND BE THE BEST DEMON YOU CAN BE!!

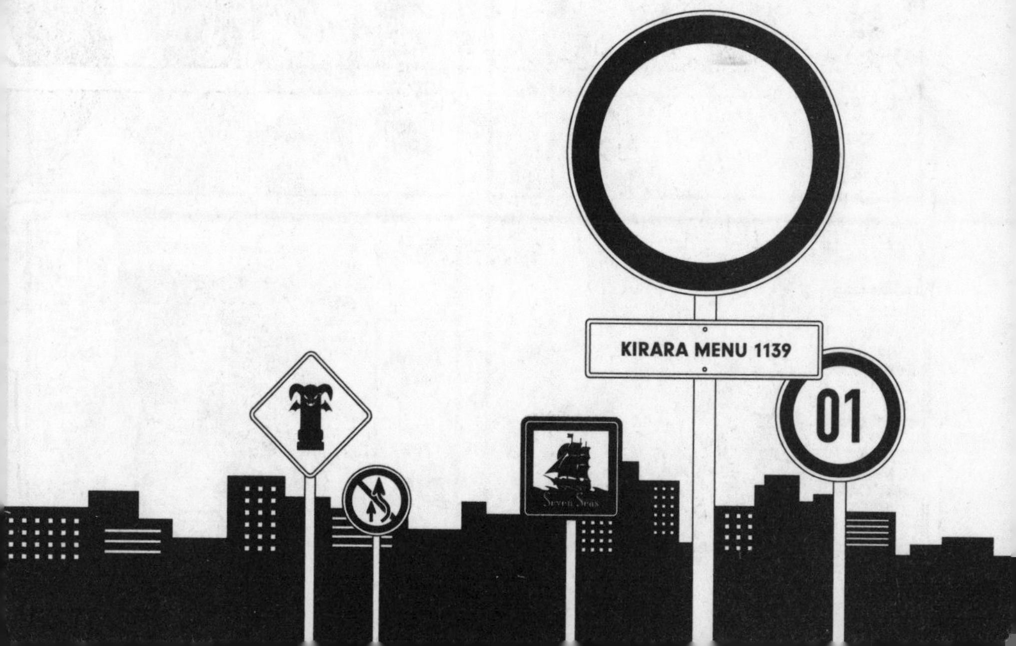
KIRARA MENU 1139
01
Seven Seas